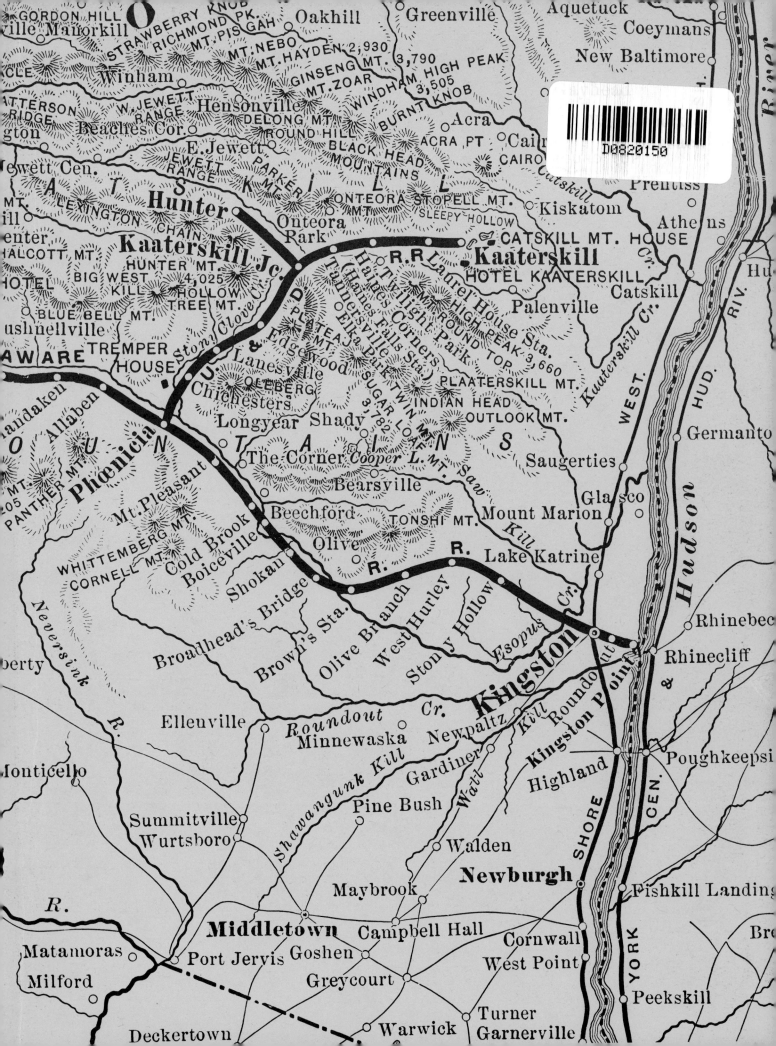

DUE DATE

MAY 2 6 1992			
MAY 2 8 1992			
	201-6503		Printed in USA

THE ULSTER AND DELAWARE

...Railroad Through the Catskills

GERALD M. BEST

Golden West Books

San Marino, California

THE ULSTER & DELAWARE
...Railroad Through the Catskills
Copyright © 1972 by Gerald M. Best
All Rights Reserved
Published by Golden West Books
A Division of Pacific Railroad Publications, Inc.
San Marino, California 91108 U.S.A.
Library of Congress Catalog Card No. 70-190176
ISBN No. 87095-041-X

TITLE PAGE ILLUSTRATION

The colorful painting by famous railroad artist Harlan Hiney, recreates a scene which was commonplace to the residents of Pine Hill, New York, when the Ulster & Delaware's summer season was at its peak. In the scene train No. 7, the *Dayline*, with passengers from New York via Kingston Point, double-heads up the steepest portion of the grade en route to Grand Hotel Summit, with the assist of a third engine at the rear.

Golden West Books

P.O. BOX 8136 • SAN MARINO, CALIFORNIA • 91108

To My Wife Harriet

After an absence of 20 years, Rip Van Winkle finds his house in ruins and is rejected by his dog Wolf, in this scene from Felix Darley's *Illustrations of Rip Van Winkle,* published in 1848. — COURTESY THE NEW YORK HISTORICAL SOCIETY

PREFACE

THE CATSKILL Mountains in eastern New York State, brought to early fame by Washington Irving's legendary story of Rip Van Winkle, were described in early guide books as the range of mountains fronting the west bank of the Hudson River from Kingston to Catskill village. They formed a rectangle about 25 x 60 miles, with the town of Stamford near the western border.

Recent syndicated articles in the travel sections of metropolitan newspapers have erroneously placed hotels such as Grossinger's and the Concord in the heart of the Catskills, whereas they are located near the town of Liberty in Sullivan County, far south of the true Catskill mountains. The famous naturalist T. Morris Longstreth tramped what he termed the Catskills from one end to the other, and he outlined the boundaries as follows; "On the east by the nearly vertical wall extending from High Point on the reservoir, parallel to the Hudson and about ten miles from it, to Mt. Pisgah about thirty miles north and west. On the southwest from High Point along the valley north of the Shawangunk Range to Napanoch, west from there to Livingston Manor, so as to include the wild region of small trees and ponds. On the west a rough line from Livingston Manor up to Stamford through Arena, Andes and Bovina Center. On the north by an arc from Stamford to Livingstonville and Mt. Pisgah."

The range of mountains extending southwest from Kingston all the way to the Delaware Water Gap is a part of the Appalachians known as the Shawangunks as far as the New Jersey State line below Port Jervis and the Kittatinnys through New Jersey. The region once served by the New York, Ontario & Western Railway is a part of the Appalachian range, Longstreth's boundary point touching it at Livingston Manor and that only because he wanted to include the wild region north of there. The compiler who wrote the summer guides for the N. Y. O. & W. neatly sidestepped the issue by describing the region from Summitville through Liberty to Roscoe as the Delaware Mountains, defining them as that portion of the mountains *south of the Catskills* between the branches of the Delaware on the north and the main river on the south. A friend who has spent a lot of time in both areas has a definition which should satisfy everyone. The area fronting the Hudson and for several miles west from the summit of the cliffs should be called the "Wilderness Catskills." The part from Ashokan Reservoir west to Stamford should be, and is, called the "Central Catskills." The Delaware Mountains area, which some wag dubbed the "Sour Cream Sierras," could be called the "Jewish Katzkills."

Having thus tried to locate the true Catskills for those who have never been there, I can state that they consist of a series of mountain peaks ranging in height from a few hundred feet to the highest, Slide Mountain, 4,204 feet, with many others above 3,500 feet. None of them are like the craggy peaks of the Rockies, but have gentle slopes covered with trees, except Stony Clove gorge and the cliffs facing the Hudson River; even they are partially forested. It is a land of rushing streams, waterfalls and the narrow valleys created by them through millions of years. As a schoolboy, I first saw the Catskills from the train window while going from Port Jervis to Kingston with my father. At that time the mountains seemed to be so much higher than they appear to me today. However, as a child anything looks larger!

At Kingston we called on a gentleman who lived in a mansion — Samuel Decker Coykendall —, for my father was tracing the Decker family history and Coykendall had offered to help him. I sat restlessly for an hour in the spacious living room while the two men discussed the Deckers and the town of Wantage, New Jersey, where Coykendall had been born. He spent his youth in my home town, Port Jervis, which was probably why he was so friendly to us. I came away with a lasting impression of a dignified, gracious man and little did I dream that half a century later I would research the history of the Ulster & Delaware Railroad, of which Coykendall was then president. I learned that the fortunes of this railroad, except for ten years, were controlled by three generations of one family. The first was Thomas Cornell, the second Samuel D. Coykendall, (Cornell's son-in-law), and the third Cornell's grandson, Edward Coykendall. Interviews with retired employees have provided a wealth of information about the last 35 years of the Ulster & Delaware as an independent company, but Edward Coykendall, the man who could have supplied the most information, died in 1949. I began my research for this book in 1955.

Historian Winfield Robinson, gathering material for a paper on the Ulster & Delaware for the Railway & Locomotive Historical Society, spent a week in 1936 interviewing every retired employee of the Ulster & Delaware who was willing to talk. In Kingston he was received by Edward Coykendall, then president of the Rondout National Bank.

Coykendall said that all the Ulster & Delaware records were turned over to the New York Central in 1932 and that he did not have one single item

regarding the railroad; not even a picture. When pressed for a few recollections he stated bluntly that he did not want to talk about the Ulster & Delaware, period! A letter to F. E. Williamson, president of the New York Central, received a prompt and courteous reply. He said that the New York Central received no records of any sort about the Ulster & Delaware as a corporation, nor any of its historical records; only the inventory of equipment, buildings, land, etc., when the railroad was taken over by the New York Central in 1932. He ended by suggesting that Robinson get in touch with Edward Coykendall. Having thus received the complete runaround, Robinson abandoned the project. I am fortunate to have his notes and correspondence with Williamson. There was a good reason why Edward Coykendall was touchy about the Ulster & Delaware, and the story is presented in the text.

I first rode this railroad in 1912, though I have lived in California most of my life, but I have revisited the railroad a number of times. These visits are all very pleasant memories of a shortline which had many of the characteristics of a trunkline; of a family railroad which served an area containing some of the finest mountain scenery in the country.

The author is indebted to a number of institutions and individuals in the course of preparing this history. For making available their vast files of New York State newspapers and books, I wish to thank the Henry E. Huntington Library, San Marino, California. To Miss Caroline Matzen, Librarian, Kingston Public Library, my special thanks for the use of the library's microfilm files of the Kingston and Rondout newspapers. To Cornelius E. Cuddeback of Port Jervis, my appreciation for the hours he spent reading the Port Jervis newspapers in the files of the public library there. And the assistance of Alton M. Weiss, editor of the *Catskill Mountain News*, Margaretville, New York, was of great value, especially with regard to the Delaware & Northern Railroad.

Without the help of Raymond S. Baldwin of Oneonta, who worked over 50 years for the Ulster & Delaware and its later owner, the New York Central, I would have missed many colorful episodes in the history of his beloved railroad. He has been generous with pictures, extremely patient with the hundreds of questions I have asked him in the past five years, and I am beholden to him in many ways. Recently he celebrated his 91st birthday. Through Baldwin I met George Emmett of Kingston, retired master mechanic at Rondout and Kingston, who helped me straighten out some knotty problems. Equally helpful was Edward L. May, both with photographs and help in reconstructing the equipment rosters. John B. Hungerford of Reseda, California, spent part of his boyhood in the Catskill region and has made available his collection of guide books, timetables and pictures from that area.

George Phelps of Arcadia, California, has a wealth of material about the U. & D., as his uncle, Lancelot Phelps, was its last superintendent, and has been generous in making it available for my use. John F. Sherman of Kensington, Maryland, grandson of one of the Ulster & Delaware's most colorful engineers, Henry Sherman, has some of his grandfather's souvenirs which I have used. George E. Burnett of Kingston, retired U. & D. engineer who spent all his working years on that railroad, has been my Kingston correspondent, helping me overcome the handicap of living 3,000 miles away and, during my Kingston visits, wading through the jungle wastes of the old Rondout yards and shop area with me. To artists Harlan Hiney for the oil painting on the dust jacket and to Manville B. Wakefield for the chapter headings, my special thanks.

To my old friend, Everett L. DeGolyer, Jr., Secretary of the DeGolyer Foundation of Dallas, Texas, "muchas gracias, senor" for the use of photos from the library's collection. Photographs have been generously loaned to me by John P. Ahrens, Thomas B. Annin, M. B. Cooke, Henry Eighmey, Robert R. Haines, Harold L. Goldsmith, A. Gibson Hague, George F. Holdridge, Edward L. May, Milton E. Pulis, the Steamship Historical Society of America, Inc., Thomas T. Taber, the late Frederick A. Lewis and the late Walter A. Lucas. We are all fortunate that the famous Rocky Mountain photographer, William Henry Jackson, came to the Catskills in 1902 on behalf of his Detroit Publishing Co. and exposed 200 of his glass plate negatives, photographing hotels and mountain scenes for use by the hotels and railroad companies. They are now safely deposited in the Library of Congress and many of Jackson's photographic gems are reproduced in this book. If I have left anyone out, or their photos are incorrectly credited, I assure them that it was unintentional.

For the use of his railroad research library, which complements mine, thanks to Don Duke. And last but not least, to Harry Eddy, Librarian, Bureau of Railway Economics, Association of American Railroads in Washington, D. C., for his diligence in digging up ancient boiler explosion reports, annual reports and a host of other data, my deep appreciation.

— GERALD M. BEST.

Beverly Hills, California.
April 28, 1972

Reminiscent of Thomas Cole's 1844 painting, William Henry Jackson photographed North and South Lakes on a glass plate negative in 1902, with the Hotel Kaaterskill on South Mountain, and High Peak, a thousand feet higher, in the background. — LIBRARY OF CONGRESS

TABLE OF CONTENTS

The world-famous Catskill Mountain House. In the days before photography, stylized engravings were the rule. In this scene the hotel is made to look larger and the cliffs steeper than they actually were in order to impress prospective tourists. — AUTHOR'S COLLECTION

1

EARLY TRANSPORTATION TO THE CATSKILLS

HEN THE monopoly held by Robert Fulton's North River Steamboat Co. was broken in 1824 the Hudson River was open to competition for the first time. Though sailing vessels on the Hudson were still in the majority then, side-wheel and propeller driven ships of many companies were soon carrying passengers and freight to Albany and intermediate points. For the first time the Catskill Mountains were within reasonably easy access to residents of New York City.

At first the river steamers had no competition either from railroads or stage lines, as the journey by steamer from New York to the villages on the west bank of the Hudson near the Catskills could be made within the daylight hours in summer. In the middle of the third decade of the 19th Century there was only one hotel of any importance in the mountains west of Catskill village of a size to accommodate a number of visitors. This was the Catskill Mountain House which opened for its first season in 1824.

Perhaps the best early description of this famous hostelry is contained in the annual issues of the *Appleton Railroad and Steamboat Companion*, a guide which described in detail all the railroads and steamship lines within the states of the Atlantic seaboard. Quoting from the 1847 issue, from the chapter devoted to a passage up the Hudson

from New York to Albany — "The Village of Catskill, 111 miles from New York and 34 from Albany, is seated on both sides of Catskill Creek, near its junction with the Hudson. Coaches, so arranged as to be at the steamboat landing on the arrival and departure of the boats, run regularly to and from the mountain for the conveyance of the passengers, and also to enable those who are so inclined, to visit the different falls in the vicinity. The time required for ascending to the Mountain House, a distance of 12 miles, is usually four hours, and the price one dollar — half the time being sufficient for return. The journey up the mountain, though a safe one, is rather trying to timid persons; the road for two-thirds of the distance from the landing being very uneven, and the remaining distance a steep ascent in a zigzag direction to the top. The Catskill Mountain House is 12 miles from Catskill Landing, upon the summit of one of the principal mountains, known as 'Table Rock' at an elevation of 2,500 feet above the Hudson. This hotel, erected by the citizens of Catskill at a cost of $22,000, is 140 feet long and four stories high, with a piazza extending across the front, supported by a colonnade. It is placed at a convenient distance back from the verge of the precipice, in order to allow carriages to drive up in front to set down and receive passengers. A few feet from the building the rock terminates in a

A single drivered engine built by H. R. Dunham, of the type used on the Canajoharie & Catskill, is shown in this line drawing copied by Walter Lucas from an original drawing in Hodge's 1840 publication, *The Steam Engine.* — AUTHOR'S COLLECTION

fearful precipice, from the brow of which the inexperienced beholder starts back in uncontrollable alarm."

Appleton describes the mountains rising to the west of the hotel and the two lakes, beyond which are the Catskill Falls which descend 250 feet in three cascades. He stressed the fact that the mountain air was particularly healthful; that it was many degrees cooler in the summer than the river valley below, and that the trip was well worth the effort. He called the falls the "Catskill Falls," whereas today the Dutch spelling of Kaaterskill is used. To this day the native pronunciation of this name sounds like "Cauterskill." In the Guide there is no mention of any other hotel in the Catskill region, for the Catskill Mountain House enjoyed a monopoly at that time.

Before the above story was written, a railroad had been built west from Catskill village, through the valley of Catskill Creek a distance of approximately 26 miles to the village of Cooksburg. Called the Canajoharie & Catskill Railroad, incorporated April 19, 1830, it was built between 1837 and 1840 with money raised partly through stock subscriptions and a loan of $200,000 from the State of New York. Using wooden rails on which strips of wrought iron 2¼ inches wide and ⅝ inch thick were fastened, the railroad builders used the generally accepted principle of track construction employed by other railroads in the State, which by 1837 extended most of the way from Albany to

Buffalo. When the railroad reached Cooksburg, all of the money advanced by the State and the stockholders had been spent, and only one-third of it had been completed. Powered by one locomotive turned out by an incompetent builder in New York City named Dunham, the railroad was doomed from the start. Failure of a wooden bridge across Catskill Creek at High Rock on March 4, 1840, precipitated the train into the creek, though the engine was already off the bridge when it collapsed. One man was killed, and the railroad was out of business until the bridge could be repaired. The Greene County Historical Association has some of the reports of expenditures on the railroad after the accident, and it is evident that trains ran on the line through 1841.

During 1840 and 1841, various schemes were proposed to tie the Canajoharie & Catskill to the Hudson & Berkshire Railroad on the east bank of the river by means of a ferry between Catskill and Hudson, but nothing came of them. The traffic generated by the farmers, the tanners and the lumber mills of Catskill Creek valley was insufficient to meet expenses, let alone pay off the loan. Having defaulted on the interest in 1841, the comptroller of the State of New York seized the property and auctioned it off on May 20, 1842, the highest bidder being the Catskill Bank, which paid $11,600. All usable material was salvaged and the locomotive was used for years as a stationary engine at Catskill Point icehouse. This ended railroad building on the Hudson's west bank between Albany and New York for a decade, except for the New York & Erie's main line which started at Piermont, within sight of Manhattan Island. One heritage the Canajoharie & Catskill left for others 40 years later was the roadbed, which was in due time used for some distance by the Catskill Mountain Railroad in 1882.

In 1847, the Hudson River Railroad began construction of a standard gauge line from New York City to Albany along the east bank of the river. This railroad had adequate financing and its prime objective was a connection with the series of railroads which stretched across the State from Albany to Buffalo. The old strap-iron rails having been outlawed several years earlier, the "T" rail of wrought iron was used. Poughkeepsie was reached from New York at the end of 1849, the work then starting south from Greenbush (later Rensselaer), until the rails met on October 2, 1851. Oakhill Station, 110 miles from the 30th Street

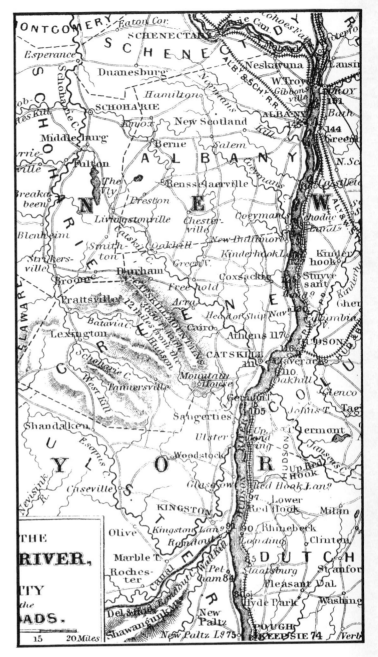

The 1857 map, illustrated above, shows the Hudson River Railroad on the east bank of the river, from Poughkeepsie to Greenbush, opposite Albany. The New York & Harlem Railroad on the extreme right ended at Chatham Corners where it connected with the Albany & West Stockbridge Railroad. (ABOVE-LEFT) An early woodcut of a Hudson River Railroad train crossing an arm of DeKoven's Bay en route to Albany. (LEFT) The first railroad station at Greenbush, New York, was circular, with an observation tower in the center of the roof. Horses were often used to switch freight cars when steam engines were not available.
— AUTHOR'S COLLECTION

station in New York City, was built directly opposite the village of Catskill and ferry service was soon established. The morning train from New York required 3 hours 41 minutes, to make the trip and enabled passengers bound for the Catskill Mountain House to arrive there before supper, with a convenient train in the other direction for those returning from the mountains. Oakhill Station soon became Catskill Station and eventually was called Greendale. By 1900, fast expresses from New York to Saratoga and Montreal made scheduled stops at Greendale to let off passengers bound for the Catskills. At Rhinecliff, 21 miles down river from Oakhill Station, the ferryboat *Rhine* had been carrying passengers since 1815 to Columbus Point, a four-mile stagecoach ride from Kingston. In 1852 the *Rhine* was replaced by the side-wheel ferryboat *Lark*, and the latter in turn was replaced by the *Transport* in 1881.

The Hudson River Railroad was a success from the start and within three years was carrying over a million passengers a year, an enormous figure for the times. It had no physical connection with the railroads at Albany until in 1866 a bridge across the Hudson replaced the ferries. It controlled rail transport in the Hudson River valley for 32 years and, except for the New York & Erie Railroad's branches at Piermont and Newburgh, there were no railroads south of Athens on the west bank of the river for many years. When the Dutch settled in the Esopus valley the slopes of the Catskills were heavily forested with hemlock and oak trees. Their bark provided the tanner with his tannin, no other source of this chemical then being known. Within 50 years, the Catskills were almost completely denuded of the forest primeval. By 1870, second-growth trees had enabled the mountain slopes to recover from this ruthless exploitation and the region was ripe for a new type of development, the summer hotel.

Since Rondout will be mentioned many times in this story, a brief history of the city will help explain its importance to Kingston and to freight traffic on the river. By April 1828, the Delaware & Hudson Canal had been placed in operation from Honesdale, Pennsylvania, to a point on Rondout Creek called Eddyville, a distance of 108 miles. Three miles north of Eddyville was a hamlet called The Strand, or Kingston Landing, directly below the town of Kingston, and here were located the

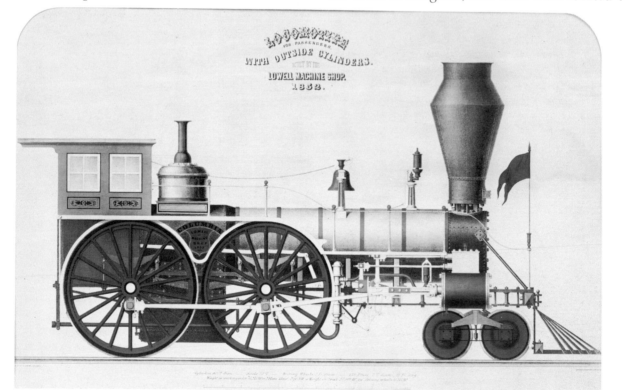

One of the earliest of the Hudson River Railroad engines was the *Columbia*, a high-speed racer with seven-foot driving wheels. Like all locomotives of the 1852 period, the wheels and cab were painted in bright colors and the boiler jacket and brass work highly polished. — AUTHOR'S COLLECTION

Hudson River Railroad No. 86, built by Schenectady in 1869, the year the Rondout & Oswego Railroad construction began, poses at the 31st St. shops in New York City. (BELOW) The canal terminal at Rondout, with the Delaware & Hudson Canal Company's office in the brick building at the right. — AUTHOR'S COLLECTION

canal company's main offices, boat construction yards, docks and homes for the workers. The town was renamed Bolton and when its population reached 10,000 it was incorporated as the city of Rondout in May 1849.

Completion of the Hudson River Railroad caused a lively passenger traffic to develop between Rhinecliff on the east bank and Rondout. This required a ferry ride to Columbus Point and a trip to Rondout in a stagecoach over a bumpy road. In 1852 Columbus Point was abandoned and the ferry came into a new slip in Rondout. This change also shortened the stage ride to Kingston by a mile. Within 20 years, Rondout and Kingston had grown together to such an extent that the former was absorbed into Kingston on May 29, 1872, though the name Rondout, as a ward of the city, is used to this day. In 1866 a horsecar railroad was built from Rondout ferry to the center of Kingston over a devious route of three miles. The grade for the first 500 yards was so steep that two extra horses were used as helpers and the cars were forever derailing due to the flimsy construction of the track. In 1894 an electric trolley line replaced the horsecars.

Train time at Big Indian station, circa 1890. A westbound passenger train with engine No. 4 at the head end is passing an eastbound express, before beginning the steepest part of the climb up Pine Hill. — EDWARD L. MAY COLLECTION

2

IRON THROUGH THE CATSKILLS

THE FIRST railroad to be built west from the Hudson River through the heart of the Catskill range was the Rondout & Oswego Railroad which was chartered April 3, 1866, to build a standard gauge railroad between the two cities for which the railroad was named. Just as it was with the Canajoharie & Catskill, the promoters of the Rondout & Oswego set their sights at a city far distant from their real objective, a connection with the Albany & Susquehanna Railroad. This railroad had already been completed from Albany southwest to Unadilla, 99 miles, with its final destination at Binghamton, New York, 140 miles from Albany, where it would connect with the Erie Railway. Built to the Erie's broad gauge of six feet, the Albany & Susquehanna was completed December 30, 1868.

The man who guided the destiny of the Rondout & Oswego during its first four years was Thomas B. Cornell, enterprising owner of the Cornell Steamboat Co. of Rondout and owner of that most beautiful of river boats, the *Mary Powell*. Cornell was born at White Plains, New York, in January 1814 and by the time he was 34 he and an uncle had bought the steamboat *Norwich*, then operating as a night boat for freight and passengers between Rondout and New York City. Soon Cornell was operating a small fleet of side-wheel towboats, eventually incorporating his interests in a company bearing his name. His principal business was towing barges on the river, particularly coal barges loaded with anthracite coal brought to the storage piles near Rondout by the Delaware & Hudson Canal Co., of which Cornell became a director in 1868. The passenger and freight steamers were of secondary importance and Cornell sold the *Mary Powell* at the end of the 1868 season.

As first organized the officers of the Rondout & Oswego Railroad were Thomas Cornell, president, and John C. Brodhead, treasurer of Ulster County, the vice-president and construction superintendent. The directors, besides Cornell and Brodhead, were Henry A. Samson, Edgar B. Newkirk, H. Schoonmaker, James G. Lindsley and L. N. Heermance of Rondout and Kingston; N. W. Watson of Shokan; Isaac W. Longyear of Shandaken; Orson M. Allaben of Margaretville; E. J. Burhans of Roxbury; F. R. Gilbert of Stamford and R. T. Hume of Harpersfield. These men were actually representatives of the townships through which the railroad would pass and which, before actual construction began, pledged themselves to subscribe to common stock in the railroad to the amount of $1,500,000. This money was raised by the sale of township bonds, of which the town of Kingston was the largest subscriber, selling $600,000 in bonds and receiving in return 6,000 shares of stock in the railroad.

19

Portrait of the Honorable Thomas B. Cornell, the man who guided the destinies of the Rondout & Oswego Railroad and the Cornell Steamboat Company.
— NEW YORK PUBLIC LIBRARY COLLECTION

The steamer *Mary Powell*, once owned by Thomas Cornell, sailed the Hudson for over half a century. This graceful, wood hulled sidewheeler was built in 1861, and contained a vertical walking beam engine powered by two boilers located outside the superstructure. She was lengthened in 1862 and her 1,560 horsepower made her one of the speed queens of the Hudson. — STEAMSHIP HISTORICAL SOCIETY OF AMERICA

The *Norwich*, built in 1836, was used by Thomas Cornell in passenger, freight and tugboat operations on the Hudson River. — STEAMSHIP HISTORICAL SOCIETY OF AMERICA, INC.

Side-wheel tugs were soon replaced by propeller vessels such as the *Edwin H. Mead* of the Cornell Steamboat Company. — STEAMSHIP HISTORICAL SOCIETY OF AMERICA, INC.

Cornell personally bought $25,000 worth of stock and took part in active solicitation of stock subscriptions. He revealed that the railroad would be built only as far as Colliersville, 108 miles from Rondout and six miles north of Oneonta, where a connection would be made with the Albany & Susquehanna Railroad and with the Cooperstown & Susquehanna Valley Railroad, then under construction. The Rondout & Oswego would thus have a direct line to Cooperstown, the center of a rich farming region in Otsego County, and at the same time connect north and south with the Albany & Susquehanna. As a director of the Delaware & Hudson Canal Co., Cornell knew that plans were afoot to extend the company's steam railroad north from the Carbondale area to a connection with the Albany & Susquehanna at Nineveh. He was also aware that pressure would then be brought on the latter railroad to install a third rail from Nineveh to Albany if they were unwilling to change the broad gauge permanently to standard. Cornell wanted to be in on the transport of coal by rail, an eventuality which he foresaw would eliminate the canals forever.

Construction began slowly, nothing being done except the surveys and the acquiring of the right-of-way until grading began in earnest in the spring of 1868 at Rondout. The first few miles of the railroad were in some ways the most difficult; the line had to be laid out in the form of a giant letter "S" and climbed 190 feet from Rondout station to the eastern edge of Kingston on the bluffs above the river in less than three miles. In this section was the railroad's only tunnel, underneath an intersec-

The only tunnel on the Rondout & Oswego was under Hasbrouck Ave., between Rondout and Kingston. — RAYMOND S. BALDWIN

The eventual goal of Thomas Cornell was to build his railroad all the way to Oneonta. This dream came true, although not in his lifetime. In this scene, a southbound Delaware & Hudson passenger train pauses at the original Albany & Susquehanna station in Oneonta.—AUTHOR'S COLLECTION

tion of streets at Hasbrouck Avenue. For three miles west of Kingston the grading work was easy through the meadows on each side of Esopus Creek, which was crossed by means of a wooden Howe Truss bridge until a group of low hills had to be traversed through a narrow brook valley, with a two percent grade and a considerable amount of shale rock excavation. From West Hurley, 10 miles from Rondout, the grade went three miles west to Olive Branch, then southwest into the valley of Esopus Creek, which it again crossed at Brodhead's Bridge, work ceasing for the winter at this point.

In June 1869, a secondhand inside-connected locomotive named the *Pennsylvania* and eight platform cars were landed at Rondout, together with 1,000 tons of iron rail from England. Crossties were in plentiful supply and the tracklaying crew which started from Rondout in early June had high ambitions to catch up with the grading crews. They were doomed to disappointment, for construction work at Hasbrouck Avenue held them up until mid-August when the *Pennsylvania* steamed through the heart of Kingston. From that time until October 1 the tracklayers averaged 2,000 feet per day, reaching milepost 20 near the town of Shokan on September 30. During 1869 the graders reached Shandaken, milepost 33, and, as the winter proved to be mild, the tracklayers were five miles west of Boiceville, near the town of Mt. Pleasant, in March 1870. A new locomotive, the

Wm. C. More had been received from the Dickson Works in November 1869, additional freight cars arrived and 20 miles of the track had been ballasted by May 1870. Frank J. Hecker, former Union Pacific roadmaster, was made the operating superintendent and on May 25, 1870, the first regularly scheduled passenger train was run. Hauled by the *Pennsylvania*, the train consisted of a baggage car and a passenger coach. It left Rondout at 6:40 A.M., and went as far as Mt. Pleasant station, 24 miles from Rondout, returning in the late afternoon. For days after that first train the coach was filled with curious locals anxious to see the railroad's progress, and for many of them, a first train ride. In June a third locomotive and more rolling stock arrived and freight train service to Shandaken started September 1. A considerable traffic in bluestone developed, this being quarried near West Hurley from great bluish colored sandstone deposits and cut into slabs which could be used for sidewalks, curbs, gutter linings and building stone. The sidewalks of most eastern cities were made of bluestone squares until the development of con-

An early woodcut drawing from Van Loan's *Catskill Mountain Guide* shows Overlook Mountain and the Overlook House as seen from West Hurley. A Rondout & Oswego passenger train is steaming west towards Phoenicia. (BELOW) Rondout & Oswego's *Wm. C. More* No. 1 stands in front of Hamilton House in West Shokan. This locomotive was for years the road's only freight engine. — ROBERT SCHMIDT COLLECTION — COURTESY TOM TABER

Artist's impression of Horseshoe Curve on Pine Hill, before the denuded slopes had been reforested.—JOHN B. HUNGERFORD COLLECTION

crete put the bluestone quarries out of business. Even so, Kingston today has many bluestone sidewalks in the residential districts.

Early in 1870, Thomas Cornell came under fire from the townships west of Shandaken which had bonded themselves for large sums in order to have the railroad go through their towns by 1871 at the latest. Instead of devoting all his time to the Rondout & Oswego, he had become involved in two other railroad projects. One was the Delhi & Middletown Railroad, organized to build a railroad from Delhi in Delaware County to Andes, Union Grove, Margaretville and Dean's Corners where it would connect with the Rondout & Oswego. This infuriated the towns west of Dean's Corners and they clamored for Cornell to resign if he could not spend all his time in their behalf. As a further aggravation in July 1870 Cornell organized the Rhinebeck & Connecticut Railroad. As owner of the Cornell Steamboat Co. his primary interest was to make work for his tugboats, towing barges of

coal from the D. & H. canal terminal to outlets along the Hudson River. Rhinecliff, on the east shore of the river opposite Rondout and the river port for Rhinebeck, two miles inland, was an ideal place to start a railroad to connect the river port with a network of railroads which joined at Boston Corners on the Connecticut State Line. Cornell did not consider this project to be in any way detrimental to the Rondout & Oswego as it was financed entirely by people living on the Hudson's east bank.

The annual meeting of the Rondout & Oswego was held on September 20, 1870, and in his annual report Cornell stated that the railroad was in running order to Shandaken, 32 miles; that six miles were graded up Pine Hill and three miles were graded from the summit downhill towards Dean's Corners. He said that since the townships were not favorable to his continuing in office he thought it best to resign, and he did so forthwith. He stated that he owned $25,000 in paid-in stock and would

24

continue to be interested in the railroad's progress, but would take no further part in its construction.

The directors then elected John C. Brodhead president and Cornell left the meeting. From that date, for nearly five years, the affairs of the railroad were a duplicate in miniature of the financial and political life of the Union Pacific Railroad. Cornell devoted his time to the surveys and planning of the Rhinebeck & Connecticut Railroad, and for close to a year he disappeared from the news of the day in the Kingston papers. Pressure to build the Delhi & Middletown was removed by the construction of the branch of the New York & Oswego Midland from Walton to Delhi, and the former was never built. Work on the Rondout & Oswego continued. The graders built a magnificent horseshoe curve on a 3.2 percent grade on the side of Belle Ayr mountain and passed over the summit at an elevation of 1,885 feet. From the summit the grade descended at 3.08 percent for three miles to Griffin's Corners station, then by an easier 1.4 percent grade four miles down the mountain to the valley of the Bushkill and its junction with the Delaware's East Branch at Dean's Corners, later called Arkville. A mile and a half down river was Margaretville, a prosperous farm community which had contributed a great deal towards the cost of the Rondout & Oswego. It would have been a convenience for Margaretville if the railroad had gone through the town, but this involved three extra miles of construction and with the cost per mile running way above the estimates, doubling through Margaretville was out of the question. Not for 35 years would Margaretville have a railroad of its own.

On March 6, 1871, the railroad had its first serious accident. A construction train hauled by the locomotive *Pennsylvania* was returning to Kingston from the west end of the road. When it was a mile west of the Kingston depot the engine derailed and was ditched. A car loaded with heavy logs overturned, killing brakeman Michael Gannon and seriously injuring the engine crew. The cause was found to be worn flanges on the locomotive's driving wheels and because of this and other wear and tear the engine was never repaired. The wreck was only one of president Brodhead's worries that spring of 1871. A bill had been introduced in the New York State legislature making it mandatory for all railroads within the State to use rail of 70 lb. weight on mountain grades with sharp curves. Curiously enough, this bill was sponsored by Thomas Cornell. Whether it was vindictiveness on Cornell's part or concern for the safety of the railroad's passengers is not evident in the news dispatches, but the signing of the bill by the Governor forced the Rondout & Oswego to halt all tracklaying when they reached Big Indian, at the foot of the grade up Pine Hill. Here they waited for three months while the 70 lb. rails were ordered, manufactured and delivered.

The rails arrived late in June, and since the grade was ready, the tracklayers made good time. The road was ballasted and open for business to Dean's Corners on September 11, with the railhead two miles beyond there. The annual report published September 15 listed seven locomotives, nine passenger and baggage cars, and 90 freight cars of various types in service. During 1871, 113,763 passengers and 25,000 tons of freight were

Rondout & Oswego No. 7, built by Danforth in 1870, was mistakenly called a freight engine. It had no tender, a ton of coal being carried inside the oversized cab, with the water stored in side tanks underneath the running boards. It was probably used principally for switching in the Rondout yards. — THOMAS TABER COLLECTION

In this original wet plate negative scene, an Erie Railway train is testing the Wallkill Valley's bridge over Rondout Creek near Rosendale, on the day of its official opening in 1872. Note the crowd of stovepipe-hatted officials at the upper left, watching the test. Others are standing on the locomotive and the bridge supports. Below the third span is Lock No. 7 of the Delaware & Hudson Canal. — AUTHOR'S COLLECTION

carried, bringing in a net revenue of $50,000. By the time taxes and bond interest were deducted there was nothing left to add to the construction account, which was nearing zero.

Following the release of the annual report a campaign of vilification against Brodhead and certain of the directors was launched by the *Rondout Daily Freeman*, and in the course of this the *Freeman* exposed shortages in Brodhead's accounts as county treasurer and accused him of misappropriation of railroad bonds. The *Freeman* was definitely pro-Cornell, since he was its principal owner, and Cornell no doubt instigated the frequent editorials attacking Brodhead. Work on the railroad during this period slowed almost to a halt, the track being opened for traffic to Halcottville, milepost 53, on December 15. On that day Brodhead resigned as county treasurer, and S. D. Coykendall, Cornell's son-in-law, was appointed to the post. In January 1872 the railroad was opened to Roxbury, milepost 59, and Thomas Cornell was offered a directorship as a replacement for General George H. Sharpe, who had joined the board a year earlier. Cornell refused to serve on the same board with Brodhead and a few weeks later became president of the Wallkill Valley Railroad, which had been building from Montgomery towards Kingston but which had been stalled by factional difficulties of the same character as those which plagued the Rondout & Oswego.

In February 1872, in a move probably caused by desperation, the directors leased the uncompleted railroad to John A. Greene & Co., contractors, for two years. They were to operate it, continue the construction, and pay the interest on the bonds, the last of which had been sold to keep the construction crews going. On April 10, president John A. Brodhead resigned and was replaced by General Sharpe. The Farmers Loan & Trust Co. of New York, which represented a number of the bondholders including Thomas Cornell, insisted on new management. At this point, William B. Litchfield stepped into the picture. He was a contractor engaged in building the Syracuse & Chenango Valley Railroad and, when it was found that the Greene & Co. contract was illegal, he proposed to take over the unfinished contracts and extend his railroad from Syracuse beyond its original goal of Earlville, New York, to Oneonta and a connection with the Rondout & Oswego. General Sharpe introduced a bill in the New York State assembly

reorganizing the Rondout & Oswego and changing its name to the New York, Kingston & Syracuse Railroad. The Governor signed the bill on May 9, 1872, and the new company floated a new $4,000,-000 consolidated mortgage bond issue, the proceeds being used to pay off the old bond issues and provide another two-million to complete the railroad.

Litchfield continued grading the railroad north of Roxbury in the spring of 1872, following the Delaware's East Branch to its junction with the Bear Kill, then passing through a spectacular cleft in the Moresville range at the village of Moresville, milepost 65, later known as Grand Gorge. The grade made a 90 degree curve to the west and down into the valley of the Bear Kill. From this point through South Gilboa past the twin Mayham ponds, sources of the Bear Kill and the Delaware's West Branch, to the summit involved a two percent grade for nearly seven miles, reaching an altitude of 1,846 feet at the top. The descent into the valley of the Delaware was easy for the graders and, having passed Stamford, they began a new climb to the summit of a range of hills north of the town, past Harpersfield to a point near West Harpersfield where the work ceased for the winter. Litchfield must have had a very small tracklaying crew, for the first passenger train to reach Moresville arrived on August 8, 1872. The track was laid in front of the new station in Stamford on November 18, but heavy rains interfered with the ballasting operations and the first passenger train to reach Stamford left Kingston on December 12. Great excitement prevailed in Stamford on that day, cannons were fired and a band added its music to the roars of the crowd surrounding the station when the train pulled in.

Litchfield ceased all tracklaying at Stamford, even though six miles of grade past Harpersfield was ready for the rails. How different the history of the railroad might have been had Litchfield added that six miles, but having finished 75 miles at an average of $40,000 per mile, a total of $3,245,921 had been spent, more than had been raised from bond sales due to the depressed value of all railroad securities at that time. Another million would be needed to extend the line to Oneonta. How to raise this sum was to remain the unanswered question for over a quarter of a century.

At the end of July 1872 the Farmers Loan &

Trust Co. of New York began proceedings to fore-close on the bonds of the New York, Kingston & Syracuse Railroad because the interest on 900 bonds had not been paid. President Sharpe and Litchfield insisted that they had been paid up to date. It is difficult for the historian to condense into a few words the battle which was waged in the newspapers during August and September of that year. Suffice it to say that the first salvo was fired by Sharpe and Litchfield in the form of a suit brought against Thomas Cornell, S. D. Coykendall and treasurer Anthony Benson charging the grossest of malfeasance when they were officers of the railroad, such as misappropriation of bonds, theft of money from the treasury, etc., and the full text of this suit was reprinted in the August 29, 1872, *New York Herald*. The *Herald* had the good grace to print both Cornell's and Benson's denials of all the allegations the following day. Cornell said in his statement that he had been threatened with this suit if he did not at once persuade the Farmers Loan & Trust Co. to drop their foreclosure proceedings. Since all the statements made in the suit were untrue, and that he had nothing to conceal, Cornell refused to intercede with the bank. The *Rondout Freeman* squared off to defend Cornell and the *Rondout Journal* became the mouthpiece of General Sharpe and Litchfield. The probability of a libel suit against the latter two gentlemen must have brought them to their senses, for an armistice was privately reached by all parties concerned. The suit against Cornell was postponed, the foreclosure suit was not pressed by the bank, and the battle of words gradually ceased.

Litchfield operated the railroad as lessee through most of 1873 without doing any construction work, and since the earnings were not sufficient to pay the railroad's debts, things soon came to a head. Three creditors of the railroad, the Spuyten Duyvil Rolling Mills of New York, Ernest Caylus & Co. of the same city, and the Danforth Locomotive & Machine Co., obtained judgment of $147,000 against Litchfield and the sheriff of Ulster County moved in. The directors of the railroad had by this time become disenchanted with Litchfield and agreed with the Farmers Loan & Trust Co. that he must go. Litchfield was told to turn over all his contract papers and documents to a representative of the Farmers Loan & Trust Co. and, when he refused to do so, to quote the reporter, "he attempted to make forcible resistance but was overpowered and compelled to submit." He was rudely kicked out of the company's office and his lease of the railroad was cancelled. By compromise, the creditors were paid in part and, to satisfy the bondholders, the railroad petitioned for a receivership.

On November 28, 1873, E. M. Brigham of the Farmers Loan & Trust Co. was appointed receiver. He made further payments to the creditors, operated the railroad through 1874 and paid $90,000 in back interest. The panic of 1873 was by then having its effect, resulting in a 30 percent drop in the receipts of the New York, Kingston & Syracuse Railroad in 1874. Litchfield's dream of a railroad from Syracuse to the Hudson River collapsed like a punctured balloon, for the Syracuse & Chenango Valley Railroad became bankrupt in 1873, and, though it reached Earlville in 1874, Litchfield lost all he and his brother in Cazenovia had invested in it. Years later it became a branch of the West Shore Railroad and has long since been abandoned.

On June 12, 1875, at the request of the bondholders, the New York, Kingston & Syracuse Railroad was placed on the auction block in New York City and bought by the Farmers Loan & Trust Co. for $750,000. Immediately after the auction the railroad was reorganized as the Ulster & Delaware Railroad, with Thomas Cornell, president, Samuel

NEW YORK, KINGSTON AND SYRACUSE R. R.									
E. M. Brigham, Receiver.				F. J. Hecker, Gen. Supt., Rondout, N. Y.					
Pas.	Exs.	Pas.	Mls	*June 8*, 1874.	Mls	Pas.	Exs.	Pas.	
A. M.	P. M.	A. M.		(*New York time.*)		A. M.	P. M.	P. M.	N. B.—Trains marked + run daily, except Sunday; § Sunday only.
§6 00	†2 40	†7 00	0	lve...**Rondout**¹..arr.	74	10 15	5 30	5 45	
6 15	2 57	7 14	4	.....**Kingston**².....	70	9 57	5 15	5 30	
6 35	3 18	7 32	9	.....West Hurley....	65	9 32	4 57	5 10	
6 44	3 28	7 41	12	.....Beaverkill.....	62	9 20	4 47	4 59	
7 00	3 45	7 56	17	.....Olive Bridge....	57	9 02	4 31	4 43	
7 05	3 49	8 00	18	.......Shokan.....	56	8 57	4 27	4 39	
7 12	3 57	8 07	21	.....Boiceville......	53	8 49	4 20	4 32	
7 23	4 12	8 17	24	...Mount Pleasant...	50	8 37	4 10	4 21	
7 31	4 22	8 25	27	.....**Phœnicia**³....	47	8 27	4 02	4 12	
7 44	....	....	32	.....Fox Hollow.....	42	8 10	....	3 59	
7 50	4 41	8 41	33	....Shandaken.....	41	8 04	3 45	3 54	
8 08	5 00	8 58	36	.....Big Indian.....	38	7 53	3 37	3 45	
8 23	5 18	9 12	39	.....Pine Hill.....	35	7 35	3 23	3 30	
....	5 27	....	41	......Summit......	33	7 24	....	....	
8 43	5 41	9 30	44	...Griffin's Corners..	30	7 13	3 05	3 11	
8 55	5 56	9 41	48	..**Dean's Corners**⁴..	26	6 59	2 53	2 59	
9 02	6 04	....	51	....Kelly's Corners...	23	6 47	....	2 50	
9 07	6 10	9 51	53	....Halcottville.....	21	6 41	2 40	2 45	
....	6 21	....	57	...Stratton's Falls...	17	6 29	....	....	
9 23	6 32	10 06	59	.....Roxbury.....	15	6 22	2 28	2 30	
9 39	6 55	10 21	65	.....**Moresville**⁵.....	9	5 59	2 12	2 14	
10 05	7 25	10 45	74	.....**Stamford**⁶.....	0	†5 25	†1 45	§1 45	
A. M.	P. M.	A. M.		[ARRIVE] [LEAVE]		A. M.	P. M.	P. M.	

CONNECTIONS.—¹ With New York Central & Hudson River R. R. also, with steamers on the Hudson River. ² With Walkill Valley R. R. ³ With stages for Hunter. ⁴ With stages for Margaretville, Andes and Delhi, daily, except Sunday. ⁵ With stages for Gilboa, Prattsville, and Windham Centre, daily, except Sunday. ⁶ With stages for Hobart.

In this 1874 summer timetable of the New York, Kingston & Syracuse Railroad, Dean's Corners had not been changed to Arkville and Grand Gorge was still called Moresville.—AUTHOR'S COLLECTION

Decker Coykendall, vice-president, and Anthony Benson, who had been the treasurer until General Sharpe fired him in 1872, got his old position back. Cornell had owned over $500,000 of the bonds since 1870 and had obviously been working very closely with the Farmers Loan & Trust Co. ever since. The stockholders of the old company found themselves in possession of worthless paper representing a loss of over a million dollars which laid heavily on rich and poor alike, for the bulk of the stock purchases had been made by the townships as previously related. The holders of the seven percent bonds fared much better; they received $1,250,000 of stock in the new company and retained approximately the same amount of the bonds which the new company agreed to honor. For tax purposes the railroad was now valued at $2,000,000, about 60 percent of its cost.

In the five years since Cornell had left the Rondout & Oswego, he had built two railroads. The Wallkill Valley Railroad had been completed to Kingston in 1872 and, on April 4, 1875, the Rhinebeck & Connecticut Railroad was opened to Boston Corners. Now Cornell was ready to devote his time and energy to the Ulster & Delaware, with the help of his son-in-law, Samuel Decker Coykendall and the latter's brother George, who became superintendent of the U. & D. Samuel Coykendall had become associated with Cornell in 1859 at the age of 23 and had married Cornell's daughter Mary.

Cornell found himself saddled with a 75 mile railroad which went uphill or down throughout its length. Except for a few sections near Kingston,

there was not a single respectable tangent in the whole railroad; just one curve after another and most of them on grades as high as 3.2 percent. To haul the trains there were seven locomotives, two of which were classed as freight engines and the other five were passenger engines. The latter had low tonnage ratings on the big hills and trains of any size had to be double-headed or pushed from the rear. Eastbound trains from Arkville to Summit climbed 517 feet in seven miles; westbound trains climbed nearly 1,100 feet in 14 miles between Phoenicia and Summit, so helpers were needed on both sides of the mountain whenever there was heavy traffic. Though there were grades west of Arkville to Stamford, they were all well under two percent and engines hauled their trains usually without assistance.

During the summer of 1875 there were two passenger trains each way daily from Rondout to Stamford; one in the morning and a so-called "Express" in the afternoon, the latter making the trip in 4 hours 45 minutes, with 19 stops, whereas the morning train, which was nameless, covered the distance in one hour less running time, with three less stops. There was one train each way on Sunday. The afternoon westbound train left after the northbound Hudson River steamboat from New York had docked at Rhinecliff and passengers destined for the Catskills had ferried across the river to Rondout. The return train made connections with the southbound river boats by leaving Stamford at 7 A.M. River boats of any size could not dock at Rondout; hence the necessity of using Rhinecliff as a land point for Kingston. Kingston

Erie Railway No. 99, Hinkley-built in 1851, was the Wallkill Valley's first locomotive, used in work train service. This early photograph was made at Montgomery, New York in 1871. —WALTER A. LUCAS COLLECTION

Point was not to come into being for 20 years, as we shall see.

During the first five years of Cornell's second try with the Ulster & Delaware he almost completely reorganized it, from the employees and their duties to the rails and roadbed. Most of the original English wrought-iron rails were replaced with 70 lb. steel, especially between Rondout and West Hurley, and operating expenses were curtailed wherever possible. The latter included the layoff of some of the shop employees at Rondout, resulting in a fire which completely destroyed the shops on April 26, 1876, with a loss of $20,000 on buildings insured for $13,000. Arson committed by discharged employees was given as the cause of the fire, as was the destruction by fire of the wooden bridge across Esopus Creek two miles west of the center of Kingston on June 7, 1876. The western section of the railroad was isolated for 10 days until a temporary trestle could be hastily erected. The fire was blamed on striking employees at a bluestone quarry near West Hurley who sought to prevent the railroad from handling shipments from the quarry.

At this point the Wallkill Valley Railroad became so involved with the Ulster & Delaware through Thomas Cornell's activities that its position should be briefly outlined. A group headed by F. S. McKinstry of New Paltz, New York, organized the Wallkill Valley Railroad in 1866 to build a line from Montgomery, New York, terminus of the Erie Railway's Goshen branch, to Kingston, a distance of 33 miles. After a little over 12 miles of track had been laid north of Montgomery work ceased late in 1869 due to lack of financial support by the communities along the proposed line. The road had been built to a gauge of six feet to conform with that of the Erie, and the only rolling stock it owned was one second-hand engine bought from the Erie and a few flat cars.

The Erie agreed to operate the railroad with its own equipment, but gave it no financial assistance. Early in 1872, a number of Kingston businessmen, including Thomas Cornell, became interested in the railroad which resulted in Cornell becoming the road's president in charge of completing the line to Kingston. The railroad was leased to the Erie for operating purposes on January 1, 1872, and construction north of New Paltz was immediately begun. The countryside through which the

railroad was to pass gave Cornell only one problem, and that was the crossing of Rondout Creek at Rosendale. Here the valley narrowed so that it was a tight squeeze for the Delaware & Hudson canal to share the available space with the creek. To cross this chasm, it was necessary to build a steel bridge with a centerspan of 105 feet, 150 feet above Rondout Creek. While the bridge sections were being built at Paterson, New Jersey, Cornell sublet the contract for the Rosendale-Kingston section to Dolby & Co., which completed the railroad to Greenkill Avenue in Kingston on November 7, 1872, a few days before the bridge was finished. Within a week the track was laid to the new station on Union Avenue in Kingston and the Erie began running trains direct to Goshen, where connections were made with through trains east and west. Starting with the summer season of 1873, the Erie and the Wallkill Valley ran through parlor cars and coaches from Jersey City to Kingston and the Ulster & Delaware trains all stopped at Wallkill Valley Junction for transfer of passengers. Kingston now had a direct rail connection with the outside world, but it was the world of the broad gauge Erie and there could be no interchange of freight cars with the Ulster & Delaware, nor could the repair facilities of the latter at Rondout be shared.

Having finished the Wallkill Valley, Cornell resigned as president but retained his directorship and devoted all his time to completing the Rhinebeck & Connecticut Railroad. The Erie went into receivership in 1875, and as an economy move, discontinued running the Wallkill Valley trains through to Goshen. It was therefore necessary for Kingston residents to change trains at Montgomery and again at Goshen, causing hours of delay on a journey to New York. This inconvenience sent most of the summer boarder business back to the river boats, but there was another factor which contributed to the annual operating losses. In February 1875 a freight train broke through a wooden bridge near Walden, several cars falling into a stream and wrecking the bridge, but on September 1, 1875 another bridge wreck involved an excursion train heavily loaded with passengers. The train was returning to Kingston from a camp meeting and while crossing a wooden bridge near Shawangunk, five passenger cars were derailed as the bridge gave way, two of the cars rolling over and seriously injuring 26 passengers while 50

An unissued stock certificate of The Ulster & Delaware Railroad Company, printed in 1875, recently came to light. The stock steel engraving of a railroad scene could very well depict the Ulster & Delaware between Rondout and Kingston except for the double track in the foreground. — AUTHOR'S COLLECTION

others were cut and bruised. The damage suits from this wreck, and notice of cancellation of the lease by the Erie in January 1877 placed the Wallkill Valley directors in an untenable position. Notice of sale of the railroad at auction was posted in March 1877, and on June 5th the railroad was sold to the bondholders committee, represented by Thomas Cornell, for $128,000.

The Erie had begun narrowing its broad gauge main line to standard gauge in 1876, but did nothing about changing the gauge of its branches. The Wallkill Valley directors had purchased two new standard gauge locomotives from Danforth in June 1876, to the identical design of the passenger engines on the Ulster & Delaware, but they were held at the factory for over a year. After the Wallkill Valley Railroad Company was formed at Rondout on July 2, 1877, with Thomas Cornell as president, plans for narrowing the gauge were announced immediately, the gauge change taking place during the week of September 21st. A third rail for the Erie broad gauge cars was left in place from Montgomery to New Paltz, but freight cars loaded on the Ulster & Delaware or points north of New Paltz had to be unloaded at a transfer platform in Montgomery.

After the change in gauge, all Wallkill Valley trains terminated their runs at Rondout, and Cornell's "Man Friday," James H. Jones, superintendent of the Rhinebeck & Connecticut and head of the Rondout shops, now became superintendent of the Wallkill Valley. For five years from 1877 this arrangement continued and locomotives of the Rhinebeck & Connecticut in need of repairs were brought over to Rondout on Cornell's barges. The Erie was finally persuaded to lay a third rail between Montgomery and Goshen and in October 1879, a year after its main line was so equipped, the bottleneck of the gauges was eliminated. Jones had his troubles when the Wallkill Valley trains began using the Ulster & Delaware tracks from Kingston to Rondout. On June 22, 1878, a Wallkill Valley gravel train ran through a switch which had been left open by an Ulster & Delaware freight which was switching at the junction of the two roads, and the trains collided head-on. Both engines were badly damaged, a fireman was killed and three other trainmen were injured. New operating rules eliminated this hazard, for there were no further accidents at this point.

To handle milk shipments from dairies along the Ulster & Delaware and the Wallkill Valley, Cornell bought three milk cars, and used the old steamboat *William Cook*, called the "Milkmaid" by local residents, to transport milk to the New York market. When the *William Cook* broke down in 1880, the old side-wheeler *Armenia* replaced it. Milk shipments over the Ulster & Delaware grew until by 1900 over 30,000 tons of milk a year were hauled. This was small compared with the New York, Ontario & Western, which hauled five times as much in 1900, but then the N.Y.O. & W. was five times as large as the Ulster & Delaware.

Cornell spent nearly $300,000 in the first five years of his stewardship for improvements to the track and roadbed. Passenger traffic rose from 83,000 in 1875 to 111,000 in 1880, with the freight above 100,000 tons for the first time. The 1880 fiscal year showed a $12,000 surplus, the Ulster & Delaware was solvent, bond interest was being paid on time, and traffic was on the increase. All this was accomplished with the rolling stock Cornell found on the road in 1875. He did not buy any new equipment except the three milk cars during those years, preferring to make-do until the railroad was on a paying basis.

The year 1880 produced a change in Cornell's life pattern, and in that of the Catskills. Somewhat reluctantly Cornell agreed to run for Congress on the Republican ticket in the 1880 elections. He had already served one term in 1867-1868 and this time he made very few campaign speeches, yet was elected in the Garfield landslide by a large majority. Cornell's interest in the Ulster & Delaware and the development of the Catskills as a summer playground for city dwellers did not wane with his departure for Washington, and he kept in touch with developments at home through correspondence with Samuel D. Coykendall and by frequent weekend visits.

In an age when the one-night guest was unknown, vacationing New Yorkers flocked to the Catskills with loads of Saratoga trunks, grips, and hatboxes as they moved in for the season. The Catskill Mountain House was the monarch of the cliffs facing the Hudson River. It commanded a beautiful view and was surrounded by acres of park, wooded walks and lakes. — LIBRARY OF CONGRESS

3

COMPETITION

URING THE summer of 1880 the Catskill Mountain House was in its 57th season. Except for the smaller Laurel House and the Overlook Mountain House, the Catskill Mountain House was the monarch of the cliffs facing the Hudson — a great white building standing 2,250 feet above the river. It commanded a view of 10,000 square miles, if one may believe the hotel's advertisements, and was surrounded by thousands of acres of parks, wooded walks, carriage roads and lakes. The relatively open area in back of the hotel had been called Pine Orchard, because of a growth of small pines there, and which had been removed when the hotel was landscaped.

Most patrons of the hotel rode the Hudson River steamboats to Catskill Landing and went thence by stage to the hotel. The last few miles were over a steep and winding road with a brief level stretch while passing through Sleepy Hollow, legendary domain of Rip Van Winkle — a rough and bone-shattering ride at times, the price hotel patrons had to pay to reach such a scenic spot. Some rode the Hudson River Railroad trains to Catskill Station, then ferried across the Hudson to Catskill village to board the stages, though the bulk of the

passengers preferred the river boats because one transfer of baggage was saved.

The Catskill Mountain House was owned by Charles L. Beach of Catskill village. He bought it in the mid-1840s from a group of Catskill citizens who had built it in 1823-24 and opened it in the latter year. Born in 1808, Beach spent his early years working for his father, Erastus Beach, who owned and operated stage lines in the Hudson River valley. Accumulating a modest fortune by the time he was 35, Charles Beach bought the Mountain House from the surviving founders and proceeded to rebuild and enlarge the hotel until it could accommodate 400 guests.

Having passed the age of 70, Beach was now enjoying the fruits of his labor. He was on very friendly terms with Alfred Van Santvoord, president of the new Hudson River Day Line, which operated a splendid fleet of white ships which included the *Mary Powell*, once owned by Thomas Cornell. In a season, Beach could count on serving hundreds of families who came up-river in Van Santvoord's side-wheelers and often stayed the entire summer season. As the 1880 season closed on September 1, Beach heard some very disturbing news. He was no longer to enjoy the distinction of owning the only large summer hotel in the Catskills, for two new hotels were to be built before

"The Laurel House and Cauterskill Falls" was the title of this early woodcut. —AUTHOR'S COLLECTION

This woodcut of the Hotel Kaaterskill from an 1884 summer guide is the product of a wild flight of imagination by the artist, for he shows a train climbing up the face of the cliff below the hotel. — AUTHOR'S COLLECTION

the next season opened, one of them right in his own backyard.

The less threatening of these projects was planned as a magnificent structure to be built on Monka Hill, a short distance north of Summit station on the Ulster & Delaware. It was to be called the Summit Mountain Hotel, with rooms for 450 guests and would be ready in less than a year. This would be the third large hotel built near the Ulster & Delaware's line, the others being the Overlook, accommodating 150 persons near the summit of Overlook Mountain north of Woodstock, and the Tremper House, with rooms for 250 persons, in the village of Phoenicia. Though this new hotel would not have the view of the Hudson River valley enjoyed by patrons of the Overlook or the Mountain House, it would stand on a terrace near the peak of a hill 250 feet higher in elevation than the Mountain House. Its modern facilities, running water in each room, suites with private bath, and rail transportation available from the Hudson River almost to the doors of the hotel, would attract patrons who valued creature comforts more than a river view. Renamed the Grand Hotel before it opened, the architect and contractor was James A. Wood, who designed the Tremper House, and the hotel company was headed by D. C. Overbaugh, a Kingston coal dealer. Thomas Cornell backed the project by subscribing to a fourth of the $100,000 bond issue which was sold to raise money for immediate construction, work on the foundations starting in mid-September of 1880.

The Summit Mountain Hotel would be competition enough for Beach, but at a meeting with friends in Saugerties, halfway between Kingston and Catskill, Philadelphia millionaire George Harding announced his plan to build a new hotel at Sunset Rock, on South Mountain a mile south of the Catskill Mountain House. Harding stated that he had been a regular patron of the Mountain House for 18 years, had spent $4,000 or more each season at the hotel, and that lately he had met with many discourtesies from Beach, culminating in an open rupture a short time ago. Harding said he would build a new wagon road from Palenville, at the foot of Kaaterskill Clove, to the hotel site and was studying the feasibility of building a railroad from either Saugerties Landing or Malden, on the Hudson River, to Palenville.

Work was begun on the wagon road on September 1, and surveyors appeared at Sunset Rock the

Stony Clove Notch viewed by the artist from the south side, with the wagon road sharing the narrow opening with the railroad. —JOHN B. HUNGERFORD COLLECTION

same day to lay out the site of the hotel on land which Beach had not had the foresight to buy. The businessmen of Catskill village and the owner of the Catskill Mountain House shared the general alarm at these developments, especially when Harding's agents released a press statement that the hotel would have rooms for 1,000 persons. At a meeting in Catskill towards the middle of September a plan was crystallized to build a 3-foot gauge railroad from the river at Catskill to South Cairo and from there along the foot of the mountains to the village of Palenville, intersecting the Mountain House road near the beginning of the steep climb up the face of North Mountain. This would halve the time necessary to travel from river boats to the hotel and, by continuing on to Palenville, probably head off Harding's plan to build his own railroad to Palenville.

Articles of incorporation of the Catskill Mountain Railroad were filed on September 16, 1880. During the rest of the year capital stock totalling $77,800 was paid in, Charles L. Beach was elected president of the proposed railroad, and in May 1881 a $200,000 issue of six percent, 20-year, first mortgage coupon bonds was sold. Surveys were made and work was begun on the railroad grade by rehabilitating the abandoned grade of the Canajoharie & Catskill from Catskill village to a point near South Cairo. Here the survey left the old grade and continued southwest towards the base of the mountains, to the terminus at Palen-

ville, 15.73 miles. There were to be no tunnels on the new railroad and only a few heavy rock cuttings. Three bridges would be required; across Catskill Creek at the old railway crossing, another at Cooke's Dam and a third at Van Hoesen's Falls.

In the meantime, Thomas Cornell had not been idle, for in October 1880, no doubt after a conference with George Harding, he hired surveyors who laid out the line for a railroad from Phoenicia on the Ulster & Delaware, north through Stony Clove Notch to the town of Hunter, with a branch from a point near the Notch to a terminal one mile west of the Catskill Mountain House and directly below the site of Harding's new hotel. Newspaper accounts stated that this railroad would be 3-foot gauge the same as the Catskill Mountain Railroad. Whether Beach and his group chose the narrow gauge before the idea came to Thomas Cornell is a matter of guesswork, but in 1880 the weekly journals of the railroad industry were filled with accounts of narrow gauge construction in the far west, in Colorado, in Mexico, and a narrow gauge trunkline, the Texas & St. Louis Railroad. There were also narrow gauge railroads in the Boston area, in the Adirondacks and in northwestern Pennsylvania. Economy in construction and operation of narrow gauge railroads was the big selling point and soon the Catskills would have no less than five of them.

Working through the winter of 1880-81 an army of men built the Hotel Kaaterskill, with George

Harding making weekly trips from Philadelphia to the hotel site. Wagon trains left Saugerties and Catskill almost daily with building material for the hotel, and in June 1881 ten wagon-loads of furniture for the Kaaterskill were going up the mountain each day. A legend has been handed down in Catskill concerning Lampman's Lumber Yard there, which furnished a considerable amount of building materials for the Kaaterskill. Some of the teamsters hauling the material to the top of the mountain would sell nails, lumber and other supplies to the farmers enroute and, quite naturally, Harding would be billed for the full amount. It was also said that when these wagons became bogged down by muddy roads, they were lightened by pitching the heaviest of the loads, usually kegs of nails, into the Clove at Harding's expense. Another tale is that the lathers finishing the interiors of the hundreds of rooms would carry bundles

The impressive Hotel Kaaterskill nearly dwarfed the old Catskill Mountain House because of its great size and commanding location. The hotel, which opened in 1881, called itself "The largest mountain hotel in the world," and offered international cuisine as well as a splendid view. The buildings on the right of the two large towers were later additions. — LIBRARY OF CONGRESS

of lath to the top floor of the hotel and push them down through the partitions, thus padding the cost. The hotel opened on July 10, but guests were limited to 400 as the wings of the building were not yet finished. The very presence of the Kaaterskill, towering above the Mountain House, must have been a great aggravation to Charles L. Beach, especially since things had not been going well in the construction of the Catskill Mountain Railroad. Grading had begun in January 1881, but there had been two stormy sessions of the directors of the railroad in Catskill and the details leaked to the newspapers. It seems that some of the directors objected to sharing in the financing of that part of the railroad from South Cairo to Palenville on the premise that this should be paid for by Charles L. Beach, since it was for his express benefit. Another group of Greene County men had organized the South Cairo & East Durham Railroad, to connect with the Catskill Mountain Railroad, and the line south of South Cairo was regarded as a branch. These differences may very well have been the reason why the announced completion date of the railroad to Palenville was not realized, for during 1881 the Catskill Mountain Railroad was graded and the bridges were built, but no equipment was ordered and no track was laid.

In the interim, the Stony Clove & Catskill Mountain Railroad was organized on January 18, 1881, with Thomas Cornell as president and most of the directors were also directors of the Ulster & Delaware. There were no factional disputes in this operation, financing was easily arranged, and the wood choppers began clearing a way for the graders up the valley of the Stony Clove in March 1881. By April there were 400 men working on the grade, most of them newly arrived Italians who found the climate of the high Catskills not as amenable as southern Italy. In April a second-hand locomotive, new platform cars and box cars and finally two new passenger coaches from Jackson & Sharp, arrived. Tracklaying began in Phoenicia and the railhead was several miles north when the Grand Hotel opened for business on June 22, 1881. The tracklayers reached Edgewood, 8.5 miles from Phoenicia, early in August and the line was opened for business on August 18. A passenger train consisting of a box car for the baggage and the two

The new Grand Hotel, located 39 miles from Kingston, was a stately structure which accommodated 450 guests. The management billed the hotel as "The Most Modern Equipped Hotel In The Catskills." A superior grill and rathskeller, a symphony orchestra and weekly tennis tournaments were major attractions. The long central section with its two-storied porch provided the rocking chair brigade with a splendid view of the countryside.—LIBRARY OF CONGRESS

new coaches met all Ulster & Delaware trains, and the stages for Hunter and other points on the mountain top met the narrow gauge train at Edgewood, cutting the travel time from Phoenicia to Hunter by over an hour. At this time, Thomas Cornell, who had been elected to Congress the previous November, resigned as president and director of the Stony Clove & Catskill Mountain Railroad and his son-in-law, Samuel D. Coykendall was elected in his place. During the two years Cornell was in Washington Coykendall was in charge of all three of Cornell's standard gauge railroads besides the narrow gauge, as is evidenced by Coykendall's signature on legal documents and annual passes in 1880 and 1881.

Labor shortages prevented completion of the railroad to Hunter in 1881. Many of the Italians disliked working on hard rock and returned to New York, but the grading up through the Notch continued and the track was laid through the Notch in December. The Italians complained about the icy cold water and refused to bathe, while the locals who were working alongside of the Italians were enraged by a new type of flea never before seen in the Catskills and which attacked the natives with great relish. Snow hampered the work, but it did not prevent the new furniture factory of H. B. Lockwood & Co. from staging a grand opening at Edgewood on March 1, 1882. Special trains on the Ulster & Delaware and the

The Stony Clove & Catskill Mountain's elusive *Gretchen* No. 2 in front of Hunter station, probably in the summer of 1882. The air compressor is mounted in an unusual place; underneath the rear of the cab. Warren Todd is the engineer with the oil can; O. E. (Doly) Hoffman, fireman, standing in the gangway; Charles Van Demark, conductor and Charles Ford, trainman are two of the three men standing by the tender. — DEGOLYER FOUNDATION COLLECTION

narrow gauge brought 200 guests to Edgewood, and those from Hunter, where Lockwood had another factory, came by train from the Notch, down the hill to Edgewood. As soon as the snow melted construction was resumed north of the Notch and the railroad was so nearly ready for traffic that a special train carrying the Reverend Henry Ward Beecher and party arrived in Hunter on June 15, 1882. Regular passenger trains began operating on June 24, but the track terminated at the east end of Hunter. The remaining mile of line and the new station were ready on August 29 when a five-car excursion train from Phoenicia arrived at the Hunter depot where a brass band and a large crowd were waiting. A second locomotive had been leased earlier in the year and four of the road's seven passenger cars, called observation cars by the press, which said they were similar to those used on the Coney Island Railroad, were delivered by Jackson & Sharp the previous April. These cars were open on the sides, with seats across their width, and were probably made from the same drawings as similar cars ordered by the Catskill Mountain Railroad. They were never enclosed and, when sold and shipped away years later, still had their running boards and side curtains. Cars of similar design have been in use for the past 12 years on the steam railroad in California's Disneyland.

The distance from Phoenicia to Hunter was 14.4 miles, with Hunter 800 feet higher than Phoenicia. A ride over this line from the passengers' viewpoint was spectacular; from an operating angle it must have been a headache that first year, until the track had been evened up and the crews had become familiar with the hazards of steep grades. The climb in the first ten miles was 1,273 feet to the source of Stony Clove Creek in Stony Clove Notch. In places the grade was 180 feet to the mile, including a rise of 140 feet in the first mile out of Phoenicia, originally over a trestle which was later filled in with rock from excavations along the walls of Stony Clove gorge. As the railroad reached the summit in the Notch at an elevation of 2,069 feet, Hunter Mountain (4,025 ft.) was directly west and Plateau Mountain (3,955 ft.) was east. The track was placed on a ledge blasted out of solid rock for some distance south of the Notch and the ride was reminiscent of Clear Creek Canyon west of Denver on the Colorado Central Railroad. After passing the Notch the line descended into the valley of Schoharie Creek, then down-stream to Hunter, 1,602 feet above sea level. Here at Hunter, stages for Hensonville and Windham carried vacationers to the many hotels and boarding houses which had been built in anticipation of the coming of the railroad.

Passengers for the Hotel Kaaterskill and points in between detrained at Tannersville Junction where waiting stages transported them to their destinations. The Hotel Kaaterskill had been completed during the previous winter and was now prepared to handle 1,014 guests. All of this activity had not been lost on Charles L. Beach and the directors of the Catskill Mountain Railroad, for in May 1882 the first locomotive, the *S. Sherwood Day* No. 1, arrived in Catskill from the Dickson Locomotive Works. Of the American or 4-4-0 type, it was equipped with Eames vacuum brakes, a system which had proved successful on trains of the New York elevated lines. Soon the excursion cars ordered from Jackson & Sharp of Wilmington, Delaware, began to arrive. Similar in construction to the "observation cars" of the Stony Clove & Catskill Mountain, they were open at the sides, with 14 seats crosswise to hold 70 passengers. Curtains were to be lowered in case of rain. The car roofs were curved slightly across the width of the cars, and they lacked a clerestory. Later these cars were fully enclosed and equipped with conventional seats, reducing the number of persons a car could seat but providing more comfort and space for luggage. Four baggage cars were delivered in June and later four enclosed coaches arrived. The freight cars were on the scene before the first locomotive was steamed up.

Artist's drawing of the Stony Clove as seen from Hunter.
— JOHN B. HUNGERFORD COLLECTION

Catskill Mountain Railroad No. 1, the S. *Sherwood Day,* poses on the trestle across the marshes west of Catskill Landing, before a wreck ruined its diamond stack. The cylinder on the top of the cab is used in connection with the Eames vacuum brake system, to reduce the noise of the exhaust steam when the brakes were released. — DEGOLYER FOUNDATION COLLECTION

Tracklaying began in earnest at Catskill Landing on June 3, 1882, and the track reached Lawrenceville, nearly 12 miles distant, in early July. Mountain House station, two miles beyond, was not reached until the end of August, but ballasting had been finished to Lawrenceville and passenger service to South Cairo and Lawrenceville was begun on July 29. Two days later disaster struck the railroad. The early morning train, hauled by the S. *Sherwood Day* No. 1 was proceeding towards Catskill from South Cairo, with the locomotive running backwards, when the engine was derailed at the crossing of the Leed's toll road a mile and a half east of South Cairo. When the dust had settled the engine was upside down on one side of the track and the tender on the other side. The first coach was slightly damaged, but fortunately the passengers and the engine crew escaped with minor injuries. The driving wheels of the engine continued to revolve at high speed and the engineer had to crawl through the clouds of steam with an iron rod, poking at the throttle until the steam was shut off. The derailment was caused by the planking of the toll road crossing being laid too close to the rails. This was an easily remedied situation, but not so with the locomotive, for it suffered an estimated $3,000 damage and it was obviously going to be out of service for the rest of the season. The other locomotive, the *John T. Mann* No. 2, operated all the trains that could be run, either passenger or construction, for the remainder of the season, which as of September 30 produced a gross income of $8,105 and a net after operating expenses of $2,716. The loss of one engine had so hampered construction beyond Lawrenceville that when work ceased for the winter on November 15, the line from Mountain House Station to Palenville was still incomplete.

The first meeting of the directors of the Stony Clove & Catskill Mountain Railroad, held on September 30, 1882, was a happy one. By this time, 32,397 passengers had been carried, 5,000 tons of freight had been hauled and the company had a surplus of over $6,000 after all interest and other expenses had been paid. The railroad had cost $278,000 including rolling stock, of which $148,000 had been financed by the sale of coupon bonds. The railroad was an assured success and the Hotel Kaaterskill equally so. Most important to the residents in the high country was the fact that the railroad would operate through the winter, whereas

The bridge at the third crossing of Catskill Creek in Austin's Glen. The man sitting on the rail in the foreground is Thomas E. Jones, General Passenger Agent. — DEGOLYER FOUNDATION LIBRARY

The first railroad bridge across Catskill Creek is still in use as a pedestrian and utility crossing. The West Shore Railroad bridge crosses in the background. — GERALD M. BEST

A later picture of the *S. Sherwood Day* No. 1, with its capped stack and new initials on the tender.
— AUTHOR'S COLLECTION

the Catskill Mountain Railroad closed for the winter in November 1882. Thomas Cornell had not run for re-election to Congress in that month and, no doubt urged by hotel owner George Harding, he organized the Kaaterskill Railroad on November 25, 1882. It would be built to 3-foot gauge, and would run from Tannersville Junction on the Stony Clove & Catskill Mountain to Kaaterskill Station, a half-mile below the imposing hotel on South Mountain. Surveyed in December 1882, grading began while the snow was still on the ground. Following east up Schoharie Creek to its junction with Gooseberry Creek, the railroad had a ruling grade of 2.5 percent but averaged only 55 feet per mile. Passing south of Tannersville, it went over a ridge into the valley of Kaaterskill Creek at Haines' Falls, to end at the west tip of South Lake,

not quite a mile west of the Mountain House. Kaaterskill Station, at an elevation of 2,150 feet, was 400 feet above Kaaterskill Junction, the new name for Tannersville Junction. Construction work progressed so smoothly, since the Italians had left for greener pastures, that the railroad opened for traffic on June 25, 1883. The first train was a special from Phoenicia with president S. D. Coykendall, his sons and their grandfather, Thomas Cornell. George Harding met them at Laurel House where they had a mid-day dinner, then the party proceeded to the Hotel Kaaterskill, returning to Rondout that evening. In justice to the Italians, they were unaccustomed to below zero temperatures and their complaints about the lack of heat and hot water in their shacks on the mountain were no doubt justified.

Kaaterskill Railroad's *Derrick Van Brummel* No. 2 at Hunter station on August 19, 1883. The engine was named after Rip Van Winkle's schoolmaster. The only crew member identified is Doly Hoffman, the fireman, who stands in the gangway. — DE-GOLYER FOUNDATION COLLECTION

Catskill Mountain Railroad No. 2, the *John T. Mann*, on the head end of the train from Catskill Landing, pauses alongside the new station in Cairo in 1885. The flat car seems to be loaded with track supplies. The freight wagon and the omnibus round out this typical rural station scene of the period. — AUTHOR'S COLLECTION

The rolling stock of the Kaaterskill Railroad included two new locomotives, appropriately named the *Rip Van Winkle* No. 1, and the *Derrick Van Brummel* No. 2, of the 2-6-0 or Mogul type, two passenger coaches and two baggage cars. Through trains were run from Phoenicia to Kaaterskill, with the cars for Hunter being detached at Kaaterskill Junction, and taken to Hunter as a separate train. The railroad had cost $159,000 and of this amount only $60,000 had been financed by the sale of coupon bonds, the balance having been paid by the stockholders. Thomas Cornell became president of the Kaaterskill Railroad and the superintendent was that "Man-of-all-work," James H. Jones. George W. Harding became a director of the Kaaterskill Railroad in 1886, but held no office on the boards of the Ulster & Delaware or the Stony

A train waits on the passing track at Edgewood on the Stony Clove & Catskill Mountain Railroad. The highway had to be moved above the railroad grade and protected by the stone wall on the left. — COR-NELIUS E. CUDDEBACK III COLLECTION

Clove & Catskill Mountain Railroads. While the Kaaterskill Railroad was under construction an installation at Phoenicia was designed to eliminate all the objections of freight shippers regarding the transfer of freight from standard gauge cars to those of the narrow gauge. A Ramsey's Patent Freight Car Transfer System was purchased, with 12 sets of transfer trucks, later increased to 21 sets. By the use of this equipment a standard gauge freight car could be hauled onto the transfer track by a horse or a mule, the car body lifted, the standard gauge trucks rolled from beneath the car and a set of narrow gauge trucks substituted, all in a matter of minutes. Though the standard gauge cars were wider and heavier than those used on the narrow gauge, the special 3-foot gauge trucks were equipped with braces and equalizers to prevent excessive swaying of the car due to the larger overhang. Box cars of the Ulster & Delaware were only 20-ton capacity, built of wood and averaging 34 feet in length. It was no great problem to move them over the two narrow gauge lines and as a result the freight tonnage in 1883 doubled that of 1882. This system was used on the East Broad Top Railroad in Pennsylvania into modern times.

On the Catskill Mountain Railroad no provision had been made for a physical connection with the West Shore and it passed underneath the latter's

A meet between Kaaterskill Railroad No. 2 on the left, and No. 1 on the right, at Kaaterskill Junction proved to be a timely excuse for the crews of both passenger trains to pose for a train-side portrait. (BELOW) The Ramsey's transfer track at Phoenicia. The track on each side of the pit was 18-inch gauge, for the flat cars which supported the car bodies during the exchange of trucks. — DEGOLYER FOUNDATION COLLECTION

tracks at least 50 feet below them. The cost of a spur to a site for a transfer platform or a Ramsey transfer system was considered too great and almost all the freight destined for points along the narrow gauge was brought to Catskill Landing by river boats. Returning to the fortunes of the Catskill Mountain Railroad, its greatest problem was financial. When all the bills had been paid, or not paid depending on priority, the cost of the railroad was $336,326. Approximately $200,000 had been raised by the sale of coupon bonds and roughly $80,000 through stock subscriptions. John Driscoll, retired master mechanic of the Catskill Mountain Lines, said in 1933 that Beach put up the balance of the money out of his own pocket. As he owned many of the bonds, he was undoubtedly the largest owner. The interest charges came to $13,000 a year, plus over a thousand in taxes. Thus the railroad's net income had to be $14,000 or more per year after all operating expenses had been deducted. The railroad carried 40,950 passengers and a small amount of freight in 1883, with a net loss of $7,000, and by the end of the 1884 season the result of the inroads made by the Ulster & Delaware and its narrow gauge lines was only too clear. The profit-and-loss column in the railroad's books

A stock certificate of the new Catskill Mountain Railway Company, printed in 1885. The engraving in the center was used on both the stock and bond certificates of this company, and bears a surprising though modern similarity to Thomas Cole's painting *River in the Catskills*, c. 1841. — GEORGE F. HOLDRIDGE COLLECTION

Catskill Mountain Railway No. 2 standing at Leed's Toll Crossing, where engine No. 1 met with an accident. Engineer Frank Ruf can be seen on the engine, in this photo by C. B. Woodward. — DEGOLYER FOUNDATION COLLECTION

Cairo Railroad No. 3, the *Alfred Van Santvoord*, with the Cairo train at Catskill Landing, waiting for train time. No. 3 was built by the Dickson Manufacturing Co. in 1885 to the same specifications as the two Catskill Mountain Railway engines. Engineer Frank Ruf, the man with the oil can, stands beneath the locomotive cab. — AUTHOR'S COLLECTION

A later-day picture of Catskill Mountain Railway No. 2 at Cairo station. A new boiler and steel cab have completely changed the engine's appearance. Note the use of raised metal C.M.Ry. lettering on the locomotive tender and the letterboards of the baggage cars and coach. — AUTHOR'S COLLECTION

showed $17,000 in red ink and it became obvious that the Catskill Mountain Railroad would eventually default the interest on the bonds. In 1884 a total of 40,000 passengers and 14,000 tons of freight passed through the Phoenicia gateway bound for destinations on Cornell's two narrow gauge lines. At the end of the year, $25,000 profit after all charges was entered in black ink on Cornell's ledgers.

There was only one way out of the dilemma for Beach and his associates — receivership. Bondholders were therefore notified that the January 1, 1885, coupon would not be paid. Foreclosure proceedings began on February 11, a trustee was appointed on March 13, and the railroad was sold at public auction on June 15. In view of the high stakes involved it is not surprising that the successful bidder was a lawyer acting for Alfred Van Santvoord, Beach and several other directors of the defunct company. The old coupon bonds were replaced with an equal amount of income bonds — that is, they would receive six percent interest, paid by check, if the railroad earned it; otherwise, nothing would be paid. A new bond issue of $50,000 at five percent was the only fixed obligation and the proceeds from this were used to pay off the floating debt, which included the most pressing bills. Later another $16,000 of income bonds were sold, probably to Charles L. Beach, to clear the books of all debts. A new company, the Catskill Mountain Railway, was organized on July 1, 1885, with Alfred Van Santvoord as president and Charles L. Beach the vice-president. The railroad

was now solvent and able to pay its own way, and that it did for many years.

As a matter of interest, the South Cairo & East Durham Railroad was never built, but the Cairo Railroad was organized April 10, 1884, to build a branch from a suitable junction with the Catskill Mountain Railroad to Cairo. Headed by Lewis Wolfe of Athens, and backed financially by many of the directors of its connecting railroad, the Cairo Railroad began construction in April 1885 and was completed in six weeks for a distance of 3.77 miles from Cairo Junction to Cairo at a cost of only $36,500. Cairo Junction was 9.4 miles from Catskill Landing and the station building erected there in 1885 is still in use as a barn close to Cairo Junction Road. A new locomotive from the Dickson Locomotive Works, exactly like the two engines on the Catskill Mountain line, arrived in June 1885 and, with the railroad, was leased to the newly organized Catskill Mountain Railway in July. The latter agreed to operate the branch, keep the locomotive in repair and to provide daily freight and passenger service from Catskill to Cairo in return for $2,700 rent. The operating railroad was to keep all the income from passenger and freight business and through many years this "short shortline" remained solvent and prosperous. A daily passenger train was operated throughout the year between Catskill and Cairo even though the seasonal traffic on the main line had ended. Freight traffic originating on this branch was in due time to prove a big income producer for the Catskill Mountain Railway.

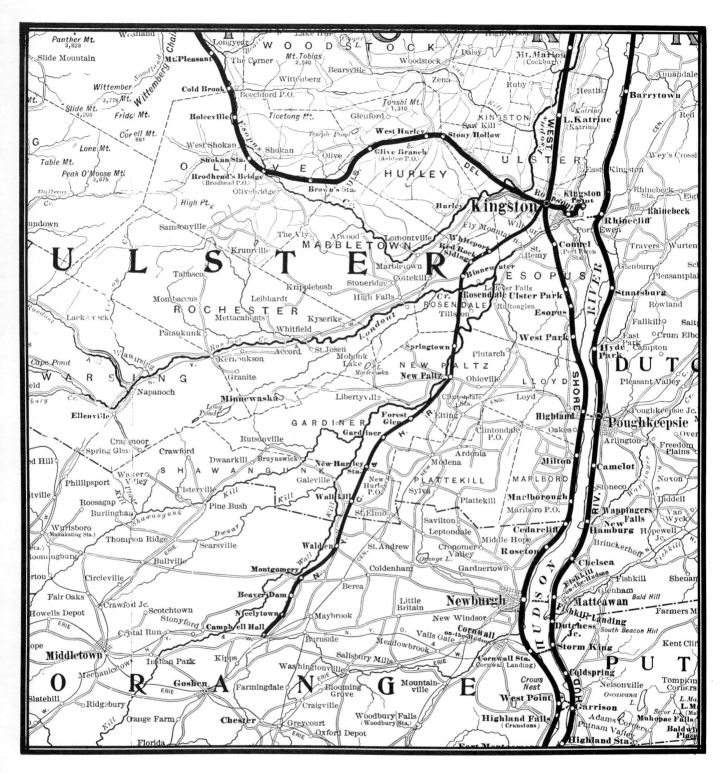

Map of the railroads on both sides of the Hudson River between Kingston and West Point shows the former Wallkill Valley Railroad with the initials N.Y.C.&H.R. for New York Central & Hudson River. The line from Montgomery to Campbell Hall, shown as a part of this branch, belongs to the Erie. This map was issued by the New York Central System in 1907. — AUTHOR'S COLLECTION

4

HUDSON RIVER RAIL MONOPOLY ENDS

THE 1885 season for the Catskill Mountain Railway ended with a profit of nearly $5,000, partly due to lower interest payments on debt and the balance on account of a development in transportation which was to affect the destinies of everyone living along the western shore of the Hudson River. This was the organization of the New York, West Shore & Buffalo Railway on February 18, 1880, that fateful year when the Hotel Kaaterskill and its allied narrow gauge railroads were conceived to plague Charles L. Beach.

As projected the West Shore Route, as it was called for short and which in due time would become its full name, was to furnish intense competition to the New York Central & Hudson River Railroad which under the guidance of William H. Vanderbilt had practically monopolized rail transportation between New York and Buffalo. The power behind the West Shore was none other than George M. Pullman. He was enraged by Vanderbilt's fostering of the Wagner Palace Car Co.'s sleeping cars which were used exclusively on the Central and its allied lines, the Michigan Central and the Lake Shore & Michigan Southern. Pullman placed his vice-president, General Horace Porter, in charge of building a new railroad along the west

bank of the Hudson from Weehawken, opposite New York City, to a point near Albany, thence west to Buffalo. Associated with General Porter were such well known men as Henry Villard, president of the Northern Pacific, Frederick Billings and other railroad executives who were not exactly close friends of the Vanderbilts. Porter and most of his associates were also directors of the newly reorganized New York, Ontario & Western Railway which was in the process of building its own line from Middletown to Jersey City in order to eliminate its dependency on the Erie-controlled New York, Susquehanna & Western, over which it had to operate through trackage rights.

All construction work on both these projects was to be performed by the North River Construction Co. which was established by Porter as a separate company, to be paid in bonds and stock of both the railroads. The N. Y. O. & W. plans did not involve building a new railroad over the entire distance from Middletown to Weehawken. There was already the Jersey City & Albany Railroad which extended from a point near Jersey City to South Haverstraw, inland from the west bank of the Hudson, a distance of 31 miles. Work on this line ceased in 1880 when the cost of tunnelling through the mountain to the west bank of the Hudson proved too expensive. Various paper railroads such

When fully developed, the Weehawken terminal of the West Shore had 17 station tracks for passenger trains. On the left, the freight cars await their turn on the car ferries which transport them to New York City, seen in the distance across the Hudson River. — DEGOLYER FOUNDATION COLLECTION

as the West Shore Hudson River Railroad were combined with the newly created New York, West Shore & Buffalo Railway. The latter reached an agreement with the N. Y. O. & W. whereby the West Shore would purchase the section from Weehawken to Cornwall when it was finished, for $10,000,000 in West Shore bonds and $2,367,000 in stock, with 99 year trackage rights for the N. Y. O. & W. From Cornwall to Middletown the North River Construction Co. would build the new line for the N. Y. O. & W.'s exclusive use. North of Cornwall, the construction company planned a new line for the West Shore to Buffalo, 376 miles.

The Saratoga & Hudson River Railroad had built a 41-mile railroad from Schenectady to Athens on the Hudson River in 1863 in an effort to divert traffic from the Erie Canal and the New York Central Railroad, bypassing Albany. Daniel Drew's Peoples Line steamboats would make Athens their terminal instead of Albany. The railroad was leased to the New York Central in 1866, purchased outright by that railroad in 1867, and for that one season the Hudson River Day Line steamboats called at Athens to connect with passenger trains there. In 1868 this service was discontinued, though a considerable freight business developed. In the following year Cornelius Vanderbilt consolidated his Hudson River Railroad with the New York Central Railroad to form the New York Central & Hudson River Railroad, and Vanderbilt thereby owned the Athens branch. In June 1876 fire destroyed the docks, station, warehouses, a steamboat, a hundred freight cars, with a loss of $400,000. The terminal was never rebuilt and the owners were glad to lease this unprofitable

branch to the West Shore, which used part of it for its main line and another section to reach Albany.

Thomas Cornell got wind of the West Shore project in 1879, long before the news was made public. He had bought the Wallkill Valley Railroad at auction in 1877 by paying $128,000 and assuming bonded debt requiring the payment of $24,000 yearly interest. Even though the line was operated economically as previously outlined, it failed to earn bond interest by $5,000 in Cornell's first two years as president. Its future did not look brilliant and when the West Shore project unfolded Cornell saw a golden opportunity to rid himself of the Wallkill Valley, get back all the money invested in it and make a handsome profit at the expense of Horace Porter's company.

The Wallkill Valley had the right under its 1866 charter to build north of Kingston to Athens, the original plan having been to provide a through route from the Erie at Goshen to the New York Central's Athens-Albany branch. Without any fanfare, Cornell sent agents out along the route to buy right-of-way, employed surveyors to work with the land agents and in the summer of 1880 hired several hundred laborers, carpenters and bridge men. Grading north of Kingston began at once, bridge material was ordered and work began on the foundations of the two principal bridges, at Glenerie Falls on Esopus Creek and the crossing of Catskill Creek just west of Catskill village. This activity did not go unnoticed and soon the West Shore surveyors and land agents invaded the country north of Kingston and began staking out their line which sometimes was within 20 feet of the Wallkill Valley Extension as it was then called. In an interview with a *New York Times* reporter Cornell announced his intention to extend the railroad to Albany in competition with the proposed New York, West Shore & Buffalo Railway. This spread the rumor that the Delaware & Hudson was behind Cornell's activities, and since Cornell was one of the Board of Managers of the D. & H. Canal Co. it might very well have been true. The newspapers speculated on the foolishness of building a railroad which would soon be paralleled by a double-tracked trunkline and the waste of money involved, but they were to hear very shortly that there would be no waste of effort by Thomas Cornell.

Though Congressman Cornell had gone to Washington in January 1881, leaving the prosecution of building the Wallkill Valley Extension to Samuel D. Coykendall, he kept in close touch with the proceedings. In June 1881 when track supplies began arriving in Kingston and there was much activity along the extension, Cornell met with General Porter and Edward Winslow and from this conference came the announcement on June 29 that the North River Construction Co. had purchased the Wallkill Valley Railroad and its extension. The price paid for this package was $128,000 in cash, representing the purchase price of the railroad when Cornell bought it in 1877; $250,000 to pay for the unfinished extension and $521,713 which was listed as an "adjustment account." It would not require a magician to figure out the profit Cornell netted from the transaction, and nobody will probably ever know if he was bluffing in starting the extension or really meant to go through with it. With a little foresight Cornell and his associates had disposed of a losing railroad (it lost $10,000 the first year after its sale), and it awakened the sponsors of the West Shore to the fact that in Kingston there was a man who was no Rip Van Winkle. In 1882 Cornell disposed of the Rhinebeck & Connecticut, of which he had become the sole owner through foreclosure sale and purchase at auction, to the Connecticut Western Railroad, also at a profit.

In January 1882 the 1,620 foot Haverstraw tunnel was holed through and the Jersey City & Albany Railroad was re-laid with 67 lb. steel rail. The 2,640 foot West Point tunnel was finished in November and the 4,225 foot Weehawken tunnel through the Bergen Hills was completed in De-

The West Shore bridge across Catskill Creek, with two additional piers installed in later years as the weight of the trains increased. (BELOW) One of the 100 high-wheeled passenger engines built by Rogers for mainline trains photographed in 1886 near the entrance of Weehawken tunnel. The enormous cab was of a type favored by suburban lines in New York City at that time. — SMITH PHOTO IN AUTHOR'S COLLECTION

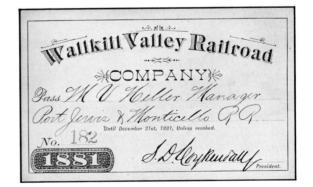

Signed by S. D. Coykendall, this pass was issued shortly before Cornell sold the Wallkill Valley Railroad to the West Shore. — AUTHOR'S COLLECTION

53

The Wilbur Bridge across Rondout Creek a short time before it was completed in May 1883. Note the large amount of falsework required to erect this huge structure. The piers for the center span, which has just been installed, are concealed behind the piling. The sailing vessel is being used to check the clearance. —HENRY P. EIGHMEY COLLECTION

cember. During January 1883 the track was finished from Kingston to West Athens, sometimes on the roadbed of the Wallkill Valley Extension and in other places some distance from it. By the end of May there was continuous track from west of Schenectady to Jersey City, except for one bottleneck. This was the great bridge at the crossing of Rondout Creek, south of Kingston and near the town of Wilbur. The structure was almost as tough to build as the Rosendale bridge on the Wallkill Valley. It was tested on May 8, 1883, by running locomotive No. 74 back and forth several times, drawing four cars loaded with stone ballast.

The bridge was 1,200 feet long and stood 150 feet above the water at the center. It cost $350,000 and a hill north of the bridge had to be tunnelled to keep the line as near level as possible.

Passenger service to Newburgh from the Pennsylvania Railroad station in Jersey City was begun on June 4, 1883. The line was officially opened for business to Kingston on June 25, the same day the Kaaterskill Railroad ran its first train. The first train from Jersey City on that day was an hour late into Kingston, too late for State Assemblyman Theodore Roosevelt to connect with the last train for Stamford. After an overnight stay in Kingston

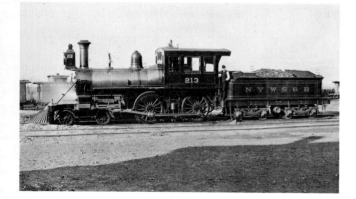

For suburban service out of Weehawken, Rogers built 20 engines like No. 213, with huge cabs which covered the steam dome as well as the back boilerhead. — SMITH PHOTO FROM AUTHOR'S COLLECTION

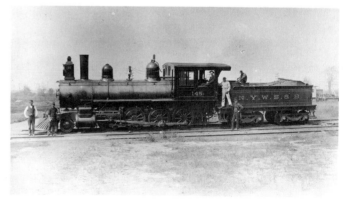

To handle the freight trains, the West Shore received 55 of these standard Consolidation type engines from the Baldwin Locomotive Works and the Dickson Manufacturing Co. — SMITH PHOTO FROM AUTHOR'S COLLECTION

he reached Stamford on the 26th, and his signature on the register of the Delaware House is still proudly displayed to mark the first through passenger of note from the big city. West Shore train service was extended to Albany on July 9, to Syracuse on October 1 and the new Weehawken terminal with ferries to West 42nd Street in New York was opened on December 15. An express with through cars for the Ulster & Delaware ran each way daily in the summer, besides a number of local trains.

The Catskill Mountain Railroad passed underneath the south end of the West Shore's bridge across Catskill Creek and the West Shore station was built on the hill just south of the bridge. A path led down to the narrow gauge railroad where there was a footwalk and a small shelter station. Though John Driscoll of Catskill said the narrow gauge railroad got little or no benefit from the West Shore, time schedules and publicity for both railroads prove otherwise. The coming of the West Shore was a tremendous boon to the Ulster & Delaware. Without it the railroad would have had to depend on the Wallkill Valley and the Erie for direct freight car service to the outside world. This route would have been too devious to attract passengers away from the river boats or the New York Central & Hudson River Railroad.

The West Shore crossed the Ulster & Delaware at grade in Kingston, thereby causing the latter's first accident involving the new railroad. On February 9, 1883, a light engine on the U. & D. was backing towards Rondout and a Wallkill Valley engine hauling two box cars was heading north. Both engineers stopped short of the crossing, as required by the rules. They each blew two short blasts on their whistles, but having been blown simultaneously neither engineer heard the other's signals. The station building obscured the view, so neither engineer knew of the other's presence. Both trains started for the crossing at the same time and when the Wallkill Valley's engineer saw what was going to happen it was too late to stop. He opened the throttle wide, saved his engine by clearing the crossing before the U. & D. engine backed into the box cars, derailing them both and injuring two brakemen. The West Shore suffered large losses due to construction train accidents between 1882 and 1884, most of them due to carelessness on the part of the train crews in not protecting work trains in both directions. The North

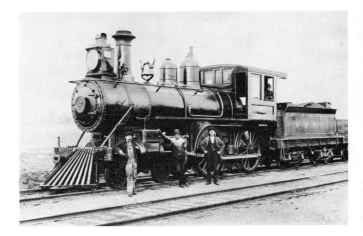

West Shore extra No. 67, with the shortened cab and capped stack, looks like a Pennsylvania Railroad engine. — HAROLD L. GOLD-SMITH COLLECTION

Engine No. 17 with a local passenger train from Kingston arriving in Newburgh. Many station platforms were wood planked to make it easier for passengers to board their trains from any one of the four tracks. — HAROLD L. GOLDSMITH COLLECTION

The Pullman Sleeping Car *Syracuse*, one of six cars built especially for the West Shore in May 1883, was photographed at the company's Detroit shop. Note the beautiful hand decoration applied to the exterior of the car. The finelining and shaded letters on the nameboard were hand-applied gold leaf. — ARTHUR D. DUBIN COLLECTION (LEFT) The interior of a Pullman Buffet Parlor Car. The buffet section is behind the glass partition in the center. The parlor chairs were the last word in luxury and each space had its own polished brass spittoon. — AUTHOR'S COLLECTION

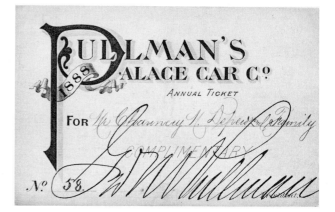

Annual pass signed by Geo. M. Pullman to Chauncey M. Depew of the New York Central proved that Pullman was not a man to hold a grudge. — AUTHOR'S COLLECTION

River Construction Co. brought thousands of Negroes from the south for the grading work, as the local supply of labor was hopelessly inadequate, and these men were the principal victims of work train wrecks.

As soon as passenger service was established to Kingston, the West Shore announced that its summer schedule would include two express trains from Weehawken which would have in their consist — "Magnificent Pullman Buffet Parlor Cars" — running direct from Philadelphia via the Pennsylvania Railroad to Phoenicia and the Grand Hotel. These new parlor cars and a number of splendidly equipped new coaches were turned out of the Pullman factory especially for these runs. In answer to questions from readers the *Kingston Freeman* stated that the buffet kitchen in a parlor car was 4 x 8 feet, glass partitioned, located between the smoking room and the drawing room. Lunch consisted of soup, sandwiches, dessert, tea and French coffee, a menu not as elaborate as that furnished by a dining car but adequate for a mid-day meal. Thirty years later on the Ulster & Delaware's buffet parlor cars you could get beef stew and apple pie, the latter with a liberal dose of brandy underneath the top crust.

In time the through car service expanded until some of the trains bound for the Catskills ran in several sections, with only a change of locomotives

The earliest known N.Y.W.S. & B. pass was issued by vice president Theodore Houston in 1883. — AUTHOR'S COLLECTION

The first summer timetable for the completed West Shore Route was issued in June 1884. Express trains required 14 hours for the journey from New York to Buffalo. Passengers bound for Chicago had to change to the Grand Trunk Railway for the balance of the journey although there were through sleeping cars from New York to Chicago. — EDWARD L. MAY COLLECTION

at Kingston. To handle this increase in traffic Cornell bought two new locomotives from Rogers and Dickson in 1882, these being the first new locomotives purchased since 1871. Six new passenger coaches were bought in that year, followed by two more in 1883. Between 1883 and 1885 six more locomotives were added. With 15 engines on the roster, the Ulster & Delaware for the first time had enough spares in the winter so that each locomotive could be thoroughly overhauled without rushing the job. The era of baling-wire repairs was at an end. Perhaps not quite, for on August 23, 1886, engine No. 3, while standing over the ash pit at the Rondout terminal after having been brought in off the road by engineer Henry Sherman, blew up and large pieces of the boiler, the bell and various other parts flew in all directions. Thomas Dagan, who was raking out the ashes, was severely injured and John Bowes, the hostler, was thrown out of the cab onto the ground. The cause of the explosion was failure of one of the boiler courses and not low water. The weakness of this part of the boiler could very well have been caused by an accident in January 1881 when No. 3 broke a side rod near Beaverkill, the flailing ends of the rod puncturing the boiler in several places and letting out all the water. These holes were probably

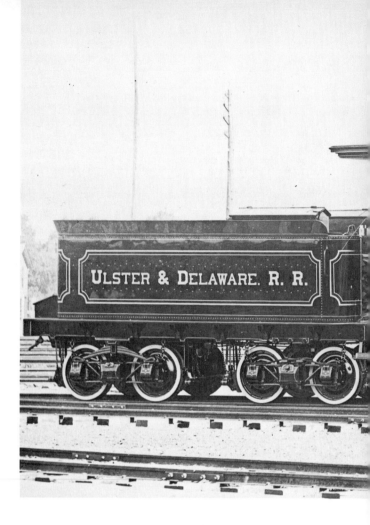

The illustration of Ulster & Delaware No. 3 shown above is nearly a perfect locomotive photograph in every detail. Brooks built this handsome Eight-Wheel passenger engine in 1887 to replace old No. 3 which had blown itself to pieces in 1886. AUTHOR'S COLLECTION (LEFT-OPPOSITE PAGE) The original No. 3, the *John C. Brodhead*, as it stood in front of Hamilton House in West Shokan when brand new. — THOMAS T. TABER COLLECTION

At Arkville, Ulster & Delaware No. 10 has in its consist one of the gothic-windowed baggage cars from Jackson & Sharp in 1870. — CHARLES E. FISHER COLLECTION

patched and the weakened boiler section gave way six years later. Both injured employees recovered fully and the following year No. 3 was replaced by a new and much larger engine from the Brooks Locomotive Works.

West of the railhead at Stamford, three and one-half miles down the Delaware, was the village of Hobart and its residents looked with longing at the railroad so near and yet so far. Cornell attended a meeting in Hobart early in 1884 and from this conference the Hobart Branch Railroad was born. Chartered March 25, 1884, the money was raised by capital stock subscriptions to which Cornell contributed generously and work was begun six weeks later. Though the descent along the river bank averaged 60 feet to the mile, there were no heavy rock cuttings nor any long fills. Following the river's north bank most of the distance, the extension crossed the river east of Hobart and ended at the foot of Cornell Avenue on December 1, 1884. Costing only $43,000, since many local farmers had contributed teams, labor and even a bit of stone masonry, the railroad was leased to the Ulster & Delaware for $3,000 yearly rent. The U. & D. furnished the train service and kept the track in good repair.

As a result of the completion of the West Shore to Kingston, the gross revenues of the Ulster & Delaware grew steadily and the surplus increased yearly until Cornell was able to pay off the $180,000 floating debt and still have a surplus. At the 1889 annual meeting Cornell said he hoped soon to be able to pay off some of the bonds and thereby reduce the heavy interest charges.

Returning to the fortunes of the New York,

West Shore & Buffalo, it was opened throughout its length, 428 miles, on January 1, 1884. There was through service via the Pennsylvania Railroad from Washington and Philadelphia to Saratoga and Lake Champlain, besides the Catskills, and sleeping cars on the limiteds furnished service from New York to Chicago via the Grand Trunk and Wabash railroads. Unfortunately, the railroad got off to a bad start. Due to a combination of inexperienced train crews, unfamiliar with a brand new railroad and a notable lack of supervision, a series of wrecks not only gave the railroad a bad name but involved the company in damage suits of serious proportions. On October 1, 1883, the two night passenger trains collided head-on near St. Johnsonville, New York, killing a passenger and several of the train crew and injuring dozens of passengers. The cause was the failure of the engineer of the eastbound train to wait at St. Johnsonville until the westbound train arrived, compounded by neglect of the conductor to notice that they had passed their meeting point. Not that the "Central" was any less culpable in the matter of accidents, but the West Shore's misfortunes always hit the front page, like those of the New Haven years later.

The double-tracked railroad had cost $101 million, almost as much as the Pacific Railroad built between 1863 and 1869. The West Shore was a too expensive railroad built too soon, and on the very day it opened officially from Weehawken to Buffalo the directors stated that they could not meet the bond interest when it came due the next time, and that a receivership was therefore inevitable. The rest is a complicated story, full of politi-

The afternoon train ready to leave for Rondout, when Hobart became the western terminal of the Ulster & Delaware. — DEGOLYER FOUNDATION COLLECTION

West Shore No. 195 on a cold winter's morning. This class was added by the New York Central in 1892 when freight trains increased in size. — HAROLD L. GOLDSMITH COLLECTION

cal manoeuvring. Receivers Russell and Houston for the railroad and Judge Ashbel Green for the North River Construction Co. were appointed June 9, 1884. Theirs was a thankless job, for the "Central" cut freight rates from Buffalo to New York in half, taking away what little freight business the West Shore had. The latter countered by cutting passenger fares from two cents a mile to one cent.

By June 1885 the deficit of the West Shore had run into millions and the bonds had dropped to less than half their face value. At this time it came to public notice that a number of Philadelphians had been buying these bonds and now had over half of them. They made an offer to the "Central's" new president, Chauncey M. Depew, whereby the bondholders would request an auction sale of the railroad, their representatives would buy it and would then lease it to the "Central" for a price. This offer was accepted by Depew, and on September 26, 1885, the Supreme Court at Newburgh, New York, set the price at $22,000,000. The auction was held and on December 11, 1885, Chauncey M. Depew notified all employees of the newly organized West Shore Railroad that the "Central" had leased it for 475 years.

It has been said that J. Pierpont Morgan had

arranged all this at a meeting between Depew and Pennsylvania Railroad officials George B. Roberts and Frank Thomson, whereby the South Pennsylvania Railroad, conceived by William H. Vanderbilt in 1883 to plague the Pennsylvania Railroad, would be sold to the Pennsylvania and the West Shore bondholders would arrange to sell their road to the "Central." It is a good story, but Pennsylvania Railroad historians state that at this meeting the West Shore was never discussed. Soon after Depew had the West Shore under his control, the Pullman cars were replaced with Wagner Palace cars until Pullman bought the Wagner Company in 1899. During the 1890 decade a drawing-room sleeping car ran from Weehawken to Bloomville on the *Half-Holiday* Special on Saturday afternoon and returned from Bloomville on Sunday nights on the *Catskill Mountain Night Express* which arrived in Weehawken early Monday morning. This was the only regular sleeping car run on the Ulster & Delaware and it was discontinued by 1900.

Most of the West Shore's trackage west of Utica was eventually abandoned and today the Hudson River line is single-tracked, freight only, and forms a part of the Penn Central System. No doubt it is in worse financial trouble than it was in 1884.

Train time approaches at Fleischmann's station on a summer day. A light engine has just passed and the stages from the hotels wait for their guests, while the baggage of home-going passengers lines the platform. — LIBRARY OF CONGRESS

5

PIONEER HOTELS

WHEN THE Ulster & Delaware was completed to Stamford in 1872 there were only two hotels in the Catskill Mountains which could accommodate 300 or more persons: the Catskill Mountain House and the Overlook Mountain House. The former, perched high on the eastern edge of the mountains, relied entirely on the Hudson River boats or the Hudson River Railroad for its connection with the outside world, plus a 12 mile carriage ride from Catskill Landing to the hotel. The Overlook was six miles by carriage from the West Hurley station of the Ulster & Delaware. A little more than a dozen years later the entire hotel picture had changed to a surprising degree and the development of the Catskills as a resort area for the many instead of the few was under way.

Though the New York, West Shore & Buffalo published a summer guide in 1883, its 1884 issue was the first to include the entire railroad system. Part of the guide was devoted to the Catskills and the anonymous individual who wrote this chapter had a splendid knowledge of his subject. His narration presented in this chapter carries the reader on a mythical train ride from Kingston over the Ulster & Delaware to the hotels in the mountains.

During the ten minutes' stop of the West Shore train at Kingston, the through Catskill Mountain cars have been transferred to the track of the Ulster & Delaware R. R., and are ready to bear their occupants on into the enchanted region of perpetual coolness and refreshing breezes, where sparkling streams dash and tumble through mossy forest and shaded glen, and wind-swept heights uplift themselves far above the heat and worry of the every-day world of the plains. The Catskills, Katzkills, Cauterskills, Kaaterskills, Katzbergs, Katzenbergs or Kaatersbergs, as they are variously spelled, or the Ontioras, as the Indians named them, do not rise directly from the bank of the Hudson, but from a plain some ten miles to the west of it and to the northwest of Kingston. As the train draws nearer, High Point, Cornell and the Wittenberg stand out in bold relief — then the several hotels of the eastern range are seen and recognized, though in the distance, and at that elevation they look like childrens' card houses. At West Hurley, the passengers for the Overlook Mountain House leave the train and enter comfortable stages for the drive up the breezy mountain-side. Overlook Mountain is the cornerstone of the Catskills, for here the trend, which of the eastern range is nearly north and south, turns at almost a right angle to the westwards.

The hotels the train passengers saw from a distance were the Kaaterskill and the Catskill Moun-

This old woodblock sketch is the only known illustration of the first Overlook Mountain House. Accommodating 300 guests in its prime, the hotel was destroyed by fire in 1873. (BELOW) The Tremper House at Phoenicia used this view of the hotel and the U. & D. station in its advertising for many years. — BOTH AUTHOR'S COLLECTION

tain House far to the north and the Overlook. Standing near the summit of Overlook Mountain at an elevation of 2,978 feet, the original Overlook was built by Artemus Sahler in 1870 and enlarged in 1871 to care for 300 persons. Sahler sold it to John E. Lasher in 1873 just before it was destroyed by fire after the close of the season. During 1876-1877 the Kiersted brothers built a somewhat smaller version of the original hotel, with rooms for 150 guests. The hotel provided such luxuries as a bowling alley, billiard tables, steam heat, gas lights, at rates from $10 to $15 a week. The Overlook was nine miles from West Hurley, up a rutty dirt road which zigzagged back and forth, passing George Mead's hotel enroute. Mead's was built in 1863, halfway up to the summit of Overlook Mountain, and later Mead built the road to the summit. His hotel was the first one south of Kaaterskill Clove, and it accommodated 75 at half the price of the Overlook. On the top of the mountain, an easy walk from the Overlook, was an observation tower 3,150 feet above the Hudson. From there the view

east and south, when the air was clear, was unsurpassed. Through the years patrons returned to the Overlook and Mead's time and again to relax amid the splendid isolation of the mountain top, far from the social whirl of the hotels north and west. In 1877 plans were announced to build a railroad to the summit of Overlook Mountain, but happily it was never built.

From West Hurley to Shokan the mountains proper are hidden from the railroad by a range of foot-hills on the right; but at Shokan, which is termed the 'gateway to the Catskills,' the road bends sharply to the north, and, still following the Esopus, plunges into the Shandaken Valley, the grandest 'clove' or notch in the mountain system, which by it is cleft in twain from north to south. One of the most important stations on the road is Phoenicia, 26 miles from Kingston. Here, on a plateau at the foot of Tremper Mountain, the Tremper House, one of the finest hotels in the Catskills, is located.

Built by Capt. Jacob H. Tremper, Jr., in 1878, the Tremper House stood on a natural bluff a quarter of a mile from the station, at an elevation of 1,000 feet. With 130 rooms in the main hotel building, besides cottages adjoining, it was an expensive hotel for the times, with rates from $14 to $25 a week. Cooled by breezes caused by the meeting of wind currents from the cloves of Stony Creek and the Esopus, the Tremper House was a favorite with New Yorkers, though its life span was less than two score years. W. C. Newton built an overgrown boarding house in Phoenicia in 1882, and in this nameless hostelry 275 persons could find food and lodging.

The Palace Hotel in Shandaken, at the entrance to the famous Echo Notch, later became the Glenbrook and had a fiery end in 1966. — AUTHOR'S COLLECTION

64

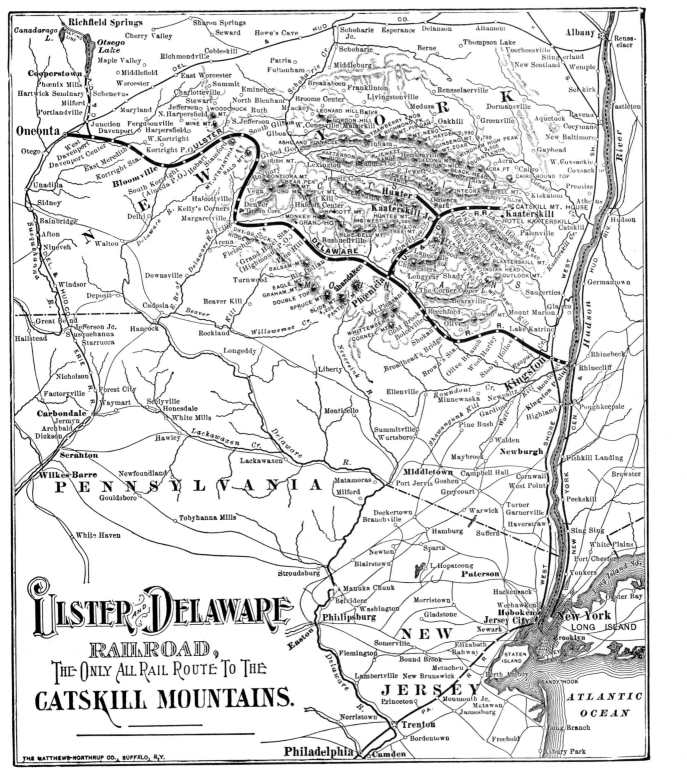

This publicity map issued by the Ulster & Delaware Railroad shows the relationship of
its Catskill lines with the West Shore Route into Weehawken and New York City. For
many years the railroad ignored the competing lines of the Beach system. This 1901
map shows the Ulster & Delaware completed to Oneonta. — GEORGE E. BURNETT COL-
LECTION

The train moves on, bearing still farther into the mountains those passengers destined for the Western Catskills. On the right are Mount Sheridan, Broadstreet Hollow, North Dome, Peck Hollow, Mount Sherrill and Deep Notch, at the entrance to which is Shandaken Centre, whence stages find their way up through Deep Notch to West Kill and Lexington, at both of which places are located pleasant hotels and boarding houses.

At Shandaken the new La Ment House had facilities for 150 and offered archery, tennis, bowling and dancing nightly, in addition to the splendid climate the 1,100 feet altitude afforded. Five years later LaMent sold the hotel to F. A. McClure, who changed the name to the Palace Hotel. In 1966, as the Glenbrook, it burned to the ground.

Three miles from Shandaken is the hamlet of Big Indian, and from this point the railroad leaves the valley and begins to climb the mountain-side, with a grade of 150 feet per mile. Pine Hill, three miles from Big Indian, has been built since the opening of the railroad, and contains naught but hotels, boarding houses and summer cottages.

In Pine Hill the largest hotel was the Guigou, built in 1880 by Theodore Guigou to entertain 250 guests, at rates from $10 to $17.50. Guigou began taking in summer boarders in 1854 when his tanning business failed, so he was the pioneer of the Pine Hill district. Then there was the Ulster, built by B. L. Rider in 1882 and the Alpine, both of which could handle 100 boarders. In 1887 the Rip Van Winkle was built on a terrace below the Guigou by the Van Loan brothers, who charged up to $25 a week for their 150 guests. By 1916 the owner was L. Cohn, the rates were cheaper, and the best of Kosher fare was in the dining room.

From this point the train rounds a magnificent curve so sharp as to receive the name of Horseshoe — of course no well-regulated mountain railroad would be without its horseshoe curve — lifts itself up the steepest grade of the line with much hoarse panting from the locomotive, and comes to a resting place at Grand Hotel Station, 1,886 feet above tidewater. To the right of the track and about 400 feet above it is the Grand Hotel, one of the largest in the Catskills and commanding a mountain view unequalled in the State.

The Grand has already been described, and it shared with the Hotel Kaaterskill the patronage of high New York and Philadelphia society. Edward A. Gillett, the first manager of the Kaaterskill, was moved over to the Grand in 1884, on loan from

The Guigou House, across the valley from the Pine Hill railroad station, was first class in every respect. — AUTHOR'S COLLECTION

The Rip Van Winkle was also on Pine Hill and close to the Guigou House. Resembling an oversized mansion, with the typical additions as business increased, the house was beautifully situated and afforded guests a fine view of Belle Ayr mountain and the valley below. — LIBRARY OF CONGRESS

Judge William Strong of the United States Supreme Court once said, "I have seen the Catskills from the Hudson River side, but this view from the Grand Hotel is the finest of all." The Grand Hotel, monarch of Pine Hill, was a magnificent sight in itself as seen from Belle Ayr mountain. — LIBRARY OF CONGRESS (LEFT) The Palace Hotel at Fleischmann's, typical mansard-roofed styling of the 1880's, is still in use in 1972. — GERALD M. BEST

The Takanassee Hotel Country Club at Fleischmann's, a product of the Sullivan County style, was closed in 1969 and destroyed by fire June 22, 1971. Built in 1922, it was the biggest of the large hotels to be built in the Pine Hill area. — GERALD M. BEST

The Alpine, in Pine Hill village, in the days when hotels expanded by building additions in the rear. While the Alpine was a popular hotel, it lacked the majesty of some of the larger establishments. — LIBRARY OF CONGRESS (LEFT) While the Alpine was not as prestigious as many of its neighbors, it survived all of them. Disappearing under the wrecker's assault in the fall of 1970, the old wooden structure ended a colorful 90-year career. — GERALD M. BEST

the Colonnade Hotel in Philadelphia. The Grand was a city unto itself, with a pharmacy, postoffice, resident physician and all the amusements the other hotels provided. A symphony (sic) orchestra, headed by Louis J. Cornu, leader of the Union Square orchestra in the winter, provided music for the daily 'tea-dansant,' and concerts with dancing afterwards, in the evenings. The rates started at $31 a week and the welcome mat was out for Gentiles only.

From Highmount, the train, greatly lightened of its burden, rolls swiftly, unaided by steam, down the steep grades of the western water shed, and after a short halt at Griffin's Corners, emerges into the valley of the east branch of the Delaware at Arkville, seven miles from the summit, where it connects with stages for Margaretville, Delhi and points down the Delaware valley.

In 1884 there were no large hotels in Griffin's Corners, but 600 tourists could find lodgings in the boarding houses close by. The station was a mile west of town, and around it grew the town of Fleischmann's, to which name the U. & D. station was changed in 1891. Later the two towns were merged as Fleischmann's. So tremendous was the growth of this area that in 1910 there were 18 hotels having a capacity of more than 100 guests and a total number of 4,200 beds were available near this one station.

At Arkville the Locust Grove House, owned by Hiram B. Kelley, was an enlargement of a summer home built by Edward Livingston, Minister to France in 1812. In his advertisements, Kelley stated that it was the former home of Lord Willoughby. Though an Irishman was the host, the majority of his 150 patrons were of German descent. On the road to Margaretville was the Hoffman House, later called the Pakatakan Inn, and where the 125

guests were principally artists and nature lovers. The Hotel Ackerly in Margaretville, built in 1845 by David Ackerly and enlarged twice by his son until it could accommodate 200, had beautiful parks and fountains facing the river to the east. The Ackerly became the rendezvous of the Columbia University football squad each September for three weeks of pre-season practice, until fire badly damaged the hotel in 1903. It was rebuilt as the Pocantico Inn and in turn was destroyed by fire in 1928.

Railroad magnate George J. Gould, oldest son of Jay Gould, bought Thomas Cornell's summer home and estate at Furlough Lake, high in the Catskills east of Arkville, in 1893 and his business car, the *Atalanta* of the Missouri Pacific Railroad, was a frequent visitor to the house track at Arkville while Gould was in residence.

Roxbury, a thriving village 58 miles from Kingston is interesting to the New Yorker as having been the early home of Mr. Jay Gould, and in it is still pointed out the country store in which he found employment as a boy. The railroad king has many warm friends living here, who speak familiarly of him as 'Jay', and relate anecdotes of his precocious shrewdness and business ability.

Roxbury never catered seriously to the summer trade by building huge boarding houses or hotels. Though beautifully situated, with streets lined with magnificent trees, there was only Shady

Lawn, owned by Dr. J. J. Keator; it accommodated 75, was strictly dry and its rates were low. A number of private homes took in "city boarders," and if you wanted to live it up you had to stay at a small year-round hotel known variously as the Mitchell, the Delaware Valley House and the Roxbury Hotel in the center of town.

At Grand Gorge, six miles beyond Roxbury, stage connections are made for Gilboa, three miles and Prattsville, six miles distant.

Below Prattsville on Schoharie Creek near Devasego Falls was the Devasego House, a stately colonial type building built prior to 1883, with a capacity of 175 boarders. Later the name was changed to Devasego Inn.

The Ulster & Delaware road finds its terminus at Stamford, a bright, charmingly located town at the foot of Mount Utsayantha, 73 miles from Kingston and 1,767 feet above the sea.

At Stamford one would expect that in 1884 there would be meager hotel facilities, for it was on the western slopes of the Catskills, a long train ride from New York. Lemuel Lamb built a small tavern at Stamford in 1813, called it the Delaware House; Fred M. Tingley added an annex later, with beds for 40, and kept it open all year. Stamford's only school was called the Seminary, run by Dr. S. E. Churchill, M. D., as an annex to his home. Back of the school was a dormitory used by children from the back country during the school terms. In 1872 two couples from Brooklyn wandered over from Prattsville on a sightseeing hike and asked Dr. Churchill if he could put them up for the night. He did, and this act of hospitality was to change the good doctor's whole life, for by the following season he had enlarged the dormitory and was taking in from 30 to 40 boarders. His business prospered, his fame as a host and as a doctor spread by word of mouth and in 1882 he started building Churchill Hall which was completed early in 1883. The new hotel attracted thousands of visitors each season and had to be enlarged twice. Only a few blocks from the railroad station, on spacious grounds, the hotel had a pavilion for dancing, separate from the main building, and a music hall with the appointments of a theater. Dr. Churchill was influential in the building of the Stamford Opera House. His hotel's annex stayed open all year and he made Stamford the social center of the western Catskills. A mar-

The Shady Lawn Hotel in Roxbury was the only hotel in that village to advertise in the early summer guides. In bold face type they announced, "Good Board, Good Beds, and Large Airy Rooms." Publicity also stated, "The hotel is just 20 minutes ride from the birthplace of Jay Gould, the most successful Financier and Railroad King the world has ever produced." — JOHN B. HUNGERFORD COLLECTION

The picturesque village of Stamford with Mt. Utsayantha in 1902. In the foreground is a mansion in the process of being rebuilt into a hospital. It has long since been replaced with a modern building. — LIBRARY OF CONGRESS

Stamford's largest hotel, Churchill Hall, was unrivalled as a health and pleasure resort. The hotel, with its circular tower and dining room on the ground floor, was within walking distance of the station. In 1890, a large annex was erected on adjoining property, connected with the main house by a covered piazza, and visible at the right of this view. The hotel contained an elaborate music hall, parlors, two tennis courts and artificial lakes for boating. (LEFT) The Rexmere, Dr. Churchill's last hotel development, as photographed by William Henry Jackson in 1902. It has changed little in the intervening 70 years, but cannot be seen from this point because the sapling trees planted by Dr. Churchill have completed masked the hotel.
— BOTH LIBRARY OF CONGRESS

velous legend centers around the doctor and an elderly, very wealthy patron who had a chronic illness. Apparently Dr. Churchill made the correct diagnosis, for during the summer he restored her to good health, and she was so grateful to him that she gave him a check for $25,000 so that he could spend the winter travelling abroad. Instead, the doctor built the Hotel Rexmere in a beautiful setting facing a series of small lakes, and though the Rexmere's guest capacity was only 150, the furnishings were luxurious, most of the rooms had baths, and the doctor's only travelling was from one of his hotels to the other.

Success brings competition and by 1889 the Grant House was built on Brooklyn Heights to accommodate 100; the Cold Spring House had been built at the east end of town; the Greycourt Inn, close to Churchill Hall, had room for 75 guests; Hamilton Hall, built by M. W. Goodell in 1889 on the edge of Churchill Hall's lawn and later sold to Dr. Churchill; the Madison, the Mountain View House, the Westholm, just to name a few, were the leaders among the 46 hotels and boarding houses which by 1890 could handle a thousand visitors with ease. Many wealthy New Yorkers and Philadelphians were attracted here, and a column of news about these guests appeared each Sunday in the *New York Times* society pages. Stamford vied with the hotels in the eastern Catskills as the most popular resort area, though it never quite succeeded in its goal.

In July 1890 Jay Gould and his daughter Helen arrived in Roxbury aboard Gould's private car, the *Bedford Penola,* and announced his intention to build a summer home there. His plans were never fulfilled, for he died in 1892 and his daughter restored the old family home as a memorial to her father. She spent part of each summer there, giving festivals for the benefit of the school she had given to Roxbury along with a memorial chapel and library. In 1894 the *Times* reported a grand ball at Churchill House in Stamford, with Helen Gould attending, the other guests including Mrs. J. K. Van Rensselaer, George B. Childs, the Misses Mackay and Roebling and many others. Those who wished to see their names in the society columns had only to go to Stamford during the 1890s and their presence would be duly reported.

The West Shore guide, after describing Stamford, returned to Phoenicia to complete the des-

The Delaware Motor Inn, once the Delaware House, first opened in 1813, stands in the center of Stamford over 150 years later.—GERALD M. BEST

The Cold Spring Apartments in Stamford, a small pioneer hotel with three additions, is remarkably well preserved in 1970. — GERALD M. BEST

cription of the hotels served by the two narrow gauge lines.

The main line U. & D. train has barely left Phoenicia before the train on the Stony Clove & Catskill Mountain also pulls out on the opposite side of the station, and bravely begins the steep ascent, in which 1,273 feet in elevation must be overcome in 10 miles of distance. The rise is often 150, and in one place 180 feet per mile; and the ride, amid the wild and beautiful mountain scenery, in the open observation cars attached to the trains of this road during the summer, is simply fascinating. The terminus of the Stony Clove & Catskill Mountain is at Hunter, but the train stops at Kaaterskill Jct., where a portion of the train is switched off to the track of the Kaaterskill Railroad. Hunter is a fine village, with unsurpassed attractions for summer boarders. Stages connect Hunter with many resorts which do not enjoy railroad facilities.

Hunter is on Schoharie Creek, many miles upstream from Prattsville and the Devasego Inn. In 1884 it had four big hotels, the largest of which was the St. Charles, earlier known as the Breeze Lawn, at 2,200 feet elevation, and with rooms for

Greycourt Inn, with its unique porches and wide front steps, faced Stamford's main street near Churchill Hall. With accommodations for 80 guests after completion of its annex, the hotel offered a magnificent view of the mountains and the beautiful valley of the Delaware. — LIBRARY OF CONGRESS

Hunter House in Hunter used this fine Walton Van Loan drawing in their advertisements. The house accommodated 200 guests on a year-round basis and offered billiard rooms, a bowling alley and a tonsorial room. (BELOW) Today, the new Hunter House stands on a hill in back of the site of the old hotel, which burned to the ground. — GERALD M. BEST

Schoharie Creek, provided its 100 patrons with every luxury of the times.

North of Hunter there were a few large hotels and many boarding houses. Of note in East Windham were Lamoreau's Summit House and Briggs' Grand View Mountain House, each with rooms for 150 persons, and the Chichester with beds for 125 boarders. In the heart of Windham Centre was The Windham, built in 1829 as the Osbornville House by Bennet Osborn. It remained in the family and was taken over by Osborn R. Coe in 1879, who enlarged it to accommodate 100. It changed names at the whim of the owner, being at various times Coe's Hotel, Coe's Mountain Home and The Windham. The most beautiful hotel in the Wind-

The Central House and Cottages was surrounded by well-shaded, ample grounds, with piazzas on three sides. Pure spring water was offered on each floor. Hotel advertisements emphatically announced *NO BAR.* — AUTHOR'S COLLECTION

200, it offered the best view of the valley and the mountains. Hunter House, built in 1883 had rooms for 200 guests. It was a five minute carriage ride from the station, and unlike most of the other hotels, was open all year. Among its attractions were a rifle range, livery stable, barber shop in the hotel and a cuisine rated well above the average for summer hotels. A short distance from Hunter House was Central House, which boasted that it had no bar, and gave the distances to the nearest Protestant and Catholic churches as a gentle hint which some hotels bared in large type — no Hebrews desired. A mile from the station on the hillside above the town was Prospect House, very exclusive, rates furnished on application, guest capacity for 200. The smaller Kaatsberg Hotel, built by Robert Elliott in 1884 on the banks of

The Kaatsberg was an attractive summer boarding house pleasantly located on the banks of the Schoharie Creek. A bathing house was on the premises for free use of guests. — AUTHOR'S COLLECTION

The Haines' Falls House was in its prime when William Henry Jackson made this glass plate negative in 1902. This popular resort was enlarged to include 160 feet of piazza fronting Kaaterskill Clove. A short distance from the hotel was Haines' Falls where the water at the main fall descended 150 feet into the gorge. The Sunset View House in the background at the left is still in use today. — LIBRARY OF CONGRESS

Windham House, oldest hotel in the Catskill region, has survived with additions and renovations, a gem of post-colonial times. Built as a farmhouse in 1800, it was rebuilt into a post road tavern. In 1869 it was enlarged and converted into a summer boarding house. Its pillars and lacy balcony railings are reminiscent of the Catskill Mountain House on a small scale and has an atmosphere of antiquity shared only by the Delaware Inn in Stamford. — GERALD M. BEST

ham area, and certainly the longest lived, is Windham House, on the main road one mile west of the village. Built as a farm house by Perez Steele in 1800, his son Stephen rebuilt it as a hotel which remained very popular for through stage coach travellers throughout his life. His estate sold it in 1867 to Sherman Munger, who enlarged it as a summer boarding house in 1869 with facilities for 75 guests. Known as the Munger House, it became Windham House after the turn of the century, and has been magnificiently restored in recent years by its present owners.

> From Kaaterskill Junction, the train of the Kaaterskill R. R., a narrow gauge road eight miles long, completed and open for travel last season, and traversing the glorious, breezy valley of the Upper Schoharie, has its terminus at Kaaterskill Station, at South Lake, within a mile of both the Hotel Kaaterskill and the Mountain House.

The first train stop was at Tannersville, at the western end of the park-like area which extends west for six miles from the great wall of Manitou facing the Hudson. Tannersville was an ideal place for summer homes, for hotels and for the clubs which began forming as early as 1883 and which by the mid-1890s were spread out along both sides of the railroad. There were not many large hotels in this region in 1884, for the great development was to take place between 1890 and 1900. There was the Elka Park Association at Tannersville, on Spruce Top Mountain's slopes two miles from the village and where the club house known as Schoharie Manor replaced the small, early clubhouse in 1891. This association was composed of New York's

Leiderkranz Society members and other leaders in German mercantile and social circles in New York, with Paul Goepel as the guiding genius. Started as a private club, hard times after the panic of 1893 caused the club house to be thrown open for summer boarders, and Schoharie Inn could handle 100 of them at any one time.

On another mountain slope the Onteora Park Association had its club house, the Bear and Fox Inn, the members living in cottages surrounding the main building. The pioneer hotel for the general public was Roggen's Mountain Hotel, built in 1883 at the lower end of Onteora Park. Offering the usual tennis, billiards, boating and fishing for its 150 guests, it became Kroebel's Mountain House in 1898.

East of Tannersville the next train stop was Haines' Falls, also known as Haines Corners. The largest hotel there was the Hotel Hallenbeck, built by W. J. Hallenbeck with rooms for 100 guests. It was first known as the Hilton Hotel, built in 1878. Hallenbeck sold the hotel to R. W. Renner in 1905 and built the smaller Fenmore House. Wilson Ham's hotel in 1884 could accommodate 85 and Charles W. Haines' hotel, the Haines' Falls House, had rooms for 80 guests, later increased to 100. Much smaller, but easily the oldest, was the Vista, built by Aaron Haines in 1849 and used as a tavern until it was enlarged in 1876 to board 30. Haines died in 1883 and his daughter, Mrs. E. E. Scott, operated it for years. The last survivor of the Haines enterprises, the Vista was bulldozed to the ground in 1970. Haines' Falls did not fully develop until the mid-1890s, when Messrs. Butler and Bullock built the Antlers for the more exclusive trade, with rooms for 125 persons. Some years later L. P. Schutt, son of a former owner of Laurel House, bought the Antlers, and by 1916 S. Friedberg was catering to the Kosher trade, with 250 persons in the same hotel originally built for 125 boarders. The most spectacular of the Haines' Falls hotels was the Sunset Park Inn, standing at the head of Kaaterskill Clove above the town at an altitude of 2,600 feet. Built by C. A. Clegg, its first two stories were of stone and its rates were as high as charged by the Hotel Kaaterskill.

A mid-1890s addition at Haines' Falls was the Lox-Hurst, translated from the German as "Lynx-Forest," built by C. A. Martin, who advertised in the 1900 *Ulster & Delaware Summer Guide* as follows; "Concerning Hebrews. People familiar with the Catskills know that except at the larger hotels, Jews and Gentiles will not board at the same house. This is to be regretted; but being a fact, the houses have to take one class or the other. Therefore the proprietor begs to say that Lox-Hurst accepts Gentiles only." Martin was still holding out as late as 1916, and lox and bagels were not on the menu.

The next to the last stop of the train was at Laurel House, second oldest hotel in the Catskills, built in 1847, enlarged several times since, and in 1884 was owned by J. L. Schutt. He had just added a new wing of great architectural beauty and the hotel, standing at the head of Kaaterskill Falls, was in a class by itself. In 1884 it had a full orchestra, bowling, tennis, boating on the lake, horseback-riding, all for $15 to $25 a week. While it did not receive as much attention in the society columns as the hotels in Stamford, the Grand or the Kaaterskill, it was always mentioned. Laurel House remained in use, though with gradually diminishing patronage, until the early 1960s. Then the grim reaper in the shape of the State of New York put the torch to it in February 1967.

The train's last stop was Kaaterskill Station, and here the remaining passengers on our 1884 trip boarded carriages for either the Hotel Kaaterskill on the top of South Mountain or the Mountain House, a mile east — on the edge of Manitou's verdant wall facing the Hudson. The Kaaterskill was the creation of George Harding of Philadelphia and, to quote him from an interview in the *Times* in 1894, he had built the hotel and landscaped its vast acreage of parklands as a hobby, or

fad as he put it, and took great personal pleasure in keeping up the place. He brought Professor John A. Meyer, noted Philadelphia orchestra leader, to provide the music for dancing, concerts and a fancy dress ball each Saturday night, and the hotel teemed with activity in July and August of each year. The *Times* reporter said that the Kaaterskill's guests used to amuse themselves by hunting out Rip Van Winkle's route through Kaaterskill Clove, and while on one of these expeditions the reporter stood at the head of a waterless chasm he had been told was Haines' Falls. There was a sudden rumbling, the falls sprang to life, a man came up to the reporter and said, "Deacon Haines has turned the water on the falls. Twenty-five cents please!"

One mile east of Kaaterskill Station, standing in splendid isolation for the previous 60 years was the Catskill Mountain House, its privacy at last invaded from the rear. Guests of this hotel who came up from New York via the Ulster & Delaware and its two narrow gauge lines boarded carriages at Kaaterskill Station and paid a fare of 50 cents for the drive to the hotel. In 1884 they could (and most of them did) board the Catskill Mountain Railroad train at Catskill Landing or at the West Shore station, leave the train at Mountain House Station and endure the four-mile ride up the side of Manitou's wall to the hotel. It was a standoff as to which route they selected, but there were fewer changes via the Catskill Landing gateway. The Mountain House was seldom featured in the New

With accommodations for 100 guests, the Lox-Hurst in Haines' Falls, another of the German-built hotels, remained anti-Semitic to the end.
— LIBRARY OF CONGRESS

The entrancing surroundings of Laurel House have inspired the pens and brushes of authors and artists for over a century. The third oldest hotel in the Catskills, it was built in 1847, enlarged several times, the dormer-windowed center building being completed in 1882. (LEFT) William Henry Jackson's finest Catskill view made in 1902 shows the original Laurel House to the right of the Victorian style center structure. This historic old resort at the head of a magnificent gorge into which the sparkling waters of the Kaaterskill Falls still tumble, made a picturesque setting. To reach the great amphitheater of shelving rock above the bottom of the falls, the hotel built novel walks and trails. On the ledges of this shelf are hundreds of graffiti dating back into the 1860's. — BOTH LIBRARY OF CONGRESS

The lookout point in front of the Catskill Mountain House, as seen from the north. This world-famed view covered the Hudson River valley for over 50 miles and the hotel claimed it was "unsurpassed anywhere in the world." It was the Queen of the Catskills, and with fine cuisine and service, a nine-hole golf course, boating, bowling, an orchestra and a ballroom with an oak floor, it was in a class by itself. The hotel grounds included many miles of nature walks, some covered to permit their use in rainy weather. — AUTHOR'S COLLECTION

York City newspapers as a gathering place for society, although occasionally a reporter would mention that the Mountain House was still popular. There was an excellent explanation for this; the Mountain House had its own exclusive clientele and, except for simple advertisements in the summer guides of the railroads or steamboat lines, there was no need to report the doings of the guests or their names, as most of them shunned publicity. It would be many a year before the Mountain House would lose its place in the sun and when that finally came to pass its glittering rivals either burned to the ground or followed the Mountain House down the road to oblivion.

The Kaaterskill and the Mountain House were the only hotels east of Laurel House, and between them they could house 1,400 guests. In 1884 this represented 20 percent of all the available rooms served by the Ulster & Delaware's narrow gauge connections. There were 23,000 beds available in the area served by the Ulster & Delaware system in 1884, of which 45 percent were reached via the

Phoenicia gateway. Not included in this total were rooms for 2,000 guests in hotels along the base of the mountain slopes in Palenville, Catskill, Cairo and the valley of Catskill Creek, as these were served by the Catskill Mountain Railroad. The hotels from Kaaterskill west to Tannersville had two railroads from 1899 to 1918, and one can only guess today in determining which railroad got the lion's share of the business.

The Otis Elevating Railway was one of the novel highlights of the Catskill region. This cable line commenced operations in August 1892 and provided a rail link from the Catskill Mountain Railway into the mountains. Making the ascent in about 10 minutes, this route provided competition for the Ulster & Delaware's narrow gauge lines and was the shortest route to the Catskill Mountain House. Though this picture is out of context here, it shows the line after it was shortened and the combination steam railroad and cable line station was relocated at the base of the mountain. —PERCY LOOMIS SPERR

6

RAILS INTO THE SKY

IF THOMAS Cornell and his associates became smug in 1885 over the troubles the Catskill Mountain Railway had just passed through, it was because the Ulster & Delaware's narrow gauge children were prosperous and their business increased each year. The gentlemen were about to have a rude awakening, for like *Jack In The Beanstalk,* a new and sensational means of transportation was to connect the Mountain House with the railroad in the valley below. The directors of the Catskill Mountain Railway had become convinced that unless the stage ride up the winding road from the railroad station to the Mountain House was eliminated traffic would decrease as time went by. Of all the suggestions to overcome this bottleneck, a cable railway; a glorified version of the inclined planes used by gravity railroads seemed to have the most promise. A cable railway would be silent, clean and spectacular; certainly worth consideration.

The Otis Elevator Co. of New York City, headed by Charles Rollins Otis, was approached and soon became very enthusiastic about the idea. He helped organize the Otis Elevating Railway Co., incorporated November 25, 1885, with Charles L. Rickerson, steamboat owner, as president and both Otis and Van Santvoord on the board of directors. Charles L. Beach took no active part on the board, but his nephew Charles A. held five titles, a man of all work if ever there was one. In 1887 Otis furnished the services of his chief engineer, Thomas E. Brown, Jr., who surveyed the proposed route and furnished cost estimates. Brown had designed and installed the Eiffel Tower elevators in Paris in 1879 for Otis and was at the height of his career. There was no action towards building the line for six years and Thomas Cornell probably regarded the cable railway as an idle dream. In 1891 the company became active, a total of $157,000 in stock was subscribed and paid in, while bonds amounting to $79,000 were eventually sold. In the winter of 1891-92 contracts for grading, the machinery, cables and rolling stock were let and construction began late in January 1892. The principal contractor was Charles L. Bucki of New York. He sublet the contract for grading to Pennell, O'Hearn & Co.; tracklaying and timber work to Mairs &

81

General view of the Otis Elevating Railway from the north side, showing the original trestle work and the Bogart Road underpass. — DEGOLYER FOUNDATION COLLECTION

Looking down the cable railway from the summit, with the turnouts for coal cars in the foreground. — DEGOLYER FOUNDATION COLLECTION

Lewis and the boilers to Q. N. Evans, all of New York City. Otis Bros. & Co. supplied the cables and hoisting machinery.

Great difficulty was experienced in hauling the cables to the summit over the wagon road from Palenville. The easy way would have been to let the Ulster & Delaware and its two narrow gauge railroads deliver the cables to Kaaterskill, from whence it was but a mile to the site of the power house. This route was suggested by one newspaper commentator, but Beach had his pride and the contractor did the job the hard way. Otis sent a special cable truck from New York City, which proved too wide for the road on the turns. The solution was provided by lagging the cable reels and building special frames around them, using them simply as large wheels. A two-wheel truck, fitted to the forward end of each frame, was used to aid in guiding the necessarily awkward vehicle. This made in effect a four-wheeled cart and seven teams of draft horses hauled this weird piece of rolling stock on two trips to the summit. In some places a block and tackle had to be used to lower the cable wagon down grade, since there were no brakes and the cable reel alone weighed 11 tons. From 25 to 30 strong mountain teams were used to haul the timbers, rails, hoisting machinery and boilers to the summit, often in the face of heavy rains which turned the road into a quagmire.

Notwithstanding the infectious optimism of Charles Otis for this, his greatest achievement to date, the railroad was not ready for the 1892 season. It was tested with a live load on August 4, 1892 and was formally opened for business on August 7. The *Railroad Gazette* of August 26, 1892, has perhaps the best description of the railway, and it is presented here in condensed form.

"To those familiar with the coal inclines in the mining regions of Pennsylvania, the general character of the Otis Cable Elevating Ry. in the Catskill Mountains requires no special explanation, as the underlying principle is the same in both cases. The Otis railroad, however, is built throughout on a much larger scale and has refinements and novelties of detail which make it a noteworthy piece of engineering. The road is of the three-rail type, the middle rail being common to the two tracks. There are two cars, fixed to the cable ends, one of them making a down trip while the other makes an up trip. Halfway between the two terminals is a turnout, enabling the cars to pass each other. A cable

Guests of the Catskill Mountain House gathered near the summit of the grade during the last weeks of construction of the Otis Elevating Railway. — DONALD DUKE COLLECTION

The upper trestle near the summit in 1902, shortly before the trestle was filled in and the line shortened.—LIBRARY OF CONGRESS

Summit station from the north side. The Catskill & Tannersville Railroad tracks are parallel to the building, in the foreground. — A. GIBSON HAGUE COLLECTION

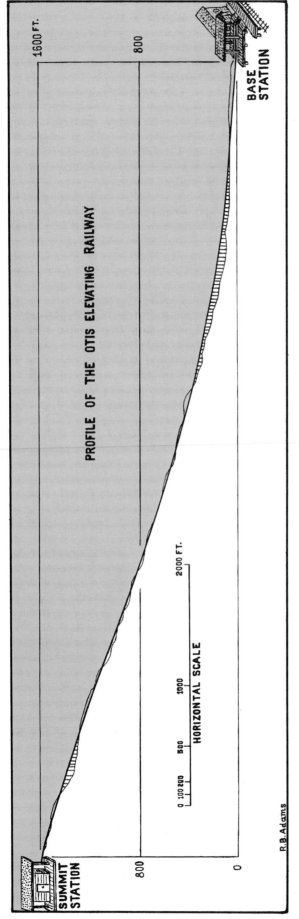

PROFILE OF THE OTIS ELEVATING RAILWAY

HORIZONTAL SCALE

R.B. Adams

passes around hoisting drums worked by reversing engines at the upper terminal station, the steam, brake and reverse levers being arranged above the engine floor, so that a good view of the line can be had by the operator.

"The road is about 7,000 feet long with a vertical rise of 1,630 feet, a maximum grade of 34 percent and an average grade of about 12 percent. The gauge of the track is 3 feet and the rail is 35 lbs. to the yard. The Otis railroad accommodation consists of two cars at each end, one for passengers and the other for their baggage. Looking up from Otis station on the Catskill Mountain Ry. one sees the mountains directly in front and perched up high on one of them, the Mountain House is plainly in view. In riding up the mountain on the road, the passenger is seated with his back to the mountains, facing the valley and moving with a speed of 700 ft. per minute. The upper station is about 300 feet north of the Mountain House.

"The hoisting machinery at the summit consists of two 12 x 30 inch Hamilton-Corliss engines, controlled not only by the regular automatic cutoff gear, but also by the throttle valve, the reverse lever and the brakes on the engines, making altogether a most unusual combination. The engines are rated at 75 HP each and are geared in the ratio of 22 to 100, to one of two Walker differential drums, each 12 feet in diameter and placed tandem-fashion. The Roebling wire hoisting cables of which there are two for each case, are 1¼ inches in diameter and are wrapped twice around each drum. Each cable is 7,250 feet long and weighs about ten tons. Ground idlers, placed 30 feet apart along the line, support the cables in going up and down the mountain. Normal speed of the engines is 86 RPM.

"The two cables for each car are fastened to a double-pivoted metal disc placed underneath the car near its middle. This disc is designed to act somewhat after the whiffletree on a wagon. So long as both cables are pulling equally, the disc remains in its normal position, but should one of them break or stretch abnormally, the disc would be turned and would throw the safety clutch into action. The latter is entirely independent of the ordinary brakes in each case and has three serrated gripping surfaces, one of which forms part of a pivoted dog. This dog is acted upon by either the disc or a special speed governor. When in action, the dog sinks its teeth into one side of the

Plan of the hoisting machinery, showing the cable drums, driving and pinion gears, the latter driven by the two steam engines shown at the top and bottom of the diagram. — DONALD DUKE COLLECTION

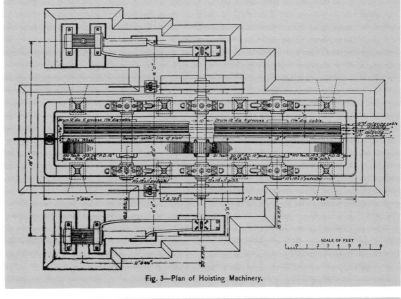

Fig. 3—Plan of Hoisting Machinery.

At the right is a side elevation of the hoisting drums and the combination flywheel and brake drum. Below, the details of the safety clutch on each car. — DONALD DUKE COLLECTION

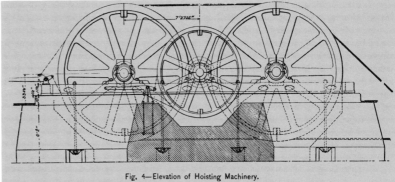

Fig. 4—Elevation of Hoisting Machinery.

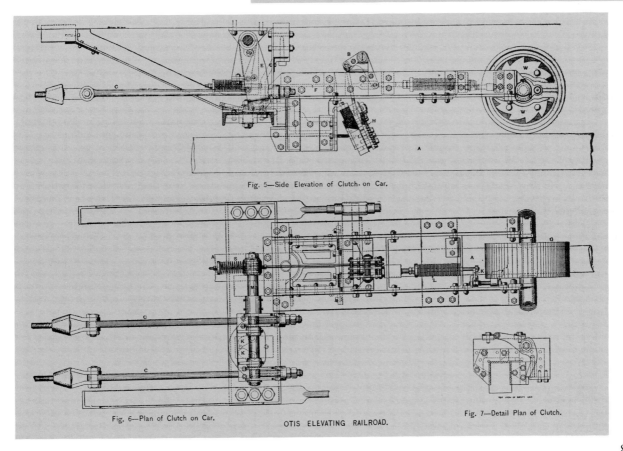

Fig. 5—Side Elevation of Clutch- on Car.

Fig. 6—Plan of Clutch on Car.

OTIS ELEVATING RAILROAD.

Fig. 7—Detail Plan of Clutch.

85

Looking down the Otis Elevating Railway, after the trestles had been filled in but before the line was shortened. In the distance through the haze, the Hudson River can be seen. — LIBRARY OF CONGRESS (BELOW) The first station at Otis Junction, with the Catskill Mountain Railway at right angles to the Otis Elevating Railway. — A. GIBSON HAGUE COLLECTION

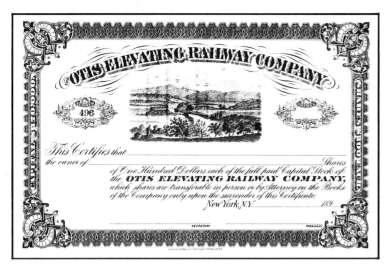

The Otis Elevating Railway stock certificates used the same view of the Catskills as the one used by the Catskill Mountain Railway. — AUTHOR'S COLLECTION (RIGHT) This is a passenger's view from the rear seat of the "down" car, after it had cleared the turnout. — GEORGE F. HOLDRIDGE COLLECTION

wooden guard rail placed between each outer and middle line of rails, and thereby draws the other serrated surfaces against the other side and the top of the guard rail. The clutch then grips the guard rail on three sides and has a holding power of 30,000 lbs. as demonstrated by actual tests.

"The speed of the cars is maintained at about eight miles per hour and the speed governor under each car is so adjusted that if the speed reached twelve miles per hour, the safety clutch would operate. The two terminal stations are connected by telephone and electric gong signals, the cars having similar signals so that a signal rung anywhere on the line is rung at all four points.

"The rolling stock consists of two passenger and two baggage cars built by Jackson & Sharp of Wilmington, Delaware, and sit permanently at an angle of ten degrees, 30 minutes. They measure 46 feet clear length, 7 ft. 6 in. wide and have a comfortable seating capacity of 75 passengers, though a maximum of 90 can be carried. The cars weigh 22,000 lbs. each, the seats are stationary, with curved backs and are stoutly braced. They are counterparts of those used by the Otis brothers in their elevators in the Eiffel Tower. The ends of the cars are glazed; the sides are open, with sliding canvas curtains. Fixed iron crossbars on one side prevent the passengers from falling out, and on the other, or entrance side, by wooden bars

which are dropped into sockets when the cars are about to start. The cars have been named the *Rickerson,* after the president of the road, and *Van Santvoord* after the proprietor of the Day Line steamers. Each car is mounted on two four-wheel trucks. The baggage cars are open, being simply platforms with sides but no tops. Steam for the Corliss engines is supplied by two vertical 150HP boilers at 90 lbs. pressure, the boiler house being located below the level of the engine house. The position was chosen so that coal could be brought up in the baggage cars on the line and dumped directly into the bunkers.

"There are three trestles with a total of 2,672 feet and a maximum height of 72 feet, containing over a million feet of yellow pine timber. The road runs through four heavy rock cuts, one of them 45 feet deep. The last 1,000 feet of the line at the east end consists simply of rails laid on cross-ties ballasted with broken stone. With the exception of the turnouts, the road runs in a straight line from end to end. The grade line is a combination of circular and parabolic curves so designed that the cars balance each other when carrying average loads, at whatever point on the line they may be."

The lower terminal of the cable railway was at a point on the Catskill Mountain Railway about one mile north of Palenville, and was called Otis Junction. Here the passengers from Catskill Landing detrained on a wooden platform and entered a shelter which was open at both ends, and where the cable car was waiting. The cable railway's track was at right angles to that of the steam railroad and there was no physical connection between the two. A siding and a "Y" for turning trains which were not to go south of Otis Junction were built and the Otis Elevating Railway was now in business.

It served the Mountain House well, although there were reports in the newspapers that some of the timid first-riders returned home by other means of transportation. For two years the cable railway's competition caused a reduction in passengers carried on the Kaaterskill Railroad, after which the latter's annual passenger total increased yearly. It was unfortunate that it was not possible for excursionists to make a one-day round trip from New York to Catskill on the Day Line steamers and thence to the Mountain House. It was possible for residents of Albany and consider-

Employees timetable of the Catskill Mountain Railway and the Otis Elevating Railway at the opening of the summer season, June 13, 1896. More trains would be added when the summer rush began two weeks later. — JOHN B. HUNGERFORD COLLECTION

able traffic developed from this area. A similar Otis railroad with a 1,630 foot climb was built a few years later at Mount Beacon, across the Hudson from Newburgh, and became popular for many years for day trippers from New York City.

For patrons of the hotels west of Otis Summit a stage ride was still required at least as far as the Kaaterskill Railroad's station. This inconvenience would obviously rob the Otis Elevating Railway of many passengers whose patronage was vital to the success of the cable railway. The best solution was to build a narrow gauge railroad to connect Otis Summit with the hotels at least as far west as Tannersville. As an opening gambit, the Catskill & Tannersville Railroad was chartered September 14,

1892, with Charles L. Rickerson president and Charles A. Beach the secretary-treasurer. After the enormous expense of building the Otis Elevating Railway it is doubtful if Charles L. Beach and his associates had any idea of following through with the proposed railroad immediately, but its incorporation had the desired effect. S. D. Coykendall of the Ulster & Delaware had no wish to see a rival railroad paralleling his most lucrative trackage on the mountain top and he suggested an alternative. After much bickering, in which each group begrudged giving aid and comfort to the rival, Coykendall's proposal was accepted by the Beach lines.

The Catskill & Tannersville Railroad would indeed be built for a distance of .93 miles from Otis Summit to the Kaaterskill Railroad's terminal at Kaaterskill Station, with a gauge of three feet, on land largely donated by Charles L. Beach. The Kaaterskill Railroad agreed to operate the Catskill & Tannersville for three years under a renewable lease, the latter to be paid half the gross receipts or $1,278 a year, whichever was greater. The Kaaterskill Railroad would retain all fares collected and maintain the track. The lease was signed in November 1892, the railroad was built in the spring of 1893 and cost $24,522. When opened for business on July 8, all Ulster & Delaware narrow gauge trains extended their runs to Otis Summit, and three additional daily trains from Otis Summit to Tannersville were run, to conform with the schedules of the Otis Elevating Railway.

To provide this shuttle service, the Kaaterskill Railroad bought a secondhand Brooks-built locomotive similar in size and type to their own engines and a combination coach. Business became so brisk on the Catskill Mountain Railway that two new passenger coaches were purchased from Jackson & Sharp in 1893 and in June 1895 locomotive No. 4 was received from the Schenectady Locomotive Works. The Beach lines, and for that matter the Ulster & Delaware Railroad, were at the beginning of their most prosperous era.

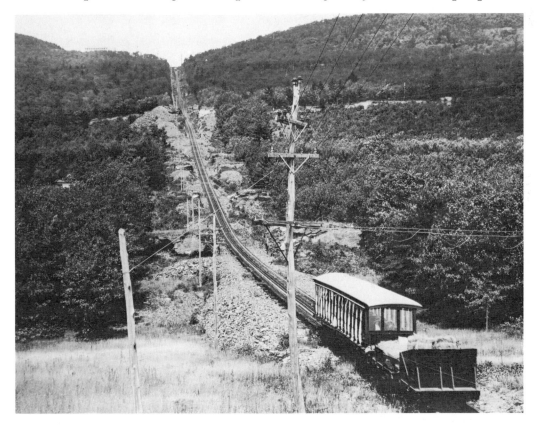

The baggage car, which is pulled by the passenger car, is loaded with hay for the livestock on the summit. This photograph shows the line after all trestles had been eliminated and the turnout moved above the deepest rock cut. — DEGOLYER FOUNDATION COLLECTION

Ulster & Delaware No. 21 rolling downgrade west of Haines' Falls in 1902. Narrow gauge spikes in the crossties indicate the haste with which the old rails were removed in 1899. — LIBRARY OF CONGRESS

7

THE ULSTER & DELAWARE REACHES ITS GOAL

ENCOURAGED BY the ease with which the Hobart Branch Railroad was built in 1884, Thomas Cornell decided that the time was ripe to try again for that elusive connection with the Delaware & Hudson at Oneonta. Cost estimates were prepared so that Cornell could discuss his plans with the townspeople along the proposed route. The unused six miles of grade northwest of Stamford, placed there by Litchfield in 1872, was still there and required only the clearing away of the underbrush and repairing erosion damage. To this six miles already graded there would be 21 miles of new grading for a total distance of 27 miles to Oneonta from Stamford via Harpersfield. But Cornell had other plans. Talks with dairy farmers and businessmen down-river from Hobart in Bloomville and Delhi convinced him that the dairies were dissatisfied with the service and the transportation charges for their products shipped over the New York, Ontario & Western from Delhi. The dairymen in Bloomville, halfway between the two railheads, favored the Ulster & Delaware, and this enticed Cornell to form a separate company to build a railroad from Hobart to Bloomville, 8.7 miles, to be leased to the Ulster & Delaware when completed.

No sooner did this plan become public in the spring of 1885 than it stirred up a hornets' nest of opposition in Harpersfield township. For 20 years the taxpayers of this township had been paying seven percent interest on the township bonds issued to pay for stock in the Rondout & Oswego. Each year they had retired three bonds at par, besides the interest. In the bankruptcy proceedings of 1875 their stock became worthless, but until 1885 the taxpayers of Harpersfield apparently did not realize it. In a period of nearly 20 years they had paid off over half the debt and fully expected that when construction on the railroad was resumed it would come via Harpersfield. They had not been alarmed at the Hobart Extension Railroad, for they considered it to be a branch of the main line and had been content that the railroad was finished to Stamford.

When Cornell announced his intention to extend the Ulster & Delaware to Bloomville and thence to Oneonta a town meeting was held in Harpersfield village, and from this meeting came a petition to the State of New York to vacate the charter of the railroad unless they built it via Harpersfield or refunded the $100,000 advanced to the railroad in 1866. The State complied with the request and brought suit against the Ulster & Delaware, the trial to be held at Delhi in October 1886. The rail-

Rondout yards circa 1890. The mainline enters the yards on the curve at upper right. The facing triple and double stub switches in the right center would be a model railroader's delight. — ROBERT R. HAINES COLLECTION

road petitioned for a change of venue to Kingston, in Ulster County, and this was granted on October 11, 1886. One newspaper commented that there was no industry along the Harpersfield-Davenport route and no extensive dairy farming, nor were the lumbering prospects good, whereas the line via Bloomville would tap a rich agricultural district. All critics of Cornell's plans agreed that it would be much more expensive to complete the railroad to Oneonta from Bloomville, but that the traffic generated would probably make the change worthwhile. As for Cornell, he figured that once in Hobart he had abandoned the Harpersfield route for all time and it is doubtful that he even considered it again.

Harpersfield's suit came to trial before Judge Alton B. Parker in Kingston on November 22, 1886. The plaintiff's lawyers failing to appear after a reasonable wait, Judge Parker ordered Cornell to state his case. Cornell testified that the present railroad company had no obligation to Harpersfield, this having been nullified by the bankruptcy sale of the New York, Kingston & Syracuse Rail-

road in 1875. He said Harpersfield should have been aware of this fact and argued that to build via Harpersfield would be much more expensive than via Bloomville, a statement open to question had a competent and informed civil engineer testified for Harpersfield. There being no arguments from the other side, Judge Parker decided for the railroad by default. A search of the minutes of the township meetings from 1885 through 1887 show that a lawyer was employed as the town attorney to represent them in Kingston, but that he pocketed his fee and never went near the seat of the trial. More was to be heard from Harpersfield later

92

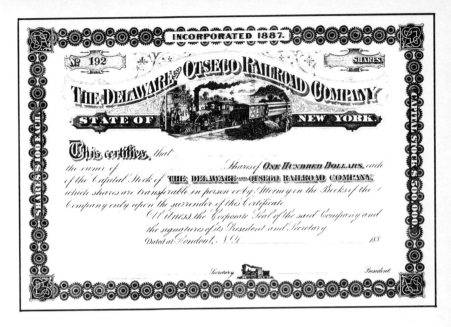

The Delaware & Otsego Railroad issued more elaborate stock certificates than those of Cornell's narrow gauge lines. The engraved illustration of the train is typical of those provided by New York City banknote companies and is not representative of a scene on the Delaware & Otsego Railroad. — AUTHOR'S COLLECTION

and from Judge Parker too, for he became the candidate for President on the Democratic ticket against Theodore Roosevelt in 1904. Though he was defeated, he soon became one of the most successful lawyers in New York City.

With the legal hurdle out of the way, Cornell organized the Delaware & Otsego Railroad on May 5, 1887. Stock subscriptions were slow at first and Cornell procrastinated for a year, until he was spurred into action by the announced plans to build a competing railroad. Organized by men in Cooperstown, the Cooperstown & Charlotte Valley Railroad proposed to build a new railroad from Cooperstown Junction on the D. & H. north of Colliersville in an easterly direction along Charlotte Creek through Davenport Center, Harpersfield (of all places), thence to Cooksburg, onetime terminal of the Canajoharie & Catskill, and down Catskill Creek to a connection with the West Shore Railroad. The Cooperstown & Susquehanna Valley Railroad, built in 1869 from Cooperstown to a connection with the Albany & Susquehanna (D. & H.), was leased to the new railroad, thus making a continuous line from Cooperstown to Catskill. One could just see the gleeful smiles of Harpersfield residents as they visioned themselves on a railroad after all, and a competitor of Cornell at that.

On the morning of March 11, 1888, all of the Hudson River valley and most of the eastern seaboard as far south as Philadelphia was visited by a storm which began with heavy rains, turning later in the day to sleet as the temperature fell. By the morning of the 12th the temperature was five degrees above zero, the wind was 60 miles per hour and the greatest blizzard of the 19th Century in the U. S. was at hand. The storm continued all through the 12th and 13th and ended on the morning of the 14th, at which time it was estimated that 40 inches of snow had fallen on the level and drifts up to 30 feet in depth were common. All the railroads within the compass of the blizzard were snowed under, and no trains ran on any railroad from the 12th to the 15th. In the Catskills, the Ulster & Delaware's narrow gauge lines closed up shop and sat out the storm. The main line was equally hard hit. On the 12th the train from Hobart, with two locomotives, became snowed in at Brodhead's Bridge, while the westbound train on that day became stalled at Mayham's cut, three miles east of Stamford. Two locomotives sent out to help the stalled train at Brodhead's Bridge derailed in a cut east of Olive Branch, but the great barrier to clearing the line was McKelvey's cut near West Hurley. The cut was drifted eight feet deep for 1,200 feet and the bucker snowplow pushed by three locomotives was useless. A relief train brought hundreds of shovelers to the cut and for three days they worked until the track was all clear.

New York City suffered from lack of food, especially milk for the children, but on the morning of the 16th the West Shore had been opened to Buffalo; later in the day the New York Central began running trains. Late in the afternoon came the cheering news from Kingston that a train loaded with cans of milk had gotten through on the Ulster & Delaware, more milk cars from the Wallkill Val-

Cooperstown & Charlotte Valley No. 4 with train, crossing over the Delaware & Hudson mainline and the highway, near Cooperstown Junction.—AUTHOR'S COLLECTION (LEFT) The milk train taking water at Hobart in below-zero weather. The caboose is the first of the Eight-Wheel type purchased by the railroad. — RAYMOND S. BALDWIN

Ulster & Delaware No. 16 coming into Bloomville terminal after a bout with the snow. This was before pilot plows came into use. — DE-GOLYER FOUNDATION COLLECTION

ley had been added and the cars were being rushed to Weehawken. This was not the last blizzard in the Ulster & Delaware's history, but it is the one which is still talked about by old-timers who as small children lived through the days when none knew if the snowfall would ever cease.

A warm spell quickly followed the blizzard and grading began on the Cooperstown & Charlotte Valley Railroad east of Cooperstown Junction, reaching Davenport Center over the very ground surveyed in 1866 for the Rondout & Oswego. Cornell spent the year 1888 raising enough money to grade his extension to Bloomville which was done during 1889 and early 1890. Money was hard to raise in Cooperstown, fortunately for Cornell, and the track of the new Cooperstown & Charlotte Valley progressed eastward for only six miles to West Davenport, though the graders built culverts, fills and rock cuttings up the valley of Charlotte Creek beyond Davenport, well into Harpersfield township, before the winter of 1889-90 set in.

Early in February 1890 the C. & C. V. tracklayers reached Davenport Center, while the graders resumed work east of Harpersfield. Suddenly all work stopped, for Thomas B. Cornell had died in Kingston on March 30, 1890, of pneumonia, in his 77th year. When his will was read he had named his wife Mary and his nephew Edwin Young as the executors of his estate. Young was attorney and general counsel of the Delaware & Hudson Canal Co. and had become vice-president of the Ulster & Delaware in 1889. Upon Cornell's death Young became temporary president and began the administration of Cornell's estate, which was valued at between three and four million dollars. Samuel Decker Coykendall ran the Cornell Steamboat Co. and the railroad properties until the estate was at

The special funeral train was a common sight during the past century. In this scene, No. 16 pauses in Arkville for water while en route to Kingston and Thomas Cornell's funeral there. Note the black crepe decorations hanging from the letterboards of the baggage car and coach.
— HAROLD GOLDSMITH COLLECTION

A construction train with four-wheel caboose No. 626 takes water at Hobart. The old enginehouse and terminal may be seen at the left. — RAYMOND S. BALDWIN

While at Stamford, the Bloomville-Rondout passenger train No. 36 pauses for a train crew portrait, including the conductor at the left, the enginemen, baggagemen, trainmen and the porter. — CHARLES E. FISHER COLLECTION

least partly settled. Cornell owned a major portion of the $2,000,000 U. & D. five percent bonds and almost all the common stock. Edwin Young sold the bonds to the Lincoln National Bank and J. D. Vermilye & Co., both of New York City, and distributed the stock among Cornell's grandchildren, his son-in-law and to his widow, assuring family control of the Ulster & Delaware. Cornell had also been the founder and president of the First National Bank of Rondout. A special election was held June 13, 1890, and Charles C. Clarke, vice-president of the West Shore, and Horace Greeley Young, Edwin Young's brother and senior vice-president of the Delaware & Hudson, were elected to the Ulster & Delaware's board of directors. According to the *New York Times* of June 14, the West Shore and the D. & H. were to jointly operate the Ulster & Delaware, but this never quite came to pass. The Youngs were as anxious as Cornell had been to complete the railroad from Rondout to a connection with the D. & H. and their influence in Cooperstown was undoubtedly what stopped all further work on the Cooperstown & Charlotte Valley. The track of the latter ended at Davenport Center and there it remained for many a year. Before Cornell's death grading work on the Delaware & Otsego was north of Bloomville on the way to Oneonta and when heavy snows halted operations for the winter, track had been laid part way from Hobart to Bloomville.

Edwin Young was formally elected president of the Ulster & Delaware in January 1891, with Robert C. Pruyn of Albany the vice-president. Pruyn was a member of a distinguished Albany family once headed by John V. L. Pruyn who helped found the Mohawk & Hudson Railroad. The railhead of the Delaware & Otsego was in front of the new Bloomville station on April 17, 1891, the grade through Wright Brook valley, five miles north of Bloomville and 400 feet above it, was complete with bridges and culverts, and considerable work had been done on the grade down the north side of the mountains into Schoharie Creek valley. With the menace of a rival railroad gone, the Youngs halted further construction until it could be financed. Expenses had been $306,000 and $190,000 of it was in the form of floating debt; i.e., unpaid bills. Settlement of the latter was reached by leasing the Delaware & Otsego to the Ulster & Delaware on May 1, 1891. D. & O. shares were exchanged for an equal amount of U. & D.

stock, and the creditors were given $125,000 in U. & D. five percent bonds and $65,000 in cash. The grade beyond Bloomville was protected by paying taxes on it as they came due and by keeping it in repair.

The celebrated Harpersfield case erupted again in 1889, lawyers for the township persuading the New York State Supreme Court to reopen the case. The court set aside Judge Alton Parker's decision and in January 1889 ordered a new action to vacate the Ulster & Delaware's charter. Five other townships along the Ulster & Delaware which shared Harpersfield's opinion that they should have at least some share in the railroad, joined in asking that the trial be made a test case for them all. The New York State Railroad Commission donated their two-cents' worth that same year by ruling that the railroad was not obligated to fulfill any contracts entered into by the defunct New York, Kingston & Syracuse Railroad. On April 18, 1890, several weeks after Cornell's death, the case came to trial in Kingston. After hearing the testimony from both sides the judge ruled in favor of the defendant railroad. He stated that, first, the action was barred by the statute of limitations and, second, that the Railroad Commission had the right under law to rule on such matters. In December 1890 the State Supreme Court affirmed the judgment and Harpersfield township, as well as all the others involved in this joint action, had to pay off the bonds with interest out of local taxes, for the railroad which, at least in the case of Harpersfield, never came their way. When the last Harpersfield bond had been paid off in 1894, the township had paid out $206,000, all raised through taxes. What a relief it must have been to the farmers of the valley when that onerous tax burden was removed. The

A favorite small town pastime in 1893; waiting for the afternoon train to arrive in Hobart.
— RAYMOND S. BALDWIN

In the view above, a busy scene at Bloomville when it was the end of the line. The afternoon train is ready to leave for Kingston. At the left, the Bloomville train ready to leave Rondout station. Departing trains backed east to the main line switch, then headed west. — RAYMOND S. BALDWIN

only notation in the township records after the case was settled was that the "Dog Fund" of 1889 be used to pay for the legal costs. The suit had indeed become a "dog!"

Under president Edwin Young a certain amount of modernization was undertaken. Two new locomotives were added and in 1893 all the old style stub switches were eliminated on the main line, though a few remained on house tracks or spurs for years. A new federal law requiring the use of automatic couplers was passed in 1893, and the Ulster & Delaware gradually replaced the Miller hooks and the link and pin couplers with the Janney type. A severe snow and ice storm which was in some ways worse than the 1888 blizzard began on February 17, 1893, and by the 22nd the drifts on the Ulster & Delaware from Shandaken to the summit were 25 feet deep in the rocky cuts. Hundreds of men shoveled their way through these drifts, and on the 23rd a train of milk cars got through to Kingston and was sent to New York to relieve the shortage of milk there. History was repeating itself after five years.

Edwin Young died suddenly on April 21, 1893, in his 37th year, and his brother Horace Greeley Young was elected in his place at a special meeting in Kingston. Joel Burdick, a D. & H. official, re-

placed Edwin Young on the board, thus keeping up the D. & H. influence. Horace G. Young and Samuel D. Coykendall agreed to a merger of the two narrow gauge railroads with the Ulster & Delaware and to ultimately standard gauge them. Under Coykendall's management the Stony Clove & Catskill Mountain had paid $6,200 a year in dividends and built up a rapidly growing surplus. The Kaaterskill Railroad had not done so well due to flood damage to the roadbed one year, but it was not in the red. The merger was effected June 1, 1893 and newly issued U. & D. five percent bonds to the amount of $334,000 were used to retire the Stony Clove & Catskill Mountain's $210,000 bond issue and reimburse the stockholders. The Kaaterskill Railroad stockholders received $8,000 in cash and $60,000 in U. & D. bonds in exchange for the Kaaterskill bonds. Although the two narrow gauge railroads were carried on the books with the old corporate names, they were for all practical purposes part of the U. & D. system. The

Ulster & Delaware narrow gauge No. 1, the *Hunter* **decorated for July 4, 1894, a few weeks before it collided with a passenger train at Edgewood. —** DEGOLYER FOUNDATION COLLECTION

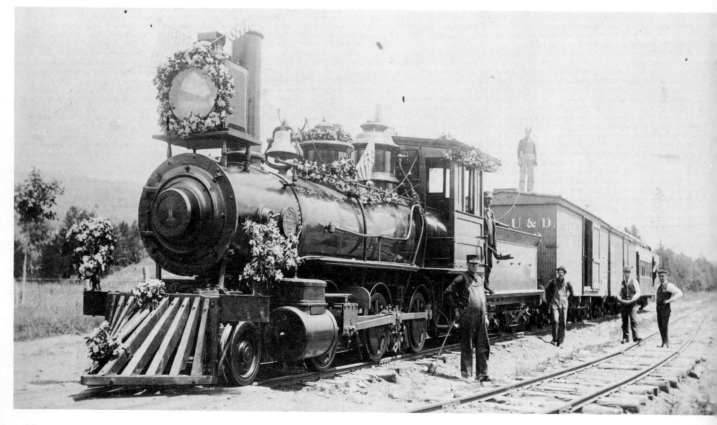

equipment was relettered Ulster & Delaware and in the latter's timetables, the two roads became "The Narrow Gauge Division."

On August 18, 1894, a calamity of major proportions was prevented by the heroism of one man. A narrow gauge passenger train had left Phoenicia for Hunter in the late afternoon and when the train was two miles north of Lanesville and a mile south of Edgewood the locomotive *Hunter* appeared, coming down the mountain alone at a speed which made it impossible to prevent a head-on collision. On the engine of the passenger train the sudden appearance of the light locomotive came as a complete surprise and, after the engineer had shut off steam, he and the fireman jumped clear, as did the crew of the *Hunter,* and all escaped serious injury. The *Hunter* turned sideways and came to rest across the track, but by forgetting to apply the brakes the engineer of the passenger train created a potential disaster, for since the passenger engine was not derailed the train began to move backwards downhill, and by the time the engine crew had picked themselves up and gave pursuit it was too late. Brakeman Porter on the passenger train quickly realized the situation, applied

The *Hunter* with westbound train No. 36 steams along the Kaaterskill branch at North Lake in 1895. — DEGOLYER FOUNDATION COLLECTION

The Hunter-Kaaterskill Junction train poses for a picture while waiting for its connecting train. The *Derrick Van Brummel's* cap on top of the smokestack seems ready to fall off. — DEGOLYER FOUNDATION COLLECTION

Ulster & Delaware narrow gauge No. 5 at Tannersville. The engineer with the derby is Charles Fuller; John Askin, fireman, at Fuller's right; Perry McDonald, conductor; Guy Mattice in the white shirt, baggageman and Geo. F. Haines, agent is at the extreme right. — GEORGE PHELPS COLLECTION

the hand brakes on the cars, climbed over the tender and into the cab of the engine where he opened the throttle and the train was brought to a stop slightly less than a mile south of the collision point. So grateful were the passengers that they collected a purse of $100 for Porter. In the session the conductor had on the carpet the next day it was brought out that he had been given a meet order to pass the light engine at Lanesville, had failed to give the engineer his copy and stuck the orders in his pocket, forgetting the whole thing. The management did not forget to fire him.

By the winter of 1894 the effect of the panic of 1893 was being felt by the railroads and the communities they served. Horace Greeley Young was called back to Albany to devote his full time to the Delaware & Hudson and, though he remained on the U. & D. board for many years, his primary interest was the D. & H. Robert Pruyn acted as temporary president of the U. & D. until the annual meeting of December 3, 1895, when Samuel Decker Coykendall became the seventh president of the railroad. Coykendall had been busy the previous five years running the Cornell Steamboat Co., the narrow gauge railroads and, after Edwin Young's death, handling Cornell's estate which had involved much litigation. Since the Coykendall family owned most of the railroad's common stock, it became a family affair for sure. Samuel's oldest son, Thomas Cornell Coykendall was elected vice-president, son Harry S. became the treasurer, Frederick K., another son, and George, Samuel's brother, became directors. Only Horace G. Young, H. C. Soop of Kingston and Charles Bray and Amos Van Etten of Rondout were left from the old board. The venerable Alfred Van Santvoord, who had come on the board with the Youngs in 1890 resigned, while Robert C. Pruyn returned to Albany and became a D. & H. manager in 1910.

Thus did the "Kingston Crowd," as one financial reporter in New York dubbed them, take over the railroad. Edward Coykendall, Samuel's third son, became the new superintendent in place of that man of many jobs, James H. Jones. Obviously the Coykendall family was going to run the railroad for better or for worse, and so they did, until changing times and the grim reaper removed them from the scene.

The Coykendalls set up a program of improvements to place the railroad in a better position to take advantage of the ever increasing popularity of the Catskills. One of Horace G. Young's last acts was to firm up the plans to build an extension from Rondout to the site of Columbus Point, there to provide a landing for the Hudson River Day Line steamers. There had been many complaints from passengers about the necessity of going ashore at Rhinecliff and taking the ferryboat *Transport* from there to Rondout before boarding the Ulster & Delaware trains. To eliminate this bottleneck, the work of building a new steamboat landing to be called Kingston Point was authorized at the 1895 U. & D. annual meeting. A railroad connection from the new landing to Rondout was also authorized, but some of the landowners held out for high prices and it was necessary to have some of it condemned in the public interest before work could start. The Kingston Board of Trade was asked to help and not only contributed financially to the project but persuaded some of the holdouts to sell

Samuel Decker Coykendall
1836-1913
COURTESY OF MARTIN HAGELE

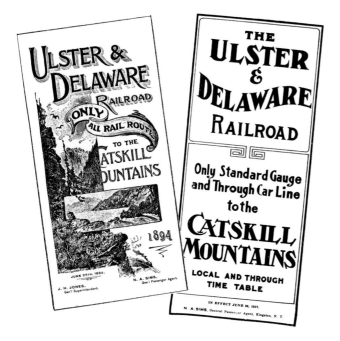

The summer Ulster & Delaware timetables for 1894 and 1917 both listed N. A. Sims as general passenger agent. — DONALD DUKE COLLECTION

their worthless swampland at a reasonable price. Just before the opening of the 1896 season in June the mile of new track was in place, the new dock was in use and the boat train for the mountains started its run at Kingston Point. This bothered the ferry owner not one bit, for he was Samuel Decker Coykendall.

The area to the west of the landing was developed as a park, with an amusement section at one end, and the place became very popular with residents of the Albany area. They came down to the Point on the Day Line's boat in the morning and returned home in the late afternoon. Kingston residents were heavy patrons of the Point in the summer, coming down the hill from the city on the trolleys of the Kingston City Railroad, which used the Ulster & Delaware tracks past the shops to a district known as Ponckhockie where the cars turned left onto their own line to the Point. No fewer than 18 open type cars were required for this traffic and the only protection they had against the U. & D. trains was a semaphore located just east of the Hasbrouck Avenue tunnel and operated from a shanty at the foot of the hill by John Lons-

Kingston Point from the deck of a Hudson River Dayliner. The Ulster & Delaware train in the background is a mixture of vestibuled and open platform type cars. — STEAMSHIP HISTORICAL SOCIETY OF AMERICA, INC.

Engine No. 22 has just arrived from the Catskills with passengers for the *Day Line*. The ladies were still wearing straw hats in 1900. — HAROLD GOLDSMITH COLLECTION

Ulster & Delaware No. 33 at the head of the *Day Line* train for the Catskills, waits for helper engine No. 18 to back down the long fill from Rondout.—JAMES BOYNTON COLLECTION

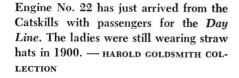

The *Albany*, southbound Hudson River Day-liner passing Poughkeepsie Bridge. — GERALD M. BEST

berry. It was all in the family, for the Coykendalls owned the electric line too. In later years after this line was sold to the Kingston Consolidated Railroad, the latter's tracks were extended down the Strand past the U. & D. shops to Ponckhockie, there to cross the U. & D. tracks and continue on the original right-of-way to the Point.

Kingston Point was only a minor improvement compared with others planned. The first was a replacement of almost all the original wooden bridges and trestles with 34 new iron bridges and to build a new repair shop at Rondout with power house and electric generator to furnish power to the new, motorized equipment. Out on the line every station was equipped with agents' semaphores to replace the old flag system. All this was done in 1897 and in 1898 two decisions were made: to standard gauge the narrow gauge lines before the opening of the 1899 season and to complete the Delaware & Otsego Railroad to Oneonta. Contracts were let for both projects in November 1898 and though there was snow on the ground, work proceeded whenever the weather would permit. On the narrow gauge, except for widening the rocky shelf south of the Notch and increasing the radius of several very sharp curves, little work had to be done on the roadbed from Phoenicia to Hunter and Kaaterskill.

The ferry boat *Transport* continued in service for many years after Kingston Point was opened. — STEAMSHIP HISTORICAL SOCIETY OF AMERICA, INC.

An overloaded Kingston City Railroad trolley car passes Rondout shops en route to Kingston Point. At the right, a westbound train climbs Pine Hill grade, with new engine No. 9 helped by Dickson-built engine No. 10. — RAYMOND S. BALDWIN

Ulster & Delaware narrow gauge No. 1 at Phoenicia in 1899. Engineer Henry C. Sherman lays an affectionate hand on the former *Hunter*, which was soon to start a new life in the Adirondacks.—DE-GOLYER FOUNDATION COLLECTION

Icicles hang from the tender as No. 5 couples onto the Bloomville-Rondout train.—AUTHOR'S COLLECTION

Ulster & Delaware engines Nos. 3 and 12 waiting for orders for a snow extra, at Phoenicia, February 14, 1899. At the right, engines Nos. 1 and 3, ready to leave Phoenicia on the same day with a westbound passenger train. — WILLIAM CONERTY, COURTESY DEGOLYER FOUNDATION

All work came to a halt on February 12, 1899 when the worst storm since the blizzard of 1888 hit the eastern seaboard. History repeated itself with rain at first, then sleet and then high winds with fine, almost powdery snow driven by 50 mile winds. February 13 saw most of the railroads in New York State snowed in; all but the Ulster & Delaware which had learned a great deal about snow fighting since 1888. Two of the older locomotives had been equipped with enormous pilot plows which extended from an inch above the track to the center of the boiler. One of the narrow gauge engines also had this type of plow and, with a second engine helping in the rear, these combinations were sent out on the line as the storm developed and the line was kept open except Stony Clove Notch. This marooned Hunter and the

A classic railroad photograph from the camera of William Henry Jackson. The scene is Kaaterskill station in 1902, three years after the conversion from narrow to standard gauge. Engines No. 23 and No. 26 have been turned around and are ready for the return journey to Rondout.
— LIBRARY OF CONGRESS

villages on the mountain top for several days with huge drifts of snow.

Anticipating the change of gauge, all cross-tie replacements on the narrow gauge after 1894 had been to standard gauge length and by 1898 only a few thousand of them remained to be replaced. New 70 lb. steel rails were laid outside the lighter narrow gauge rails, permitting trains of either gauge to pass over the four-rail sections. Progress was so rapid that the last standard gauge rail was laid at Kaaterskill Station on June 1, 1899. The new track was reballasted by June 26, 1899, and on that day, a through train was run from Weehawken to Kaaterskill, the only change being the locomotive at Kingston. Three new standard gauge Ten-Wheel locomotives for use on the branch were purchased and the narrow gauge equipment sold. The Catskill & Tannersville Railroad, now a marooned orphan, was returned to its owners by the U. & D. at the end of the 1898 season.

Starting in March 1899, the part of the Delaware & Otsego grade west of Bloomville which had been completed in 1891 was worked over and grading began on the unfinished portion. The summit was eight miles northwest of Bloomville and was reached with a grade of 1.7 percent to an elevation of 1,862 feet, only 23 feet lower than Grand

Ulster & Delaware No. 19 with a train carrying seven narrow gauge passenger cars, leaving Phoenicia for Kingston in 1899. — DEGOLYER FOUNDATION COLLECTION

Ulster & Delaware No. 23 with three new vestibuled coaches, ready to leave Phoenicia with the funeral train of the Hon. Davis Winne. Doly Hoffmann, engineer and J. Franscia, conductor. — WALTER A. LUCAS COLLECTION

Hotel Summit. The Bloomville-Kortright terrain was rugged enough, but the next nine miles down the valley of Kortright Creek to its junction with Charlotte Creek at Davenport Center involved a descent of over 600 feet in nine miles, including three crossings of the stream. Davenport Center was the eastern terminus of the Cooperstown & Charlotte Valley as previously related, and from its completion in 1890 passenger service had been furnished from Cooperstown to Davenport Center. When the U. & D. graders reached the latter place, no connection with the C. & C. V. tracks was made, the new line traversing Charlotte Creek on a steel bridge, then following the north bank of the creek to West Davenport where a connection was made with the C. & C. V., the two roads using a joint station. A mile west of there the U. & D. grade crossed the C. & C. V. tracks, then Charlotte Creek and the Susquehanna by means of two steel bridges.

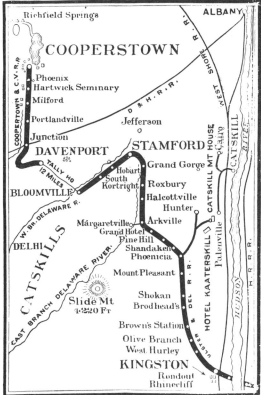

After the Bloomville extension was completed, a "Tally-Ho" provided a connection to Davenport, the east end of the Cooperstown & Charlotte Valley R.R.

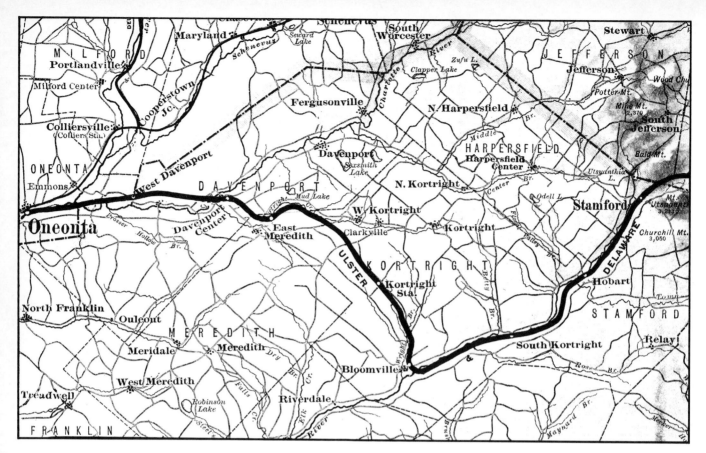

The track was laid to Oneonta early in July 1900, making a physical connection with the D. & H. a half-mile north of the latter's station. The U. & D. station was built near the junction and passengers interchanging between the two railroads had to use public transportation. The first U. & D. passenger train for Rondout, hauled by engine No. 9, left Oneonta on July 16, 1900, and by then the terminal facilities had been moved to Oneonta from Bloomville. The hotels in Cooperstown which had been operating a summer "tally-ho" stage line from Bloomville to Davenport Center since 1891 for patrons coming up to Cooperstown via the U. & D., now arranged for the C. & C. V. trains to make close connections at West Davenport, and this continued for two summers. The extra train needed for this service cost more than it earned and in 1903 all passenger service from Cooperstown Junction to Davenport Center was discontinued. The D. & H. absorbed the C. & C. V. the same year, and thereafter passengers for Cooperstown changed at Oneonta. The line from Cooperstown Junction to Davenport Center was used by the D. & H. for freight only until 1930 when the rails were pulled up and what little business there was in the valley was left to the Ulster & Delaware. In 1970 the D. & H. applied

Map of the west end of the Ulster & Delaware from Stamford to Oneonta, published shortly after the line was completed, ignores the existence of the Cooperstown & Charlotte Valley Railroad south of Cooperstown Junction. — AUTHOR'S COLLECTION

for abandonment of the Cooperstown branch, of which more later.

How did Coykendall raise the money for all these improvements? By consolidating all the companies involved into one new company, *THE* Ulster & Delaware Railroad Co. The stockholders of the old companies received share for share in the new company except those of the Delaware & Otsego, which were exchanged for new stock on a percentage basis. The new company assumed responsibility for the old bond issues and new bonds at five percent with a par value of $500,000 were sold. The consolidation was in force January 1, 1902, and as of that date the plans of Thomas Cornell were fulfilled — by Samuel Decker Coykendall.

One note about Coykendall. When the Delaware & Hudson Canal closed forever at the end of the 1898 boating season, Coykendall was assured

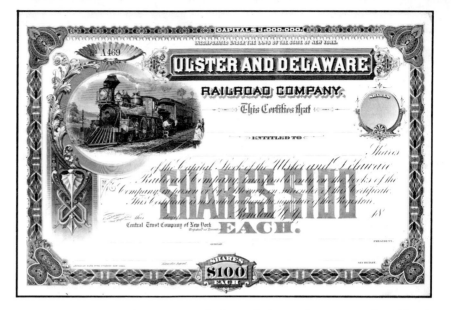

U. & D. stock certificates issued after 1901 had the word *The* placed ahead of Ulster & Delaware Railroad Company.—AUTHOR'S COLLECTION

A trainload of 11,000 Christmas trees ready to leave Tannersville for the New York market. (BELOW) The Kaaterskill-Phoenicia train crew in September 1900. Left to right; Perry McDonald, conductor; Emery Craw, trainman; Andrew Gulnick, trainman; Raymond S. Baldwin, baggageman; Henry C. Sherman, engineer. — JOHN LEIPOLD PHOTO—COURTESY DEGOLYER FOUNDATION COLLECTION

of a very good slice of the anthracite coal traffic if he could effect a connection with the D. & H. at Oneonta. The heaviest work for the Cornell Steamboat Co. towboats was lost when the canal closed and he had to have something to replace the lost business. This was the big incentive to build the Oneonta extension. When the canal property was put up for sale in 1899 the D. & H. expected that the Erie, the N.Y.O. & W. or Pennsylvania Coal Co. would buy it, but at that time they were not even interested enough to send representatives to the auction, which was held on June 13, 1899. Coykendall *was* interested and opened the bidding at $10,000. To his surprise, there were no other bidders and the whole canal property from Honesdale to Eddyville, canal bed, towpath, reservoirs, bridges, locks and all, were knocked down to Coykendall. He stated that he bought the canal primarily so that he could use it for hauling cement from his Rosendale Cement Co. and he operated the canal for two seasons from Eddyville to Ellenville, then used it only from High Falls to Eddyville until the end of the 1904 season, at which time he ceased operations, as the need for the canal had passed.

Coykendall had barely taken possession of the canal in 1899 before he was approached by the Pennsylvania Coal Co. which had been hauling its coal over its own railroad, the Erie & Wyoming Valley, from Scranton to Hawley where the cars were turned over to the Erie for delivery to tidewater. Anxious to have their own railroad to the Hudson River, they offered Coykendall a handsome price for a lease on the canal bed from Hawley to Lackawaxen, on which they planned to build

111

the Hawley & Wyoming Railroad and to lease the canal in New York State for a railroad to be called the Delaware Valley & Kingston Railroad. Besides the offer of a block of stock in the new company, Coykendall was made a director, with W. V. S. Thorne, vice-president of the Erie & Wyoming Valley, as president of the new company. The political effect on the railroads which would suffer from this competition was enormous. Thomas P. Fowler, president of the N. Y. O. & W., stood to

At the left, a 1903 advertisement in the New York *American's* summer vacation magazine stressed the through cars from New York and standard gauge to all points in the Catskills. The ad also subtly recommended the Catskills as a haven for tuberculosis victims without mentioning the dreaded name. (BELOW) The first train from Oneonta to Rondout is headed by engine No. 9, on July 16, 1900. Later this train was known as the *Rip Van Winkle Flyer*.

— THOMAS B. ANNIN COLLECTION

lose the most by this new railroad competition and took immediate action to prevent it from being built.

The Port Jervis, Monticello & New York Railroad which had been in bad financial condition for years, was taken over in 1899 by A. E. Godeffroy who organized the Kingston & Rondout Valley Railroad to build from the end of his line at Summitville to Kingston. Fowler had a branch from Summitville to Ellenville and the obvious move which he quickly made was to buy out Godeffroy and extend the Ellenville branch to Kingston. The papers were signed on March 15, 1900, and the O. & W. owned the railroad from Port Jervis to Summitville, with a branch to Monticello. The Erie regarded all this activity with considerable alarm, especially when in the summer of 1900 the Hawley & Wyoming Railroad began grading the old canal bed from Hawley towards Lackawaxen. It all came to an end on December 11, 1900, when the Erie announced that it had purchased the Pennsylvania Coal Co. and its railroad, the Erie & Wyoming Valley, the consolidation taking place on January 15, 1901. At the same time the Erie stated that it had bought all the shares of the Delaware Valley & Kingston Railroad and that it would not be built. Out of all this high finance, Samuel D. Coykendall emerged with his title to the canal intact from Ellenville to Eddyville, a fine settlement with the Erie for his Delaware Valley & Kingston Railroad stock, and a good riddance to the canal south of Summitville. For many years the old canal towpath from Hawley to Summitville was posted with "No Trespassing" signs under threat of arrest and heavy fines, signed by the Delaware Valley & Kingston Railroad. Even so, the writer used the towpath in defiance of these threats for years as a private equestrian path and for cycling.

On May 29, 1901 Coykendall sold the canal from Ellenville to Alligerville to the N. Y. O. & W. for $8,000 and later sold the section from Alligerville to High Falls to the same company, which used some, but by no means all, of the canal bed for their Ellenville & Kingston Railroad which was completed to Kingston in December 1902. In 1904 Coykendall abandoned the rest of the canal and shipped his cement by rail. The impulse which led Coykendall to buy the canal in 1899 had thus paid off handsomely, and he had proved himself to be a fitting successor to Thomas Cornell.

The abandoned Delaware & Hudson canal at Phillipsport in 1903, with New York, Ontario & Western No. 3 and train in the distance. — JOHN STELLWAGEN COLLECTION

Between 1899 and 1904, 10 engines like No. 27 were purchased. The extra large air reservoir underneath the running board provided plenty of reserve air. — DEGOLYER FOUNDATION COLLECTION

The foremost professional railroad photographer of New York City in the 1890's was F. W. Blauvelt, who made a trip on assignment to Catskill Landing to photograph Catskill Mountain No. 4 on a glass plate negative for a New York client. Named the *Charles L. Beach*, the No. 4 was built by the Schenectady Locomotive Works in 1895.

— AUTHOR'S COLLECTION

8

THE END OF NARROW GAUGE COMPETITION

HE NARROW gauge empire founded by Charles L. Beach concerned the Ulster & Delaware's management because of the severe competition for the patronage of summer boarders from Haines' Falls to Tannersville. In the winter of 1898 the directors of the Beach railroads met to discuss the joint affairs of the three companies. The Catskill Mountain Railway was relatively prosperous, with a $50,000 surplus. It had paid dividends from time to time on its income bonds, and carried 36,000 passengers and 74,000 tons of freight in 1898, nearly ten times as much freight as the U. & D.'s narrow gauge lines. The reason for this increase was a new on-line industry which began in 1890 and by 1896 had become a large customer of the Catskill Mountain Railway. This was the Catskill Shale Brick & Paving Co., located near the Hudson River in Catskill village. The source of the raw materials was on the Cairo Railroad near Cairo. Shale brick was made of a mixture of shale rock and clay, providing a brick of much better quality than the ordinary baked-clay bricks. A peak in this traffic was reached in 1899 when 100,000 tons of shale rock were hauled, producing a third of the railroad's total revenue. Several times daily a train of gondolas owned by the brick company shuttled back and forth from the shale pits to Catskill, and it was

this business which was keeping a fat surplus on the Catskill Mountain Railway's books.

With the Ulster & Delaware standard gauging their line from Phoenicia to Kaaterskill, the Beach roads would be saddled with a one-mile narrow gauge railroad. It was doubtful if the elder Beach cared one way or another at this point, for he was in his 91st year and his sons were carrying the burden of the great hotel property and the railroads created during the previous 16 years. The most important decision reached by the directors of the Beach railroads was to extend the Catskill & Tannersville Railroad from a point near Kaaterskill Station to Tannersville over a right-of-way authorized in the original charter. As laid out by the surveyors, it did not come directly into the U. & D. station at Kaaterskill, but ran north of it, diverging gradually from the other railroad until at Tannersville it was a quarter of a mile north of its standard gauge rival. It was a few hundred feet downhill from the U. & D. Haines' Falls station, but the station was called Haines Corners. They both served the same village.

The job of building the extension and providing the rolling stock was given to an outside contractor who began work in March 1899 when the snow from the great blizzard had melted. The line was opened to Haines Corners on July 1 and to Tan-

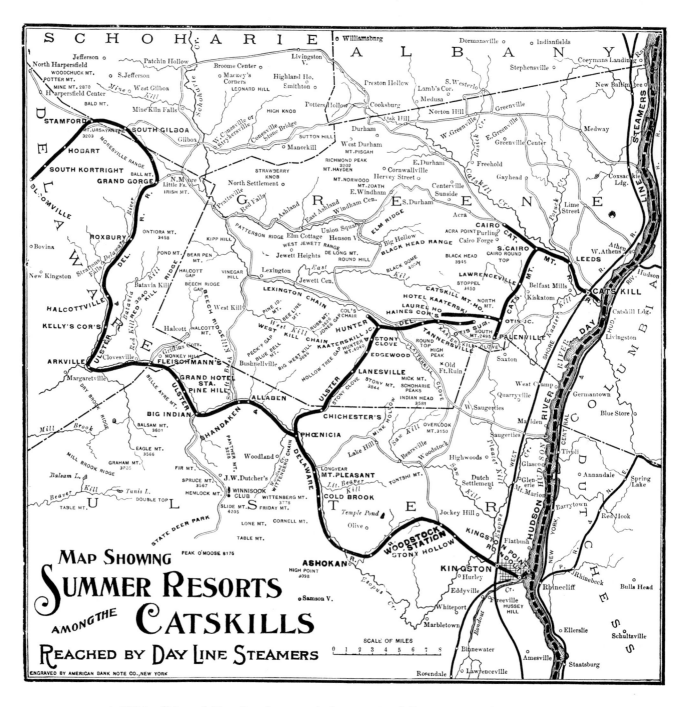

Map Showing SUMMER RESORTS AMONG THE CATSKILLS REACHED BY DAY LINE STEAMERS

SCALE OF MILES
0 1 2 3 4 5 6 7 8

ENGRAVED BY AMERICAN BANK NOTE CO., NEW YORK

A 1914 edition of Van Loan's map of the true Catskill region was first published in 1899 and shows the Ulster & Delaware terminating at Bloomville. More accurate than the official maps of the Ulster & Delaware, the Beach narrow gauge lines are shown, though the Catskill & Tannersville Railroad seems to run only as far as Haines Corners. Ashokan Dam and reservoir are not shown, but the relocated U. & D. mainline with the stations of Ashokan and Woodstock have just been added, and the old line erased. Van Loan failed to include the Delaware & Northern at Arkville, or the New York, Ontario & Western at Kingston in his 1914 revision. — AUTHOR'S COLLECTION·

nersville on August 5. It was 4.2 miles long and cost $60,000. Laid with 40 lb. rail, some of the curves were as sharp as 30 degrees, and there was one short section of five percent on a reverse curve, which the trains were able to negotiate only because of their low tonnage. Part of the cost was paid by the Catskill Mountain Railway out of its surplus and the rest by the Otis Elevating Railway, even though the latter was in financial difficulties. To operate the railroad the contractor furnished two secondhand 2-6-0 type locomotives, two passenger cars and a flat car. When one of these engines wore out two years later a new locomotive was purchased from the Baldwin Locomotive Works to carry on. The little train with its one, or at the most two cars, soon won the hearts of the summer visitors and they called it the Huckleberry Line. The railroad had a "character" all its own; the train wending its often rough way through the deep woods and the wild huckleberry bushes on the slopes west of Kaaterskill was a sight never to be forgotten. The railroad was never to pay its own way; it had to be considered for what it was — an extension of the Otis Elevating Railway.

For some years the Catskill Mountain Railway advanced $4,800 annually to meet the C. & T. payroll. Without this money the Huckleberry Line would have folded forthwith.

Although the Otis Elevating Railway now had its mountain-top feeder, it was a basket case financially. After a whopping $14,000 loss in 1898, the bond interest due on January 1, 1899, was not paid. Foreclosure by the bondholders brought forth the Otis Railway, with a valuation of about $134,000, less than half its cost. The bondholders received new coupon bonds totalling $71,000 and all the newly issued common stock. Interest dropped to $3,550 a year, a sum the railroad should be able to earn. The original stock certificates were now worthless.

117

Catskill & Tannersville 2nd No. 2, another F. W. Blauvelt glass plate photograph, was taken especially for Angus Sinclair's magazine *Railway & Locomotive Engineering.* The engine was particularly interesting to Sinclair because it was the first outside-frame engine to run in the New York region and had the smallest Westinghouse compound air pump ever built. — AUTHOR'S COLLECTION

Alfred Van Santvoord died July 20, 1901, aboard his yacht the *Clermont,* and his place on the Otis Railway board was never filled. Charles L. Beach died in 1902, in his 94th year, and all his property was left to his children. George W. Harding, the arch-enemy of the elder Beach, died a few weeks later.

After the end of the 1902 season, superintendent John Driscoll began a major change in the Otis Railway. He had already reduced the grade near the summit by digging underneath the existing roadbed, and now he began filling in most of the wooden trestles with crushed rock, especially the long trestle near the bottom of the grade, removing a hazard of increasing proportions. The last 1,000 feet of the line at the lower end was almost level and, the seats in the coach being tilted back, it must have been uncomfortable for the passengers until the grade was reached. Driscoll removed

the track in this lower section and built a new station 1,640 feet west of the old terminal. The cables were shortened in proportion, and the turn-out was moved up the mountain 820 feet, a major operation in itself. A large "Y" was installed with switches on both sides of the old station, and a spur extended on the old Otis roadbed from the apex of the "Y" to platforms adjacent to the cable railway terminal. The old station was removed, and the flow of traffic from steam trains to cable railway was made much smoother. The time of transit was cut by almost two minutes. A physical connection was made between the two railroads, and several small box and coal cars were built by Driscoll. These were hauled up the mountain one at a time, frequently continuing on to Tannersville on the Huckleberry Line and enabling the hotels to receive carload freight from the docks at Catskill Landing.

An Otis Railway train, now equipped to haul a box car in addition to the baggage car, enters the new Otis Junction station. — DEGOLYER FOUNDATION COLLECTION (LEFT) The Otis Railway and the Bogart Road bridge. The new turnout is the oval spot in the track, above the rock cut. — GEORGE HOLDRIDGE COLLECTION

This interesting promotional folder was published by the Catskill Mountain Lines in order to entice New Yorkers to use their facilities in the Catskill Mountain region. The contents contained descriptions of the sights and how they might be reached on the Catskill Mountain Lines. — AUTHOR'S COLLECTION

CATSKILL MOUNTAIN LINES

OTIS ELEVATING RAILWAY

Catskill Mountain Railway
Otis Railway ✱ ✱ ✱
Catskill & Tannersville Ry.

For the decade after the passing of Charles L. Beach the railroads from Catskill to Tannersville enjoyed their most prosperous years. The annual total of passengers carried reached a peak in 1909, with 69,000 on the Catskill Mountain Railway, 40,000 on the Otis Railway and 47,000 on the Catskill & Tannersville Railroad. The Ulster & Delaware found that it was to the mutual advantage of all the railroads serving the mountain top to sell interline tickets, for many patrons preferred to go to the Catskills by one route and return by another. The bottom dropped out of the shale brick business in 1901 and until 1906 the freight tonnage on the Catskill Mountain Railway was 10 percent of its former amount. Carloadings of shale began again in 1906 and until 1912 provided a large annual revenue, after which it steadily declined, as did the passenger traffic. Timetables and publicity for the narrow gauge lines were combined in one group and all patrons of the Mountain House were urged to use the narrow gauge in conjunction with either the Catskill Evening Lines, headed by Charles Rickerson, or the Hudson River Day Line,

Passengers detraining from a Catskill Mountain Railway train had to walk up a steep path to the West Shore's Catskill station at the left end of the long viaduct. — AUTHOR'S COLLECTION (BELOW) With a backdrop of typical Catskill Mountain scenery, a Catskill & Tannersville Railway train with second No. 1 on the head end, rolls along near Laurel House station. — GEORGE PHELPS COLLECTION

Catskill & Tannersville second No. 1 and its train crew pose for an on-line portrait near Laurel House station.—A. GIBSON HAGUE COLLECTION

with baggage always checked straight through to the hotel.

Business was good enough in 1908 so that when the last Brooks Mogul on the Huckleberry Line literally fell apart like the "one-hoss-shay," another new Baldwin like the first one built in 1901 was ordered. The bill was paid by the Catskill Mountain Railway, for there was no money in the till of the railroad on top of the mountain to pay for it. Engine No. 4, the *Charles L. Beach,* was so badly damaged in an enginehouse fire at Catskill Landing in 1908 that it had to be retired, and was replaced by an identical locomotive bearing the same name and number. The Beach railways were blessed with extreme good fortune in the matter of accidents, for though there were derailments beginning with the third day of operation in 1882, there were no disasters involving passengers, and no boiler explosions. The last derailment of any great note occurred in 1910 near Leeds, when engine No. 2 with the train from Cairo derailed on a curve, the engine overturned and one coach was derailed, with no serious injuries.

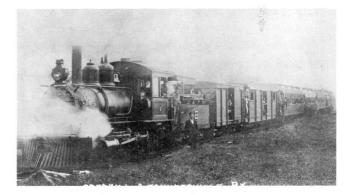

The entire roster of locomotives and rolling stock of the Huckleberry Line was needed on a holiday weekend. Even the baggage cars were jammed with passengers when the home-ward-bound crowds stormed the railroad station platforms. — AUTHOR'S COLLECTION

One of William Henry Jackson's most famous photographs shows Haines Corners station in 1902, with Catskill & Tannersville No. 2, a shiny new Baldwin engine.—LIBRARY OF CONGRESS

As a contrast to the classic Jackson photograph shown above, a 1910 view photographed by an unknown New York visitor at the same location. — AUTHOR'S COLLECTION

In 1902, few villages in America the size of Haines Falls could brag that they had two railroad stations. The Ulster & Delaware station is located in the upper right. It appears to be near train time; the order board is up and the hotel hacks are all parked at the end of the station platform. The Catskill & Tannersville station is located in the center. Compare this station with a closer view as shown on the opposite page.—LIBRARY OF CONGRESS (LEFT) The same location 65 years later. The only building remaining from 1902 is the two-story frame house to the right of the highway. — GERALD M. BEST

The rebuilt *John T. Mann*, locomotive No. 2, being turned on the turntable at Catskill Landing in 1912. (BELOW) The same engine on a work train out on the line. While the track crew shovels dirt onto the flat cars, engineer Frank Ruf, smoking the pipe, takes it easy. — BOTH AUTHOR'S COLLECTION

In 1912 the Cairo Railroad engine, having reached the end of its useful life, was replaced by a new engine built by the American Locomotive Co., a 4-4-0 No. 5 with *Alfred Van Santvoord* on the cab panel. This engine had a few modern improvements including Walschaert valve gear, and was the heaviest engine on the road. The old Cairo Railroad engine remained standing outside the engine shed at Catskill Landing and there it rusted in peace for many a year. In 1908 the Catskill Mountain Railway treated the stepchild up on top of the mountain to another passenger coach, but the parent railroad operated to the end with the 12 passenger and four baggage cars it had after 1893.

In late June 1912 the writer made his first trip over the Beach narrow gauge lines, coming up from Port Jervis by riding trains on three different railroads: the Erie, the Central New England and the West Shore, to the latter's Catskill station. The narrow gauge train, hauled by engine No. 1, came along shortly before noon and my first ride on a 3-foot gauge train was over all too soon, for we

With its new boiler greatly changing its appearance, Catskill Mountain Railway No. 1 has a full consist on this mid-day run from Catskill to Otis Junction. —WINFIELD W. ROBINSON COLLECTION

Railroad activity at Catskill Landing engine terminal. The train has just arrived from the mountains and the passengers make for the Day Line wharf, while No. 1 takes a short rest on the house track. — AUTHOR'S COLLECTION

The *Alfred Van Santvoord,* better known as engine No. 5, being turned on the arm-strong turntable at Catskill Landing during its first season of operation. — AUTHOR'S COLLECTION

Cairo Railroad No. 3, rusted and neglected, is used to support the roundhouse foreman's canoe. — AUTHOR'S COLLECTION

reached Otis Junction and I transferred to the cable car there. Away we soared up to the top of the mountain where I followed the crowd of passengers and porters with baggage to the Mountain House. It was well that I fortified myself with sandwiches prepared by my mother, for I could not have afforded a meal at the Mountain House and dinner on the train going home as well. But I walked in front of the hotel, stood at the lookout point at the jutting rock, from which I did not shrink back in "uncontrollable alarm," having climbed the face of an equally fearsome precipice directly back of Port Jervis. The whistle of an engine drew me back to the Otis Railway station, where the Catskill & Tannersville train was waiting for the passengers arriving on the next cable car. I found a seat in the last car and rode it to Tannersville, a 20 minute ride through alternate deep woods and cleared areas, and with stops at many places where there were groups of hotels. Returning on the next trip to Otis Summit, I failed to get off the train at Mountain Crest station, a few hundred feet from the Ulster & Delaware's Kaaterskill terminal, and so I had to walk back nearly a mile along the shores of the lakes, while gazing in wonderment at the great Hotel Kaaterskill on the mountain to the south.

I had time to spare when I boarded the standard gauge train for the first leg of the trip home. At Phoenicia the coach in which I was riding was attached to the Ulster & Delaware's best known train, the *Rip Van Winkle Flyer,* which had come from Oneonta, and on this train was a Pullman Buffet Parlor car. After we left Kingston and headed south along the Hudson, I had a dinner of sorts in the small dining section in the forward end of the car, my first experience of the kind and one I will always remember. I returned to the Moun-

Catskill & Tannersville rolling stock awaits loading on Ulster & Delaware flat cars, in the winter after the last run. — DEGOLYER FOUNDATION COLLECTION

A train of shale rock has come to grief at Leeds, a favorite spot for wrecks on the Catskill Mountain Railway. — GEORGE HOLDRIDGE COLLECTION

Bogart Road bridge half a century after the abandonment of the Otis Railway. The rock cut is nearly filled with second-growth trees. — GERALD M. BEST

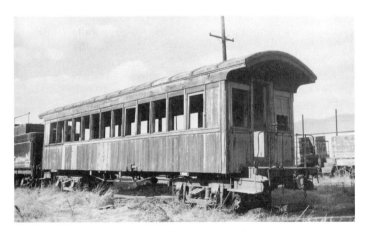

Once a Catskill Mountain Railway coach, this former Unidos de Yucatan car is in the same condition as the Bogart Road bridge. — GERALD M. BEST

tain House later with my grandfather, but it was not the same as the first glorious adventure — alone. It was 1912 before the Catskill Mountain Railway showed a loss at the end of a season since 1886. Perhaps my riding it was a jinx, but I suspect the cost of the new locomotive purchased that year was the real reason.

The advent of the automobile as a primary means of transport, and severe competition from other resort areas fostered by the Ulster & Delaware started a downhill trend. The decline began in 1912 and resulted in a combined loss for the three railroads of $16,000 at the end of the 1915 season. The bondholders were notified of the management's intention to default on interest payments, and by agreement, George H. Beach and superintendent T. E. Jones were appointed receivers. The Catskill & Tannersville was in the worst shape of any of the narrow gauges, having run up a total deficit of $40,000. The Huckleberry Line had proved to be an expensive luxury. On April 26, 1916, the Catskill Mountain Railway was auctioned for $28,000 cash, to E. E. Olcott, president of the Hudson River Day Line, Alfred Van Santvoord Olcott, general manager of the Catskill Evening Lines, and George H. Beach. The other two railroads were thrown in for their scrap value. The new company became known as the Catskill Mountain Railroad Corporation, but their time-tables listed the roads as the Catskill Mountain Lines. Summer service was limited to three trains each way daily, with a daily train each way on the Cairo branch. In September the roads shut down altogether until the following June.

At the end of the 1918 season the owners threw in the sponge. With skyrocketing prices for scrap metal, they could recover their investment and quite a bit more by junking the railroads. To continue operating them would be sheer folly. In the summer of 1919 the rails were pulled up, the machinery of the Otis Railway dismantled, and everything was eventually sold for scrap except four of the locomotives and most of the rolling stock, which went to secondhand dealers and were resold far and wide. One of the flat-roofed Catskill Mountain Railway coaches which operated on the United Railways of Yucatan in Mexico for more years than it did on the Catskill Mountain Railway now sits abandoned in a field near Pomona, California, the victim of over-enthusiasm on the part of a railfan.

Through freight trains from the west became common after 1900. Here, Ulster & Delaware No. 16 switches Santa Fe box cars at Phoenicia. — EDWARD L. MAY COLLECTION

9

THOMAS CORNELL'S DREAM COMES TRUE

SHORTLY AFTER the turn of the century, with the completion of the Ulster & Delaware to Oneonta, the railroad began demonstrating its ability to generate traffic. The standard gauging of the 3-foot gauge division soon reflected in the passenger earnings, and the number of passengers carried rose from 215,000 in 1900 to 338,000 in 1903. The coal tonnage, now coming over the line from Oneonta to Kingston for the first time, brought the freight totals from 166,000 tons in 1900 to 340,000 tons in 1903. The 16 locomotives on the roster in 1898 were increased to 24 in 1903 through the purchase of eight new engines. Between 1903 and 1907, 15 additional locomotives were added, with No. 41 acquired in 1907 being the last locomotive purchased by the Ulster & Delaware during the remainder of its existence. The last 12 new engines were the heaviest, yet they weighed only 82 tons and had less than 30,000 lbs. tractive effort; even so, they were used in both freight and passenger service, and proved their worth. The U. & D. owned only 38 passenger and 4 combination cars in its history. By paying rental to the New York Central in the summer the road could draw on the large New York Central car pool, releasing their own cars for the summer trains originating at Kingston Point, and for all winter service. The Pullman Company furnished the parlor cars when required. It was the same procedure with freight rolling stock, for the peak number of cars owned was 270, and after 1910 the average was 170. The anthracite coal traffic represented nearly 70 percent of the freight business after 1903, and this coal was hauled in cars belonging to the originating railroads or the coal companies.

There were great changes taking place in the operation of the railroad, foremost of which was the speeding up of passenger trains. Though the approaches to the curves were spiralled to a small extent, the speed limit was low compared with the N. Y. O. & W., 50 miles south. To correct this, the curves were banked for higher speeds, and the spiral approaches lengthened. By 1904 a daily express to Oneonta made the run in 3 hours 40 minutes, a reduction of 50 minutes compared with previous years. The section between Phoenicia and Kingston permitted mile-a-minute running. To protect the increasing number of summer trains, automatic block signals were installed between Kingston and Phoenicia in 1907, and by the 1908 season there were five name trains on the road. These were the *Catskill Mountain Limited*, with Pullman observation car and parlor cars, one with

The Kaaterskill Junction shelter station shortly after standard gauging was completed. With No. 22 on the Hunter shuttle train at the right, the crew poses for the camera. — RAYMOND S. BALDWIN COLLECTION (RIGHT) Locomotive No. 31 when new, at Phoenicia. Standing at the left, Claude Lockwood, flagman; above him, Thomas Jordan, hostler; on the ground at the right, William Conerty, engineer; above him, Herman Krom, fireman.—DEGOLYER FOUNDATION COLLECTION

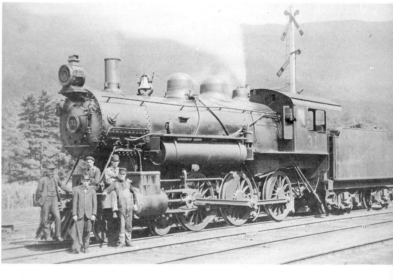

After the big Ten-Wheelers arrived on the U&D, engine No. 18 was used in helper service, and during the summer of 1912 on the Hunter shuttle train. — AUTHOR'S COLLECTION

a buffet section from Weehawken to Oneonta and Kaaterskill; the *Mountain Express,* coaches only over the same run; the *Day Line,* coaches only from Kingston Point to Oneonta and Kaaterskill, and usually in two sections to avoid switching at Phoenicia; the *Rip Van Winkle Flyer,* with a buffet parlor car from Philadelphia and parlor cars from Weekawken to both U. & D. terminals, and the *Ulster Express,* night train with coaches and parlor cars from Weehawken to Oneonta and Kaaterskill. At Kaaterskill Junction a shuttle train ran back and forth to Hunter, meeting all trains.

To dress up the appearance of the *Day Line* train from Kingston Point, ten handsome new coaches, each seating 82 persons, were purchased from the Pullman Co. in 1906. With the three vestibuled coaches bought in 1899, this resulted in the retirement of the open platform coaches to secondary runs. On holiday weekends the *Day Line* ran in several sections, and retired conductor Raymond Baldwin recalls one Labor Day when he collected 1,053 tickets and hat checks on *Day Line* No. 8 between Phoenicia and Kingston on a non-stop run made in less than half an hour.

Train watching at Kingston station in the summers of 1900-1920 must have been great fun, for in addition to the Ulster & Delaware trains, a total of

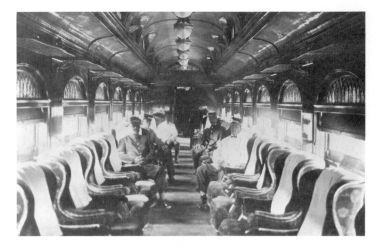

The train crew of the *Catskill Mountain Limited,* in one of the luxurious Pullman parlor cars of the period. — GEORGE PHELPS COLLECTION

The *Rip Van Winkle Flyer* coasts across Charlotte Creek bridge near West Davenport on the way to Oneonta. — MILTON E. PULIS COLLECTION

Ulster & Delaware No. 37 at Oneonta, ready for its run to Kingston on Memorial Day, 1915. —KARL E. SCHLACHTER

12 regularly scheduled West Shore trains stopped at Kingston in each direction. Some originated or ended their runs at Kingston, and these were all locals, but a number of the trains were expresses with stops only at the principal cities. Add the four daily trains each way on the Wallkill Valley branch, and Kingston station had 44 passenger trains daily except Sunday, quite a number for a non-commuter district.

Remarkably accident-free during its first 30 years, the Ulster & Delaware went through its busy years with a few serious wrecks, fatal to some of the employees but not to the passengers. In the first passenger train accident of record, the derailment of a passenger car near West Hurley was reported in September 1872, but the car bumped along on the ties until the train stopped, and the passengers escaped with only a shaking-up. In January 1873 the locomotive of the down-train on a Monday morning ran off the track at Shokan and blocked the railroad until late afternoon. The passengers were mostly on their way to attend court and took the delay good naturedly, while the hotelkeeper at Shokan depot filled their stomachs and kept them happy. The first passenger train accident to reach the columns of the New York papers was on July 6, 1884, when a train hit a large boulder which had fallen from the top of a rocky cliff a mile east of Mt. Pleasant, where the track runs close to the Esopus. The engine and baggage car got past the boulder with little damage, but the steps on one side of the second coach were bent under the trucks and the car was derailed. Fortunately the train had few passengers, and none of them was injured.

The *Rip Van Winkle Flyer* speeding along the Esopus on track which had been banked and spiralled for fast running. — MILTON E. PULIS COLLECTION

Two of the new Schenectady Ten-Wheelers climb the grade in Lockwood's Cut, east of Davenport, in 1901. — EDWARD L. MAY COLLECTION

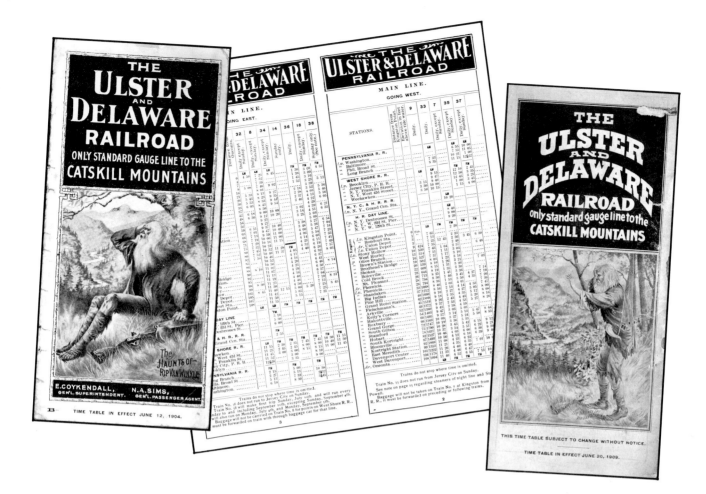

The Ulster & Delaware Railroad, for some unknown reason, never had a distinctive emblem like those of its connecting railroads. During its growth years, the haunts of Rip Van Winkle were popular as a tourist attraction, and the railroad chose to feature artwork of Rip Van Winkle as its moniker. The covers of the 1904 and 1909 timetables, shown above, feature Rip in two different poses with the same basic setting. —AUTHOR'S COLLECTION

The *Catskill Mountain Limited*, with Pullman observation car, passes a westbound train at the new station in Phoenicia. —EDWARD L. MAY COLLECTION

The twin Mayham ponds near Stamford, where ice for Kingston was harvested in the early days of the Ulster & Delaware. — GERALD M. BEST

Wonderful *Burning-of-Rome* smoke effects are being produced by this freight on the hill east of Arkville. — DEGOLYER FOUNDATION COLLECTION (BELOW) New York Central No. 2316 southbound with a coal train from the Ulster & Delaware, near Haverstraw.—AUTHOR'S COLLECTION

Raymond Baldwin recalls a similar accident in almost the same spot in the winter of 1901 when he was working as a brakeman on the ice train which hauled ice from Ben Mayham's Pond at South Gilboa to Kingston to fill the icehouses there, since the Hudson had not frozen over that year. The train was backing from Kingston to Phoenicia, with the 20 ice handlers and train crewmen huddled around the coal stove in the old flat-roofed baggage car No. 67 which was being used as a caboose, when they hit a large boulder which had fallen against one of the rails. The car was derailed, coming to rest at a tilt from the horizontal. The men all piled up in one end of the car which by this time had filled with smoke from the overturned stove, and their only light was a brakeman's lantern which was rolling around on the floor. Baldwin remembers having to stand for hours in the darkness and cold, protecting the wreck from the west until the caboose was rerailed and they could proceed west. Conductor Perry McDonald had enough of the ice trains after this incident and took another run.

Hauling anthracite coal through from Oneonta to Kingston and Rondout involved setting up new operating procedures, and the trains leaving Oneonta were made up with 22 cars loaded with 30 to 40 tons of coal each and a caboose. A helper engine was placed next to the train, behind the road engine, and this helper stayed with the train until it reached Grand Hotel Summit. At Arkville an-

other helper was added behind the caboose and pushed all the way to the Summit. There, both helpers were cut off and the road engine hauled the train to Rondout. Westbound empty trains were sometimes made up of more than 22 cars and required a helper from Phoenicia to Summit. Since the large majority of the coal cars belonged to other railroads, notably the Delaware & Hudson or to the coal mining companies, their upkeep was not always the best. The Ulster & Delaware was forced to inspect the journal boxes and brake rigging of each car turned over to them, even though the D. & H. might have done the same thing in their own yards. Derailments were inevitable, and some of them caused fatalities to the train crews. On March 19, 1913, Baldwin recalls that a coal train of which he was the conductor derailed at the foot of Pine Hill, piling 11 cars of coal in a heap, and killing brakeman Chester Rowe who had to be dug out of the wreckage. The cause was a broken journal, the most common cause of such accidents.

Coal trains running at excessive speeds were often hard to control. On the afternoon of June 14, 1907, the way freight was standing in the station at Brodhead's Bridge (later buried under water by Ashokan Reservoir) when a heavy eastbound coal train headed by engine No. 29, running at a speed of 40 m.p.h., hit the rear of the freight. The new block signals were not yet working, the station was in the middle of a sharp curve impairing the view from the west, and there was no flag protection. Seven cars of the freight train including the caboose were demolished, and six cars of the coal train piled in a heap, the engine knocking down part of the station building. Engineer E. Silkworth, fireman L. Schoonmaker and brakeman Arthur Stanton were badly bruised and burned, but all recovered. Engineer Silkworth said he was making fast time because Brodhead's Bridge was at the bottom of a sag and he had to get the momentum to climb the grade beyond. The cause was a mix-up in train orders and the engineer of the coal train was not held liable. Fortunately, there was nobody in the caboose of the freight train at the time of the accident.

The use of link and pin couplers and the lack of air brakes on freight cars was the cause of many employee accidents prior to 1890. A typical example was an accident which caused the death of brakeman Henry E. Winne and injuries which re-

No. 19 waits for train time at the Hunter terminal. On this day the shuttle train for Kaaterskill Junction consisted of one Pullman built coach and a single milk car. —DE-GOLYER FOUNDATION COLLECTION (LEFT) What a mess this coal train made when it left the rails at Brodhead's Bridge on June 14, 1907. The superintendent and other railroad officials, shown in the center of this view, supervise the cleanup operations. — HENRY P. EIGHMEY COLLECTION

Kingston passenger station served both the West Shore and the Ulster & Delaware. A West Shore train is ready to head south.

Waiting for the train at Tannersville station, with the familiar canvas-topped stages still in use. — AUTHOR'S COLLECTION

sulted in the death of a trespasser and serious injury to his companion. At the inquest, head brakeman Elmer Emmet testified that his train, headed by engine No. 1, and consisting of nine cars loaded with cut stone and several box cars, was about a mile east of Stony Hollow when they rounded a curve, and saw two men walking in the middle of the track. They paid no attention to the engineer's whistling for "down-brakes," and when the air brakes were applied on the engine, the

shock of taking up the slack in the train was so great that the rear brakeman standing on top of a box car was thrown forward and fell under the wheels. The train was not derailed, and the hearing brought out the fact that the elder of the two trespassers was stone deaf.

There were runaways on the steep grades both east and west of Grand Hotel Summit which were nightmares for the men involved, but the Ulster & Delaware's luck always saved them. Engineer

New York Central No. 2097 on a Saturday afternoon Catskill Mountains special near New Durham, New Jersey in 1919. The lack of smoke indicates the engine is either drifting or has a considerate fireman. — SMITHSONIAN INSTITUTION COLLECTION

George Earle recalls an accident at Grand Hotel Station when he was switching some cars there. The link block pin broke just as he was backing eastward out of the siding, and he was so low in air pressure that the brakes failed to stop the engine, so it ran downhill past Big Indian without derailing, and as the air built up in the reservoir he was able to finally stop on the line. Years earlier, on June 30, 1893, engine No. 6 had just finished helping a train from Arkville to Grand Hotel and was backing downhill towards Arkville when one of the main rods broke and not only disabled the air brake system but forced engineer Stewart Benson, conductor Richard Clum, the fireman and two deadheading brakemen to flee to the tender where their combined efforts on the hand brake brought the engine to a stop near Fleischmann's. That was a bad summer for No. 6, for on July 22, while backing past the Kingston station on the way home from a helper trip, it ran into the side of a string of three West Shore coaches which had broken loose from the switch engine which was setting them out in front of the station. The engineer of

No. 6 was held innocent because the towerman had given him a clear signal to cross the West Shore tracks. Faulty hand brakes on the coaches was given as the reason for the accident.

On the comic side, in October 1881 a brakeman nicknamed "Bounty," but who signed his pay vouchers as James Shenigan, was on a work train at Snyder Hollow, above Shandaken on the east side of the big hill, and was sent downhill to flag an extra freight which was due before track repairs could be completed. Bounty walked around a curve and was astonished to see a large female bear and her cubs on the track. All the bear did was growl, but Bounty turned and ran, and the extra train then coming in sight, its crew were treated to the spectacle of Bounty running uphill at top speed while the bear and her cubs took to the woods. A 300-pound bear was killed a couple of weeks later in the same area.

Raymond Baldwin recalls an episode which was talked about around Arkville for many a year. The eastbound way freight had stopped at Grand Hotel Station to pick up a car of coal which had been

New York Central's southbound *Catskill Mountain Express* is about ready to leave Kingston for Weehawken in the summer of 1914. On account of a mild depression, coaches were added to the 11 car train which was formerly all Pullman. — W. G. LANDON

137

Ulster & Delaware No. 38 and the *Rip Van Winkle Flyer* ready to leave Oneonta. Engineer Henry Sherman is at the left. — JOHN F. SHERMAN COLLECTION At the left, the Arkville station, where the *Flyer* received orders to meet the pay car special at Halcottville. — RAYMOND S. BALDWIN

Halcottville station, near the scene of the collision between the *Flyer* and the pay car special. — RAYMOND S. BALDWIN

set out on the siding for repairs. In order to get the car into the train it was necessary to make a flying switch. The hand brakes did not hold the car, it passed the west switch and after the brakeman jumped, the car disappeared down the mountain towards Fleischmann's. Arkville was quickly notified by telephone. They reported that no trains were on the hill, but that a coal train was standing on the main track at Arkville, ready to leave. As soon as word of the runaway car reached the coal train's crew, a brakeman threw the siding switch east of them and after a few minutes' wait the runaway car came into view, its brakes shoes hot and smoking from their ineffective checking of the runaway, and into the siding it went. After passing the coal train, the speeding runaway derailed into a field at the end of the siding.

Former Delaware & Northern employees tell of the time a passenger coach which had been set out on the track used by the D. & N. passenger trains at Arkville was jarred loose by a cut of cars being switched by an Ulster & Delaware way freight crew. The car rolled onto the D. & N. main line and disappeared towards Margaretville, so the agent phoned the Margaretville agent, and an engine was backed out onto the main to await the runaway. It came slowly into view, the engine backed until its speed matched that of the car, and the truant coach was brought to a stop, after which it was returned to Arkville. Raymond Baldwin scoffs at this tale, and suggests first, that the total descent from Arkville to Margaretville was less than 50 feet, and second, that the story teller must have been hitting the hard cider jug.

A coal train shook up the roundhouse forces at Rondout one night when it came down the steep grade between Kingston and Rondout, passed the clear signal just east of the Hasbrouck Avenue tunnel and came around a sharp curve to go down the last steep grade. When the switch leading to the turntable came into view, the engine crew to their horror saw that it was lined up for the turntable. Someone had thrown the switch after the train passed the signal, and in spite of emergency brake application the train hit an engine standing on the turntable and drove it part way through the brick wall of the roundhouse, damaging both engines and upsetting several cars of coal. Engineer Hutton was burned by steam but not seriously, and his fireman, Henry Diehl mourned the loss of his dinner pail, which seemed to him to be a worse

The *Flyer's* engine survived the collision with a bashed-in smokebox and other front end damage. (BELOW) Engine No. 9 had the smokebox door shoved clear into the front flue sheet. — MILTON E. PULIS COLLECTION

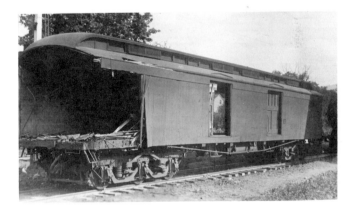

The baggage car of the *Flyer* lost one end when the engine's tender telescoped it.—MILTON E. PULIS COLLECTION

139

calamity than a few bruises. What happened to the man who threw the switch without checking the order board?

The only serious passenger train accident during Samuel D. Coykendall's regime happened on August 31, 1911, a mile west of Halcottville about 6:30 P.M. The *Rip Van Winkle Flyer,* with Henry Sherman at the throttle of engine No. 39, collided head-on with engine No. 9, which was hauling the pay-car. Edward Griffin, the agent at Halcottville, said he signalled the *Flyer* to stop, but engineer Sherman said that since Halcottville was not a station stop for his train, he was not looking at the station. When the engineers saw that a collision was inevitable they yelled to their firemen and all four men jumped. Engineer Sherman fell next to his engine just at the moment of impact and was badly scalded, trainman Lewis J. Simmons on the *Flyer* was killed, trainman Harrington was seriously injured, and trainman Edward Van Etten and paymaster Edward D. Fowler in the pay-car were injured. Though the passengers were badly shaken, none of them required medical treatment. Engine No. 9, the 4-4-0 which hauled the first train into Oneonta in 1900, was so badly damaged that it was scrapped, but the *Flyer's* engine was repaired and placed back in service. Engineer Henry Sherman of the *Flyer* was held responsible for the accident by the Interstate Commerce Commission, because he had failed to observe the train order for a meet with the pay-car at Halcottville. In justice to Sherman, the "flimsy" or train order copy handed to him at Arkville had been accidentally folded under the carbon paper, and the part regarding the meet at Halcottville was written on the printed head of the form and was almost illegible. Sherman spent the rest of his working years as foreman of machinists at the roundhouse in Rondout. He loved steam engines and if he could not run them at least he could work around them. His grandson John tells a marvelous anecdote about Henry Sherman. It seems that while still running on the road, he learned through the grapevine that what we would now call an efficiency expert was investigating the possibly excessive use of lubricants by the locomotive engineers. It is said that for many years later when right-of-way buildings between Oneonta and Kingston were torn down or rebuilt, workmen would uncover caches of oil and grease secreted by Sherman to assure proper lubrication of his beloved engine,

regardless of the outcome of the efficiency study.

On August 26, 1907, the City of New York, after several years of critical water shortage due to drought conditions, let a contract to MacArthur Brothers & Winston for the construction of a dam across Esopus Creek a few miles west of Kingston. This would create a reservoir known as Ashokan as a supplement to the other sources of water for the big city. The project had been in the planning stage for years, and now that all the land involved had been purchased by the City the work was ready to start. In the valley of the Esopus for 12 miles west of the station of West Hurley, 10 miles west of Kingston, a number of small communities were to be moved or abandoned after work commenced on the dam. A total of 11 miles of the Ulster & Delaware Railroad was to be relocated on higher ground by the contractors at New York's expense. The Ashokan Reservoir spillway level was set at 590 feet, and a new grade for the railroad was surveyed from a point a half-mile east of West Hurley to Boiceville at an average level of 620 feet. Work on the new railroad was begun in 1911 and parts of it were cut in during 1912, with the entire new line turned over to the railroad on June 1, 1913.

To construct the dam, the contractors had to build 30 miles of narrow gauge railroads, using 33 locomotives and 579 dump cars. A large portion of the construction material required for the dam was brought to the site by trucks, most of the cement coming from the Consolidated Rosendale Cement Co., owned by Samuel D. Coykendall. The stations of Olive Branch, Brown's Station, Brodhead's Bridge, Shokan and Boiceville were eliminated. The old West Hurley station was torn down, and a handsome new station was built a mile northeast of the old location, with the name changed to Woodstock. Between Woodstock and Cold Brook, on the new line, the station of Ashokan was located, 16.17 miles from Kingston Point. The new section was one mile shorter than the old line, making the distance from Kingston Point to Oneonta 107 miles instead of 108. During many months of the period from 1911 to 1913 the Ulster & Delaware trains were delayed for hours by the contractors, and the 1912 season was particularly disrupted by what seemed to the railroad company to be unnecessary delays. This resulted in claims being filed by the railroad against the City of New York for $3,000,000, in addition to the

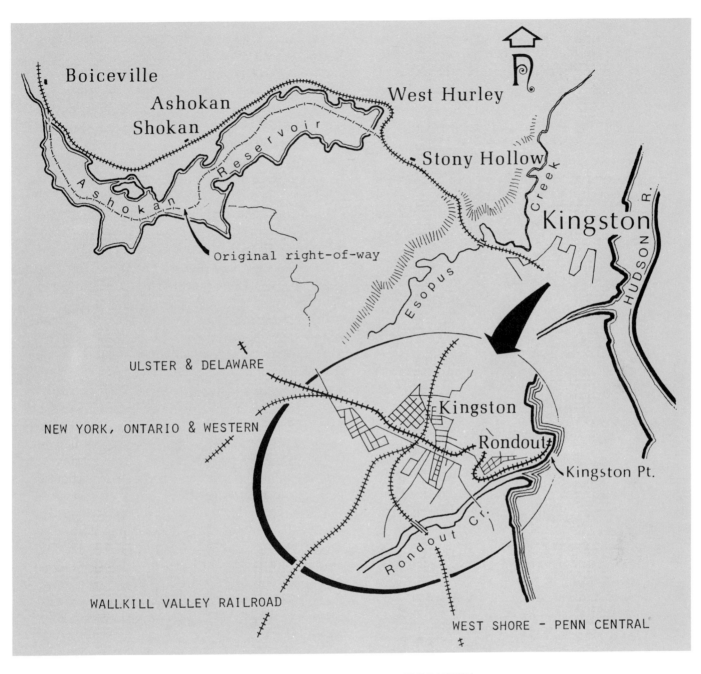

ASHOKAN RESERVOIR RELOCATION
Map of the Ashokan Reservoir project and the relocation of the mainline of the Ulster
& Delaware. From this map the reader can get some idea as to the magnitude of this
undertaking and its location in relation to Kingston.—COURTESY OF MANVILLE B. WAKE-
FIELD

The site of the Ashokan Dam, shortly after construction work began. — ROBERT R. HAINES COLLECTION

Contractor's railroad tracks criss-cross an area where earth excavations supply fill material for the dam. — ROBERT R. HAINES COLLECTION At the right, the west face of Ashokan Dam and the causeway in 1970. — GERALD M. BEST

$1,500,000 the City had already paid for the new line along the edge of the reservoir. In 1915 the case was settled out of court for $1,250,000 cash which was invested and set up as a reserve fund.

The gates of Ashokan Dam were closed on September 9, 1913, and the storage of water began. It was not until December 27, 1915, that the first Catskill water began to flow through the distribution system of New York City, and for years the City had the finest drinking water on the eastern seaboard. To augment the water supply from Ashokan, the Schoharie Reservoir was created. A dam was built across Schoharie Creek just upstream from Gilboa, on the north side of the Catskills, and was connected with Ashokan Reservoir by an 18 mile tunnel bored under the mountains to a point near Allaben on Esopus Creek. Here the water was discharged into the creek and added to Ashokan's intake. Work on the Gilboa Dam began in the fall of 1917. The reservoir, with a level 1,130 feet above tidewater, was 540 feet above Ashokan, and the water came to Allaben by gravity, not by pumping.

The Ashokan Dam itself and the work associated with it cost $13,000,000, but by the time the aqueduct and tunnel under the Hudson, the storage reservoirs and the aqueduct on the east side of the Hudson were finished the cost was over $20,000,000. When Ashokan Reservoir was filled, passengers riding the Ulster & Delaware trains were treated to a fine view as they rode along the north shore on the fastest piece of track on the whole railroad. The paint was barely dry on the station sign at Woodstock on the new line than residents of West Hurley demanded that the old name be restored. Indifference on the part of Woodstock resulted in the station becoming West Hurley again in the spring of 1915.

The new West Hurley station was the only modern building on the Ulster & Delaware during its last 30 years. — RAYMOND S. BALDWIN

Dramatic and thundering is this scene of the *Day Line* coming up from Kingston Point in 1914, and crossing the West Shore tracks at Kingston station. — W. G. LANDON

Changes in the countryside along the railroad were not confined to reservoirs and power projects. The pioneer hotels of the 1880s were gradually losing their popularity, and some of the famous hotels of the early days were either changing hands, losing their exclusive clientele or disappearing altogether. Phoenicia was a typical example. The Tremper House began its downhill journey after the economic depression of 1893-94, and in 1900 it was sold to Samuel Proskey who changed the name to Washington Inn. In 1907 the hotel was destroyed by fire, and was never replaced, for the public tastes turned towards the smaller hotels and less ostentation.

In Stamford, Dr. Churchill died and his Churchill Hall, with its satellite the Hotel Hamilton, were taken over by S. I. Brown, as was the Rexmere. Brown was a first class hotelman, and his enterprises in Stamford prospered for some years after the takeover. George Harding's Hotel Kaateskill passed into the hands of a group of Philadelphians for a while after Harding's death, was sold again and began a steady decline until its fiery demise in 1924. The Catskill Mountain House retained its reputation and its clientele of two decades after Charles L. Beach had passed from the scene, but the smaller hotels and boarding houses with modern improvements were taking the trade away from the great hotels of the 1880s. Even the Grand changed hands several times. Four years after Thomas Cornell's death, his brother Joseph foreclosed on the defaulted bonds of the hotel and bought it at public sale in 1894. He operated the Grand until the early 1900s when Samuel D. Coykendall became the owner. The high standards of the Grand were maintained for a considerably longer period than the other big hotels because it was the Ulster & Delaware's showpiece in the Catskills and it was to their interest to keep it going.

In retrospect, it seems a miracle that these great hotels could prosper in the face of remaining in idleness for at least nine months of each year, but many of them were profitable and a few pay their own way to this day. The latter is possible because in the winter the Catskills are invaded by an army of ski enthusiasts, a sport of minor importance in the days of the pioneer hotels.

At Shinhopple, Delaware & Eastern No. 5 on the north-bound passenger meets extra No. 5, the way freight, which is backing into a siding to clear the mainline. —

FREDERICK A. LEWIS COLLECTION

10

THE DELAWARE & NORTHERN RAILROAD

THOUGH it barely entered the Catskills between Arena and Arkville, the Delaware & Northern Railroad has a place in this story; first, because of the headaches it caused Samuel D. Coykendall, and second because in due time it became of considerable benefit to the Ulster & Delaware as a traffic feeder. Organized November 11, 1904, as the Delaware & Eastern, it was the brain child of Russell B. Williams, who after a long career with several railroads, became superintendent of the Scranton Division of the New York, Ontario & Western Railway. He was an intimate friend of Joseph J. Jermyn, coal mine operator of Scranton and Pittsburgh, and he envisioned a railroad from the Scranton area over a more direct route than that of the N. Y. O. & W., to East Branch on the Delaware River, thence to a connection with the Ulster & Delaware at Arkville. As Williams had no means of organizing such a company, he interested Jermyn to such an extent that the latter approached Frederick F. Searing of New York City, a dealer in railroad securities and a promoter of new railroad projects. Searing and Jermyn obtained the backing of a surprising number of influential men in the steel and coal mining industries, including Colonel

William Barbour, a director of the Hanover National Bank of New York, John W. Griggs, Governor of New Jersey, and officers of the Guaranty Title & Trust Co. of Pittsburgh.

Searing was a past master at the game of railroad promotion, and his announced intention was to build a railroad from East Branch on the N. Y. O. & W., to Arkville on the Ulster & Delaware, a distance of 37.5 miles. A branch line of 9.5 miles from Union Grove to Andes, would open up extensive tracts of timber, quarries of bluestone and create an easy means of transporting dairy products to market. Searing blandly stated that he expected that coal would be handled from East Branch to Arkville, enabling mines along the N. Y. O. & W. to get some of the Ulster & Delaware's business.

Capitalized at $1,000,000, Searing sold a considerable amount of stock and $800,000 of five percent 50-year bonds to pay for construction costs. Contracts were let in 1905. R. B. Williams resigned from the N. Y. O. & W. to become superintendent of the D. & E. Construction work, supervised by Frederick P. Lincoln formerly with the Delaware & Hudson, began at Arkville. The route passed through Margaretville where the road's headquarters had been established, and reached Union Grove, 10 miles from Arkville, at the end of 1905.

145

The first Delaware & Eastern train, loaded with rails and construction materials, heading south out of Arkville, October 28, 1905. — FREDERICK A. LEWIS COLLECTION

A busy morning at Margaretville shortly after the Delaware & Eastern was completed. — FREDERICK A. LEWIS COLLECTION

Most of the grade for the track had been there since 1870, intended for a railroad which was killed off by the panic of 1873. This was the Delhi & Middletown, which Thomas Cornell had fostered, and money for the grade was furnished by Andes township, which nearly went bankrupt paying off $120,000 in township bonds. The Delaware & Northern bought five locomotives, all Delaware, Lackawanna & Western discards averaging 23 years in age. It also bought a large amount of new freight rolling stock, much more than a railroad 37.5 miles long would need. In the spring of 1906 tracklaying was resumed, and the line was built south from Union Grove along the river on an easy descending grade. The last spike was driven in front of the N. Y. O. & W. station at East Branch, New York, and passenger service from there to Arkville was begun on November 17, 1906. The people of Andes clamored for a branch line to their town, pointing to the ready-made grade up the Tremperskill from Union Grove. This branch was built and opened for service on March 23, 1907.

All this was fine for the Ulster & Delaware and the N. Y. O. & W. That is until November 1906. Searing then let the cat out of the bag. He announced plans for a new railroad from Wilkes-

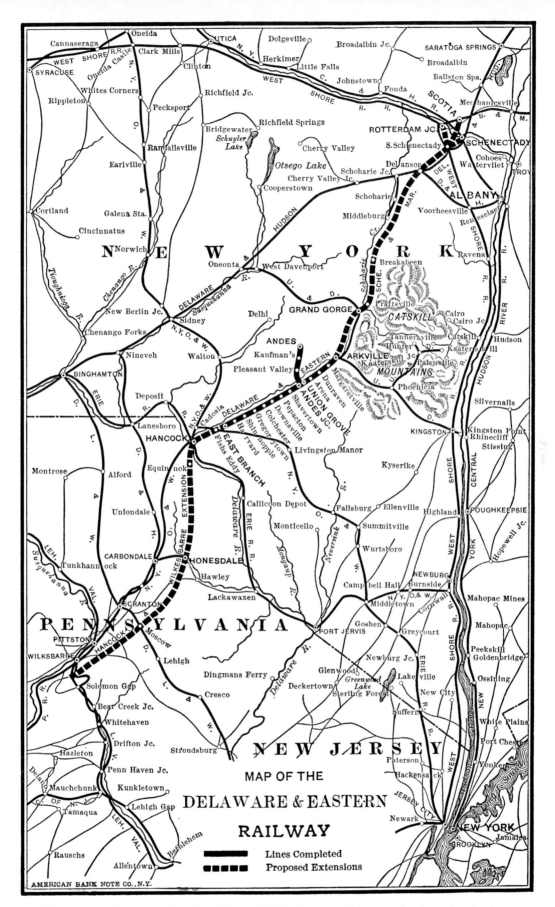

This map of the proposed railroad from Wilkes-Barre to Schenectady showed only the
Delaware & Eastern in solid lines. As planned, it was undoubtedly the shortest route
between the two terminals. — POORS MANUAL OF RAILROADS — 1908

147

Barre, Pennsylvania, to Schenectady, New York, a distance of 232 miles, to furnish fast and efficient coal deliveries to New England and eastern Canada via the Rutland and the Boston & Maine. The excuse for this railroad was that existing freight rates were exorbitant, and that competition would keep the rates down. A railroad to be called the Schenectady & Margaretville would be the northern part of the project, the Delaware & Eastern the center part, and the Hancock & Wilkes-Barre Extension Railroad the south part. On December 11, 1906, the New York State Railroad Commission granted permits to both roads to build their lines. Searing then leased the Delaware & Eastern, combined it with the two other projected railroads, and organized the Delaware & Eastern *Railway*. This was ratified at a special stockholders' meeting in New York in 1907 and the new company began selling capital stock, plus a six-million dollar bond issue. Part of the latter securities would be used to retire the existing bonds, and additional bonds to a total of over $40,000,000 would be issued.

The news of this grandiose scheme brought roars of outrage from S. D. Coykendall on behalf of the Ulster & Delaware, L. F. Loree of the Delaware & Hudson and T. P. Fowler of the New York, Ontario & Western. Coykendall and Fowler were

The *A. F. Fairchild* No. 3 is waiting in the Andes station while the track gang rerails the tender. — CHARLES E. FISHER COLLECTION

particularly disturbed because sections of this proposed railroad would parallel their main lines in a useless duplication of trackage. The three railroads combined in a joint suit against the Railroad Commission to cancel the permits. This dragged on through 1908 and was finally lost when the State Supreme Court ruled against the petitioners. The Delaware & Eastern Construction Co. was organized in New York under Searing's direction and a contract was let to W. J. Oliver & Co. to survey

Dunraven station, 23 miles from East Branch, with sections of the morning mixed train occupying the main track.—FREDERICK A. LEWIS COLLECTION

Downsville station, with the omnibus waiting for the morning passenger train, while No. 5 switches the way freight.—FREDERICK A. LEWIS COLLECTION

Shinhopple was the meeting point for the way freight and the northbound passenger, in the days when bluestone was the biggest revenue producer. — FREDERICK A. LEWIS In the view below, the Andes branch local train on Muir's Trestle a few months after it was completed. — MILTON E. PULIS COLLECTION

and grade the section from Grand Gorge on the Ulster & Delaware to Middleburgh. Nothing was done about starting the construction work during 1908, and well into 1909.

In the meantime, the Delaware & Eastern had its first serious accident. On Sunday, May 24, 1908, a passenger train consisting of engine No. 2, a milk car, a combination car and a coach had made its daily run up the Andes branch. It was customary for the train to back down the Andes branch to the main line at Union Grove, continuing backwards on the main line to Margaretville. A short distance north of Union Grove the train crossed the Jacksonburg Creek bridge, the engineer stating that he had shut off steam and was drifting at about 15 m.p.h. When about 500 feet north of the bridge, the coaches derailed suddenly and ran along on the ties and the embankment, the milk car turned on its side and the engine and tender slid down the bank into the river. The top of the engine's cab was ripped off and engineer Clair Cowan and fireman John Francisco went down with the engine. Francisco was thrown into the river, but Cowan was pinned down by the wrecked cab and only his face was above water. Francisco crawled into the cab and for several hours held Cowan's head in his arms, the conductor and several passengers helping pry a copper pipe leading to the steam gauge to permit the engineer to raise his head slightly. There Francisco sat, up to his own neck in the river, until a special train arrived from Margaretville. A chain was placed around the engine's steam dome, and after one false try when the chain broke, the engine was turned just enough to permit men to free Cowan from his watery prison. He had been there just five hours; outside of a pair of badly mashed feet, he had no other injuries and was back to work in a few weeks, though he complained for years afterward that he could not walk barefoot. Francisco was the hero of the valley, but when questioned about it recently he said it was the longest bath he had ever taken in his life. The cause of the wreck was the subject of many arguments, but the best guess was that a spread rail derailed the rear truck of the coach, the track was torn up and complete derailment of the train ensued.

During the year following the accident the railroad operated at a loss, and apparently did not pay its taxes, for the township of Hancock sent constable Arthur Bullis to East Branch where he at-

The first Delaware & Eastern locomotive into East Branch, standing on a New York, Ontario & Western siding as the local girls admire the *H. M. George.* — FREDERICK A. LEWIS COLLECTION (BELOW) The mainline N. Y. O. & W. varnish headed by No. 141 meets the waiting Delaware & Eastern train, in this rare photo from *To The Mountains By Rail.*—COURTESY MANVILLE B. WAKEFIELD

tached engine No. 1 for $700 in unpaid taxes. John Francisco recalls that it was the custom of the freight train crew to stay overnight at East Branch, leaving the engine on a siding near the bridge across the Delaware River, and when they showed up at 6 A. M. one Saturday in the first week of May 1909 they found their engine chained to the rails and padlocked, with constable Bullis standing in the cab's gangway, flourishing a six-shooter. The management in Margaretville was notified and the crew were told to take the day off. The constable kept steam up on No. 1 and obviously expected a rescue attempt, for several of his deputies joined him. Another engine was sent for the freight train, and things remained peaceful until about noon on Sunday, when superintendent Wagenhorst and 15 men, all riding the tender of engine No. 3, arrived on the scene. Breaking the padlock the constable had placed on the switch, the rescue crew backed No. 3 in on the siding, and ignoring constable Bullis in the cab, broke the padlocks on the chains around the driving wheel rims. Not trusting the MCB couplers, they chained the two engines together, and to quote the *Catskill Mountain News* — "Bullis, who had kept steam up on the captive engine, threw the reverse lever and there began a tug of war between the two steel giants that would have been well worth going to East Branch to witness. The drive wheels slipped, sparks flew, the engines puffed and sputtered, the men on both sides used cuss words, and there was excitement galore. All East Branch was out to see it." Bullis probably took special pleasure from all this uproar, for he was a discharged employee of the Delaware & Eastern and had his own axe to grind.

The rescuers after failing in several attempts to jerk the prisoner loose, during which there was a wrestling match between the deputies and the rescuers for possession of the chains, fireman John Francisco again became the hero by solving the problem very neatly. During a lull in the hostilities, Francisco sneaked along the side of the rescue engine's tender with a large pipe wrench and unscrewed the relief valves from the fronts of the steam chests on the captive engine. When another battle of the giants began, steam came roaring out of the holes in No. 1's steam chests, engineer Clair Cowan on the rescue engine gave it full throttle, and Francisco began oiling the track as the two engines moved towards the bridge across the Delaware. When it was obvious that Bullis and his men had lost the battle they jumped off their engine. The aftermath was the arrest of Bullis on charges of assault and threatening engineer Cowan with a revolver. The constable was soon out on bail, and Hancock township countered by arresting superintendent Wagenhorst and several of his men on a charge of riot. The matter was settled when the Hancock tax collector realized that the expense of trying all of the men involved might be more than the taxes due, and in time the railroad paid the taxes and No. 1 did not have to sneak in and out of East Branch any more.

In the fall of 1909 the promoters of the Schenectady & Margaretville, claiming to have raised sufficient money to begin construction, authorized Oliver to start grading at Grand Gorge. Oliver also got the contract to build two steel trestles and two tunnels. A trestle at Grand Gorge which was to outshine the Lyonbrook, Cadosia and Liberty

Delaware & Northern No. 4 at East Branch in 1915. The wavy track at the right is due to wrinkled film negative, not poor track maintenance. — KARL E. SCHLACHTER

Delaware & Northern No. 1 was one of three engines bought in 1911. It is ready to leave East Branch in June 1915, with the daily mixed train. — KARL E. SCHLACHTER

trestles of the N. Y. O. & W. would leave the south slope of the Bear Kill valley at Grand Gorge. It would then cross over the Ulster & Delaware and the Bear Kill, curving east to the north ridge almost 180 feet above the town of Grand Gorge. Grading began on the north side of Bear Creek at the north end of the projected bridge, and descended 50 feet to the mile for nearly five miles to the junction of the Bear with Schoharie Creek a mile below Prattsville. Here, in order to avoid a very sharp 210 degree curve to the north, a tunnel was to curve through Pine Mountain and emerge above Devasego Falls on Schoharie Creek. Some grading work was done in the valley of the Schoharie as far as Breakabeen. Land for stations at Gilboa and North Blenheim was purchased, and a right-of-way secured through these villages.

From East Branch to Hancock the route was surveyed parallel to the N. Y. O. & W. on the hill a hundred feet above the latter, crossing the Delaware a mile south of Hancock and running along the south bank to Equinunk, 10 miles downstream, thence south through Honesdale to a crossing of the D. L. & W. at Moscow, then southwest to Wilkes-Barre. It all looked fine on paper, and work continued north of Grand Gorge through the winter of 1909-1910. In February 1910 contractor Oliver stated that he had ceased all work and would neither order the bridge material nor start boring the tunnels until he was paid $250,000 for construction work already completed. Apparently sensing the fact that he was not going to be paid, he simultaneously brought suit in the New York State Supreme Court for the same amount of his claim. On February 25, Andrew M. Moreland and Walter B. Trowbridge were appointed receivers of the Delaware & Eastern by the U. S. District Court, and a bondholders' committee assisted them in an effort to save at least a part of the investment. In March the brokerage firm of Searing & Co. closed its doors and declared bankruptcy. Thus did Williams' and Searing's dream of railroad

Taking water at Downsville, No. 3 had a new steel cab in this 1915 picture. — KARL E. SCHLACHTER

The *Red Heifer* was this Brill-built motor car which handled most of the passenger traffic in the last 16 years of the Delaware & Northern's life. (BELOW) Express and mail are being transferred from the westbound U. & D. milk train to the *Red Heifer*. — BOTH GEORGE PHELPS

empire die on the vine, no doubt to the vast relief of the three railroads from which it would have siphoned off considerable traffic. The collapse of the Delaware & Eastern ended efforts to build new railroads from the Pennsylvania coal regions for all time. Investors with long memories recalled the West Shore's debacle, and did not flock to buy securities as Searing thought they would.

The receivers borrowed Jabez T. O'Dell, vice-president of the Bessemer & Lake Erie, as an expert to appraise the Delaware & Eastern. In his report, which was full of caustic comments, he stated that the railroad had been built so cheaply that it was falling to pieces; that it could not possibly make money. It was taking in $2,100 a mile, cost $2,500 a mile to operate, and this ratio could not be changed without extensive and expensive improvements. Unable to refinance the railroad, the receivers marked time by cutting expenses to

the bone. A year and a half later, encouraged by increased traffic, the bondholders reorganized the company as the Delaware & Northern Railroad, with Moreland as president. All the new directors came from Pittsburgh, most of them representing banks holding bonds in the old company. They accepted preferred stock in lieu of bonds, and advanced money to place the railroad in first class condition. The roadbed was reballasted, additional locomotives and shop equipment purchased and surplus equipment sold. Overstocked with freight cars which had been bought for use on the Schenectady & Margaretville, the D. & N. sold most of them to other railroads. A good percentage of the freight cars, all brand new in 1906, had spent four years on sidings.

The reorganized railroad managed to meet expenses from 1911 through 1918; the biggest money maker was the dairy business, the road owning seven milk cars and using cars from its connecting railroads when needed. The bluestone quarries were closing down, and the traffic in finished lumber did not live up to the glowing prospectus turned out by Frederick Searing. Whenever there was a surplus, it was paid to the preferred stockholders, the last dividend of $15,000 being paid in 1918. Losses began to mount up after 1919, and on March 16, 1921, president Moreland and superintendent J. J. Welch were appointed receivers. The railroad was operated as economically as possible, and the very unprofitable Andes branch was abandoned in April 1925 and the rails sold for scrap.

The shops and engine terminal at Margaretville shortly before the Delaware & Northern was abandoned. Engine No. 10 is the only sign of life in what was once a busy scene. — GEORGE PHELPS

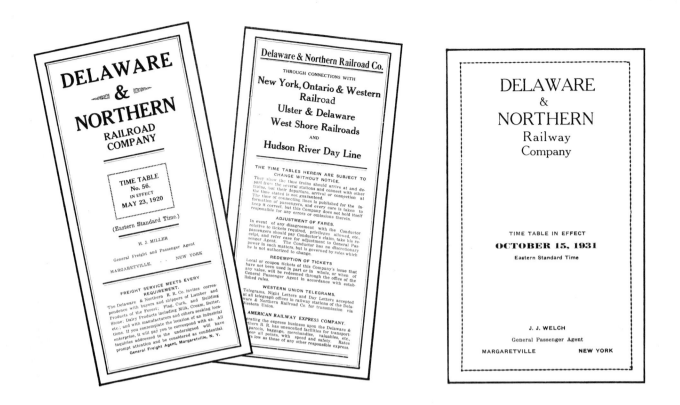

DELAWARE
&
NORTHERN
RAILROAD
COMPANY

TIME TABLE
No. 56.
IN EFFECT
MAY 23, 1920.

(Eastern Standard Time.)

H. J. MILLER

General Freight and Passenger Agent

MARGARETVILLE.   NEW YORK

FREIGHT SERVICE MEETS EVERY
REQUIREMENT.

The Delaware & Northern R. R. Co. invites correspondence with buyers and shippers of Lumber and Products of the Forest; Flag, Curb, and Building Stone; Dairy Products including Milk, Cream, Butter, etc.; and with manufacturers and others seeking locations. If you contemplate the location of an industrial enterprise, it will pay you to correspond with us. All inquiries addressed to the undersigned will have prompt attention and be considered as confidential.

General Freight Agent, Margaretville, N. Y.

Delaware & Northern Railroad Co.

THROUGH CONNECTIONS WITH

New York, Ontario & Western
Railroad
Ulster & Delaware
West Shore Railroads
AND
Hudson River Day Line

THE TIME TABLES HEREIN ARE SUBJECT TO
CHANGE WITHOUT NOTICE.

They show the time trains should arrive at and depart from the several stations and connect with other trains, but their departure, arrival or connection at the time stated is not guaranteed. The time of connecting lines is published for the information of passengers, and every care is taken to keep it correct, but this Company does not hold itself responsible for any errors or omissions therein.

ADJUSTMENT OF FARES.

In event of any disagreement with the Conductor relative to tickets required, privileges allowed, etc., passengers should pay Conductor's claim, take his receipt, and refer case for adjustment to General Passenger Agent. The Conductor has no discretionary power in such matters, but is governed by rules which he is not authorized to change.

REDEMPTION OF TICKETS

Local or coupon tickets of this Company's issue that have not been used in part or in whole, or when of any value, will be redeemed through the office of the General Passenger Agent in accordance with established rules.

WESTERN UNION TELEGRAMS.

Telegrams, Night Letters and Day Letters accepted at all telegraph offices in railway stations of the Delaware & Northern Railroad Co for transmission via Western Union.

AMERICAN RAILWAY EXPRESS COMPANY.

Operating the express business upon the Delaware & Northern R. R. has unexcelled facilities for transport of parcels, baggage, merchandise, valuables, etc., between all points, with speed and safety. Rates as low as those of any other responsible express.

DELAWARE
&
NORTHERN
Railway
Company

TIME TABLE IN EFFECT
OCTOBER 15, 1931
Eastern Standard Time

J. J. WELCH
General Passenger Agent

MARGARETVILLE   NEW YORK

The 1920 and 1931 Delaware & Northern public timetables reflect the shrinking passenger business. At the right, engine No. 7, an old Buffalo, Rochester & Pittsburgh Ten-Wheeler works out its last years on the way freight. — J. H. DEAN

Lima-built Mogul No. 10 was the last engine purchased by the Delaware & Northern, as well as the heaviest. — AUTHOR'S COLLECTION

The *Red Heifer* stops at Downsville where the busy creamery is a symphony of steam and smoke. The road foreman's Ford railcar is on the station track. — GEORGE PHELPS

Attempts at cutting wages resulted in walkouts of the employees, and a compromise was finally reached. A new gasoline motor car was purchased to replace the steam passenger trains, saving $30,000 a year. This unit carried mail, baggage, express and passengers, and was affectionately called the *Red Heifer* by the residents along the line.

In 1928 the losses were so great that the directors, headed by J. J. Jermyn, petitioned for abandonment. An angel in the person of Samuel R. Rosoff of New York City came along at this time. He had built a highway in the valley ten years earlier and was familiar with the railroad and the people of the villages it served. He bought the railroad on December 20, 1928, for $70,000, and reorganized it as the Delaware & Northern *Railway*, running it on a shoestring through the depression years. At this time, New York City was preparing to build a dam across the East Branch of the Delaware near Downsville to create a reservoir to augment the water supply of the big city. Rosoff felt that the railroad was needed to haul supplies for the dam, after which it could be moved to higher ground. Litigation involving New York, the I. C. C. and the railroad ensued, and was settled

when Rosoff agreed to sell the railroad to the city whenever the right-of-way was needed for the reservoir. Rosoff endeared himself to the people of the valley by running a school train each way daily except weekends and vacation times, and spent a considerable amount of his personal funds in keeping the railroad going. In 1939 he sold the railroad to New York City for $200,000, but additional court suits dragged on until finally, on October 16, 1942, notice of abandonment was tacked on the doors of the stations. The work of removing the rails and the bridges was hampered by spring rains, and it was not until the summer of 1943 that the last lot of ties had been cleaned up and shipped to a railroad in Michigan. The equipment was sold for scrap, and little remains today to show that there ever was a railroad from Arkville to East Branch.

As an afterthought, the failure of the Schenectady & Margaretville saved New York City a considerable sum, for when Schoharie Reservoir construction was begun in 1917, had there been a railroad in the valley at that point it would have been relocated high up on the mountainside at a cost far greater than the relocation of the Ulster & Delaware at Ashokan.

155

Back in the days when steam was still king of the rails, Ulster & Delaware trains Nos. 509 and 528 pass at Stamford. At this time, the milk trains had only a combination car on the end. — RAYMOND S. BALDWIN COLLECTION

11

THE RISE AND FALL
OF THE
ULSTER & DELAWARE

IN THE first 13 years of the 20th Century, Samuel D. Coykendall watched the surplus account grow from $467,000 to $885,000, with all bond interest paid on time, and no debts for new equipment or other purchases. According to an analysis by Moody's at the end of 1912, the Ulster & Delaware would soon be in a position to retire some of the bonds due in 1928. This was good business practice, for after 1901 the interest payments were $140,000 annually. A well managed railroad with the Ulster & Delaware's prospects naturally would set aside funds to retire the bonds gradually. This was what the bondholders of the railroad expected as the surplus approached the million dollar mark.

The best laid plans, as the saying goes, were thrown awry when Samuel D. Coykendall at 75 years of age died suddenly on January 14, 1913, at his home in Kingston. Coykendall was a wealthy man by any standards of the time. He owned a majority of the stock in the Ulster & Delaware and the Cornell Steamboat Co., and owned outright such properties as the Grand Hotel, the Consolidated Rosendale Cement Co., the Hudson River

Bluestone Co., a large ice business, the Grant House in Catskill and an interest in the Rondout National Bank.

His oldest son, Thomas Cornell Coykendall, who had been the vice-president of the Ulster & Delaware since 1895, became president pro-tem. At the annual meeting in December 1913 the directors by-passed Thomas Coykendall and elected his younger brother Edward, returning Thomas to the vice-presidency. Edward had been superintendent of the railroad and a director since his father assumed control in 1895, and knew the railroad perhaps better than any of his relatives. As the minute books of the company are not available, one can only imagine the jockeying for position on the part of the Coykendall family at that meeting. Of the board of directors, six out of ten were Coykendalls. Horace Greeley Young was still on the board, well along in years and shortly due to retire from the Delaware & Hudson. R. O'Sullivan became the superintendent of the U. & D. Probably the most illustrious member of the family, Frederick K. Coykendall, a graduate civil engineer with a Master's degree, chose to remain with the Cornell

Steamboat Co. of which he had been the manager since 1900 and, after his father's death, the president. He left the business of running the family railroad to Edward, and rose to become Chairman of the Board of Trustees of Columbia University, which office he held until his death November 18, 1954. Frederick Coykendall remained as a director of the U. & D. but devoted his time to other family enterprises. Harry S. Coykendall, treasurer of the U. & D. since 1895, died soon after his father, in 1914, and his brother Frank was appointed in his place.

The effects of the change in management were soon apparent. The year 1913 was to be the best year since 1909, the passengers carried reached a peak of 676,000 and at the annual meeting a three percent dividend on the common stock was declared, the first ever paid by the railroad. Cash in the banks totalled over a million dollars, and the 18 stockholders, most of them relatives or descendants of Thomas Cornell, collected $57,000. It did not seem like a large amount, but the directors voted this dividend each year for eight years, until the total paid out was $456,000. In justification of the dividend, who could have foreseen in 1913 the drastic changes in passenger transportation which would take place after World War I? Most important of all was the eventual demise of anthracite coal as a fuel for heating homes, in favor of natural gas, crude oil and electricity. Another point was that the stockholders had never received a penny in dividends. To be sure, its ownership gave them control of the railroad, and provided a good living for several members of the Coydenkall family, but to quote Edward Coykendall years later, his job was "no bed of roses."

Edward Coykendall had to guide the railroad through the difficult time of relocation during the building of Ashokan Dam and reservoir, and kept the trains moving, though many of them were delayed time and again during the busiest part of the summer season. This was largely compensated by the $1,250,000 cash settlement made by the City of New York in 1915, and gave the railroad a very comfortable cash balance against eventualities.

One of these occurred on the afternoon of June 16, 1916, when eastbound train No. 18, due in Arkville at 5:31 P.M., collided head-on with a light engine which was westbound on the main track a half-mile west of Arkville station. The cause was

Edward Coykendall, from a portrait probably made in 1895 when he became superintendent of the Ulster & Delaware. — COURTESY MARTIN HAGELE

Stony Clove Notch after the blizzard of March 3, 1914. The deepest of the drifts had to be shovelled out. — A. GIBSON HAGUE COLLECTION

On the right, the trains from Oneonta and Kaaterskill meet at Phoenicia after the 1914 blizzard. (BELOW) The Hunter train at Kaaterskill Junction, where the snowdrifts had been 15 feet deep. — BOTH A. GIBSON HAGUE COLLECTION

A meet on March 4, 1914 at Kaaterskill Junction, with the Hunter train on the right. — DEGOLYER FOUNDATION COLLECTION

The last coach of the Phoenicia-Kaaterskill train barely clears the steep walls of the cut at Stony Clove Notch. — A GIBSON HAGUE COLLECTION

the absent-mindedness of engineer Ferris Layman of engine No. 29, who had fireman Merrel Hoag and flagman B. Brannen in the cab with him. Layman was handed an order to meet extra No. 20, the inspection engine with superintendent O'Sullivan aboard, at Arkville before proceeding west. The orders were changed and the new order read that No. 29 would meet extra No. 20 at Roxbury. After receiving the order Layman started the engine west, apparently not hearing the shouts and hand signals from the agent who knew that the regularly scheduled train No. 18 was due any minute, and the collision resulted several minutes later. Layman of No. 29 suffered broken bones but recovered quickly; flagman Brannen came out of the wreck with hardly a scratch, but fireman Hoag was buried underneath the coal in the tender and died of internal injuries a short time after he was rescued. On the passenger train, engineer Harry Lauren on engine No. 22 was burned slightly by steam, fireman Eugene Riley was not injured but tore his jacket to ribbons on the reverse gear in his haste to jump off the engine. The mail clerks, Neil Flynn and Bill Armstrong, were badly knocked around, as was Otto Mayes, the rear brakeman. Conductor Raymond Baldwin, sitting in the first coach, was not hurt but found his hat several seats ahead of him when he stood up. No passengers were injured, for luckily the train was running at slow speed preparing for the Arkville

By 1915 the West Shore's trains were being hauled by fast Atlantic type engines such as No. 960, shown leaving West Point in 1915. — GERALD M. BEST

stop. While both engines were damaged, they were rebuilt and continued in service for many years after the accident.

After this incident, the Ulster & Delaware went merrily along, slumbering a bit through each winter and springing into action each May. During World War I, the U. S. Railroad Administration operated the road for two years and two months, beginning January 1, 1918. Ulster & Delaware trains terminated their runs at the Delaware & Hudson station in Oneonta during this period, and the U. & D. station was called East Oneonta. Non-operating income from investments and rentals to Uncle Sam kept the railroad solvent and the surplus growing. Not one new passenger car was bought after 1906, the system of renting cars from the New York Central in the summer proving very profitable for both railroads. Except for the three steel baggage cars, the U. & D. cars were all of wood construction, and were kept on the boat trains from Kingston Point to the mountains and return. In the winter they handled all passenger traffic.

The number of passengers carried dropped from the peak in 1913, especially during the war years, though the decline was halted for several years by the abandonment of the Catskill Mountain Lines. Passenger receipts, due to increased fares, did not run parallel to the number of passengers carried, and the best year of passenger income was 1921. After that, the yearly total of passengers steadily dwindled, though coal shipments remained good through most of the 1920s. When George Beach died in 1918, the management of the Mountain House was left in the hands of his daughter Mary Van Wagonen and her husband John. Though the Van Wagonens struggled to maintain the high standards of nearly a century at the Mountain House, great changes were taking place on the top of the mountain, and through the central Catskills as well. The slowly creeping tide of Jewish ownership had reached the Hotel Kaaterskill, and what had happened in Sullivan County earlier was now extended to the Catskills. The era of the cheap two-week vacation was at hand. It was possible for New Yorkers in the low income brackets to enjoy a respite from the heat and crowded conditions of the city, and hotels which had accommodated a limited number of guests in luxury were now rebuilt to handle twice that many in cramped quarters, which did not bother the boarders one bit, as they lived this way the year around.

In September 1924 the Hotel Kaaterskill was destroyed in a fire which illuminated the Hudson River valley in a Dante's inferno fed by millions of board feet of lumber, and though the Mountain House remained open for some years afterwards, the Ulster & Delaware had lost its largest customer.

The relatively accident-free World War I years through 1921 made for an excellent safety record, but on May 26, 1922, it was marred by the worst accident in the railroad's history in which six employees were killed. A work train, running backwards westerly from Halcottville towards Roxbury was struck by an eastbound coal train. The work train, with conductor G. B. Mattice and engineer A. J. Pelham, was working on the line east of Roxbury, with orders to protect themselves against an eastbound coal train after 11 A.M. They also got an order to back up to Stamford to straighten a sagging telegraph pole. Deciding to take care of the last order immediately, both the conductor and the engineer forgot about the coal train and began

When coal train extra No. 27 derailed near Roxbury, the tender went down the bank. — RAYMOND S. BALDWIN COLLECTION

The big hook pulls No. 27 back on the rails, as it still carries the white flags of an extra. — RAYMOND S. BALDWIN COLLECTION

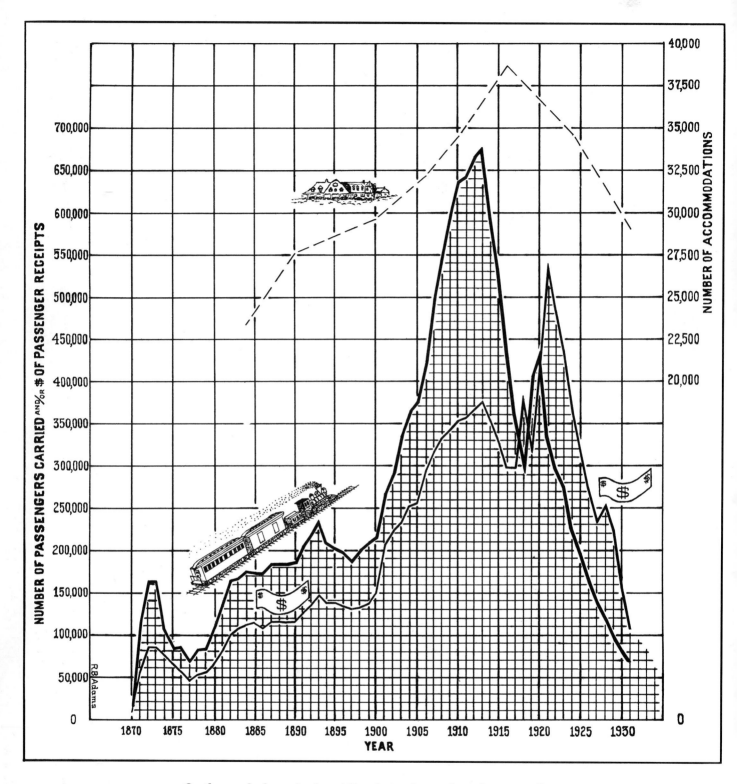

On the graph chart, the dotted line shows the number of accommodations available from 1884 to 1932. The heavy black line indicates the number of passengers carried during the railroad's life, and the light black line marks the passenger receipts in dollars.

backing towards Grand Gorge. The coal train, with engineer Charles Neebe, fireman Frank Morse and conductor J. Redmond came around a sharp curve and they saw the caboose of the work train moving towards them. Standing on the back platform of the caboose were conductor Mattice and his two brakemen. When they saw the coal train, they jumped off, but six trackmen inside the caboose, supervisor William Lafferty, O. North, Fred Chase, Fred Borst, F. Louden and Abraham Johnson were instantly killed. The enginemen on the coal train were only slightly injured, as their train was running slowly, but the wooden caboose was crushed into matchwood and its riders did not have a chance. The cause was obvious — failure of the work train crew to take siding at Roxbury before 11 A.M.

A year after this accident, the last dividend was paid to the stockholders, and what a whopping melon it was. With the surplus at $800,000, and the invested reserves of $1,250,000 received from New York City in 1915, there was more than enough to retire or refinance the bond issue due for redemption in 1928, and thus the rating of these bonds was high and the railroad's credit was excellent. Instead of leaving this reserve intact, the whole amount was paid January 3, 1923, to the 18 holders of the 19,000 shares of common stock, as a 65.78 percent dividend. Add the nine previous years of three percent dividends and the lucky stockholders had received almost the entire par value of their stock. The rising chorus of criticism from Wall Street was soon heard in Kingston, and quite logically so. In the following two years the bonds of 1928 dropped in price from 91 to 60, with the junior income bonds falling from 62 to 36. The rating of the senior bonds fell from gilt-edged to speculative, and the junior bonds were rated as a poor risk. Ownership of these bonds was spread over a large group of investors, and trading in both issues was active as the owners tried to salvage what they could of their investment before the bonds dropped any lower. It was obvious that the stockholders did not own any of the bonds, or they would never have declared such an enormous dividend.

Moody's *Manual of Railroads* for 1927 expresses the sentiment of financial experts better than the author can. The U. & D. 1926 annual report published in 1927 showed a loss of $111,697 for the year, after bond interest had been paid. Moody's had the following comment:

"The Ulster & Delaware operates 129 miles of road from Kingston to Oneonta, N. Y., and Phoenicia to Kaaterskill. Its route is through the Catskill Mountains and as a result, the grades are steep and the curves are pronounced. Little freight is originated and most of that received from connections consists of anthracite coal, 266,454 tons, or 67.5% of the tonnage in 1926. In recent years the company's business has been steadily declining, due to severe automobile and auto truck competition. As this is apt to continue, it is unlikely that any increase in traffic will come about. Equipment owned is in small amount and according to figures from the A.A.R., not in the best condition. Until 1923 the position of the U. & D.'s funded debt was generally felt to be secure, due to the substantial liquid assets held in the treasury, which, it was assumed, would be used to aid in the refunding operation in 1928 when the first mortgage bonds mature. Since the distribution of such assets to the stockholders to the amount of $1,250,000 in dividends, there has been doubt expressed as to the outcome of the company's 1928 refunding program, especially in view of the poor record made during the past few years. There is no great question but that rather large risks are involved in holding either the 1st Consolidated or the 1st Refunding mortgage bonds, although it must be pointed out that their position would be greatly improved should the recent applications for a larger division of freight rates on business jointly handled with the West Shore receive the approval of the Interstate Commerce Commission."

Moody's had ample cause for alarm. Though the railroad earned operating expenses through 1929, it showed a deficit of $108,000 after all charges had been paid, the loss being made up by drawing on the rapidly shrinking surplus.

When the major bond issue became due and payable June 1, 1928, the management served notice of default but agreed to continue to pay interest as it came due. Operating expenses were earned in 1929, but in 1930 they fell short by $9,000. As if to herald the end of an era, the Ulster & Delaware had its second and last boiler explosion that year. On August 23, 1930, engine No. 24, on passenger train No. 9, blew up at Milepost 14 near Ashokan at 8:15 A.M., killing engineer John Scully and fireman Lester Reed. The engine turned upside-down in the ditch and the first three cars of

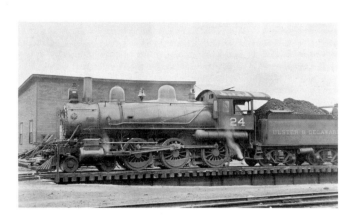

Ulster & Delaware No. 24 at Oneonta in May 1915. — KARL E. SCHLACHTER (BELOW) The end of the road for No. 24 when its boiler exploded in 1930. — EDWARD L. MAY COLLECTION

the train were derailed, but the 18 passengers and the train crew were not injured. Even the fingerling trout in the New York State Conservation Commission's car *Adirondack* were not disturbed. The cause of the boiler explosion was low water, and due to the destruction of the water glass, gauges and other cab fittings, it was impossible to determine why such an experienced engine crew had fallen victims of the explosion.

In 1931, the end of the Ulster & Delaware was in sight, for the surplus was down to $104,514, and with the country entering a severe depression, the New York Central was approached to find out if they were interested in buying the railroad. They replied that they were not. A few months later the situation changed, for in 1930 the "Central" had petitioned the Interstate Commerce Commission for the right to absorb their principal

leased railroads, the Michigan Central, the Big Four and the Lake Shore & Michigan Southern into the parent company. The I.C.C. bargained that it would agree to this merger if the "Central" would buy the ailing Ulster & Delaware at a fair price. A three-man commission was appointed, and after a thorough study of the railroad, two of the arbitrators returned a valuation of $4,100,000, or two-thirds the original cost, while the third arbitrator, a "Central" man, contended the line was worth only $1,813,333. The high figure was not accepted by the "Central" and neither the I.C.C. nor the U. & D. would accept the low figure. Late in 1930 the "Central" agreed to pay whatever the I.C.C. ruled was the "commercial value" of the railroad. In 1931 this was set at $2,500,000, which figure was accepted by both sides. To facilitate the deal, H. H. Flemming of Kingston, general counsel and secretary of the U. & D. was appointed re-

No. 23's tank has been relettered with the name of its new owner, the *New York Central.* (BELOW) No. 23 with its new number 803, at Kingston in 1936. — GERALD M. BEST

ceiver, a legal step to protect the bondholders and to enable delivery of the railroad without interference from stockholders, whose shares quite naturally would become worthless.

Effective February 1, 1932, the railroad became the Catskill Mountain branch of the New York Central. Owners of the five percent 1st mortgage bonds were offered $760 per bond by the receiver, with holders of the income bonds being offered $480 per unit, not a bad settlement considering that it occurred in the middle of a nationwide depression. Over three-fourths of the bonds were turned in by their owners in settlement at these prices, but the stockholders of the Ulster & Delaware were not to get off the hook so easily. The holders of 354 of the five percent bonds had deposited them with the Central Hanover Bank & Trust Co. of New York, and this bank, as trustee for these bonds, brought suit against the 18 stockholders of the U. & D. to recover the entire $1,250,000 which they had received as a special dividend in 1923. The suit dragged through the courts until 1937, which explains why Edward Coykendall was reluctant to discuss the Ulster & Delaware with Winfield Robinson in 1936. The State Supreme Court finally ruled that $151,145 be paid to the holders of the 354 bonds, and after deducting legal and court fees, the trustees ac-

Rondout station and the shops in the winter of 1931, a short time before the terminal was closed forever. — GEORGE PHELPS

Nos. 815 and 809 double-head a railfan excursion en route from Weehawken to New York via Kingston, Oneonta and Albany in September 1936. The train is ready to back around the curve to the former U. & D. tracks before heading west for Oneonta. — M. B. COOKE

cepted $92,500 in full settlement. The bond holdouts thus got a total of $982 for each $1000 bond. The balance of the bonds were not affected by this settlement, as their owners had signed a release in accepting the 1932 payment. Thus did the company originally formed by Thomas Cornell disappear from view.

As the property of the New York Central many economies were effected on their new branch. Ten of the 29 locomotives were scrapped, including No. 24 which had never been rebuilt after the boiler explosion, leaving 19 to be relettered New York Central on their tenders. All of the passenger equipment was soon condemned, except the three steel baggage cars and a few of the vestibuled coaches, the latter reduced to the lowly status of maintenance-of-way boarding cars. The entire Rondout terminal, shops, roundhouse, coaling station and other locomotive facilities were abandoned and torn down, former U. & D. locomotives were based at the old West Shore's roundhouse in Kingston, and shopwork was all done elsewhere, mostly at West Albany. The summer trains from Weehawken to the Catskills were continued, but there was one less train in 1935. Surprisingly enough, an effort was made to better the service in 1939 by increasing the number of trains, to no avail; the Kaaterskill and Hunter branches were losing money, and in 1940 the I.C.C. approved the abandonment of the branches. The rising tide of ski enthusiasts in the 1930s caused the development of a number of ski runs in the mountains west of Phoenicia, and special ski excursions from Weehawken to the ski areas were heavily patronized before World War II. During the war, in the

summer there were three weekend trains to Arkville, one going through to Oneonta, and after the war until 1948, all three trains terminated at Oneonta. Between summers one train a day was the rule, with the milk cars added ahead of the postal car and a combination coach.

In 1946 the author made a long-planned trip from Oneonta to Kingston to see for himself what changes had taken place in the Catskills and the railroad since 1939. To save space, I will use the first person singular to describe this trip. Arriving in Albany from the west on an early morning train, I breakfasted in the station and then boarded a Delaware & Hudson train for Binghamton, riding in an old wooden coach which took me right back to my boyhood. Arriving in Oneonta, I taxied over to the New York Central station a half-mile

A stranger in the Catskills. The engine on the left is New York Central No. 1013, a 4-4-0 used on the Hunter shuttle, meeting former Ulster & Delaware No. 40 at Kaaterskill Junction. — RAYMOND S. BALDWIN COLLECTION

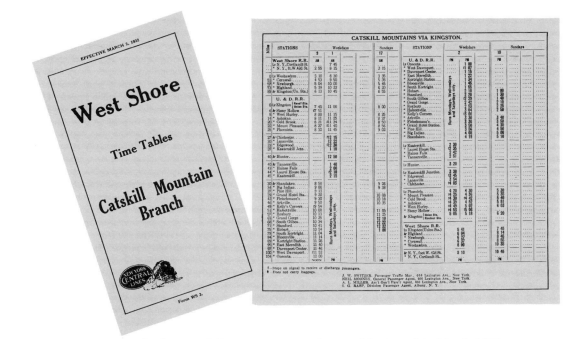

The first Catskill Mountain Branch timetable, issued in March 1932, shows one train a day each way between Kingston and Oneonta, with tri-weekly service to Kaaterskill and Hunter. — EDWARD L. MAY COLLECTION

north. Armed with photo permits and expected by the train crew because of them, I was greeted by conductor Raymond S. Baldwin and introduced to the agent, who sold me a ticket to Weehawken.

Outside, Train No. 528, headed by engine No. 815 (old U. & D. No. 38), consisted of the mail car and a combination coach, the latter with its passenger section next to the engine, a most satisfactory condition for "stack music" listening. The train crew including the conductor were clad in overalls instead of the spick-and-span blue of former years, because they were all going to be very busy switching milk cars in due time, but the engine except for minor changes looked just as it did when I first saw it in 1912. Pulling out promptly at 10:35 A.M. on a beautiful clear, cool October day, we passed the old roundhouse with its lone occupant, the spare engine which was very dead at the time. We loped along through the western approaches to the Catskills, No. 815 making very

In July 1941 westbound train No. 535 was so light that No. 800 required no helper at Arkville. — T. A. GAY

167

SKI SPECIALS

After a heavy fall of snow in February 1936, the Kingston station platform was a cold place to trainwatch. In this scene looking south, a train bound for Albany on the West Shore Route stops just short of the Catskill Mountain branch crossing. (RIGHT) A "Ski Special" which followed the Albany train from Weehawken double-heads out of Kingston on the former U. & D. line. — BOTH M. B. COOKE

Crisp morning cold holds the plumes of coal smoke and hot steam as Oneonta-Kingston train No. 518 leaves Arkville with engines Nos. 30 and 34 at the head end. (LEFT) No. 36 helps push a "Ski Special" out of Arkville in February 1936. — BOTH M. B. COOKE

New York Central Nos. 30 and 34 with train No. 518 shown above, tops the summit at Grand Hotel station. — M. B. COOKE

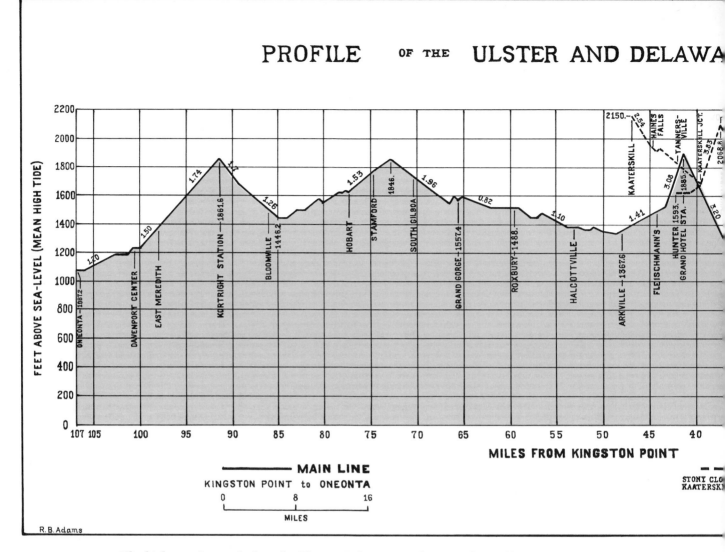

MAIN LINE
KINGSTON POINT to ONEONTA

0   8   16
MILES

R.B. Adams

STONY CLO
KAATERSKI

The highest point reached on the Ulster & Delaware, as shown in the profile above, was Kaaterskill Station, 2,150 feet. The mainline at Summit Station was 1,885 feet above sea level, higher than either of its rivals to the south, the Erie and the New York, Ontario & Western.

easy work of hauling the two-car train. I was the only paying passenger that morning, although others came aboard later in the day. The leaves of the trees had turned so that as we climbed through the dense woods, the scene was a veritable riot of color, a sight seldom seen where I live. I stood out on the platform of the combo, with the door open and the tank of No. 815 towering over me, to watch our winding passage up Kortright Creek to the summit near Kortright Station, then downhill to Bloomville and the West Branch of the Delaware.

We reached Hobart at 12:20 P.M. and conductor Baldwin, after checking with the agent, told me I had plenty of time for lunch. They were due to pass the westbound train there, and it was still switching at Stamford. Three cars of milk at the

great Sheffield Farms creamery in Hobart were not yet fully loaded, so Baldwin told me to walk up Cornell Ave. to Main St., turn to the right, and across the street I would see an old hotel with white, colonial style pillars, where I could have a fine lunch. Should the train be ready to leave before the 1:30 P.M. estimate, the engineer would blow several long blasts on the whistle, as a sign for me to stop eating, pay the check and head for the station; — he said, "Don't run, just walk — running right after a big meal is bad for digestion!" When I mentioned that I had hoped to catch the 5:04 P. M. southbound local on the West Shore out of Kingston, Baldwin said we would never make it, but for me not to worry; he would get me to Weehawken almost as soon as the local would. Deciding not to spoil my appetite by stewing over

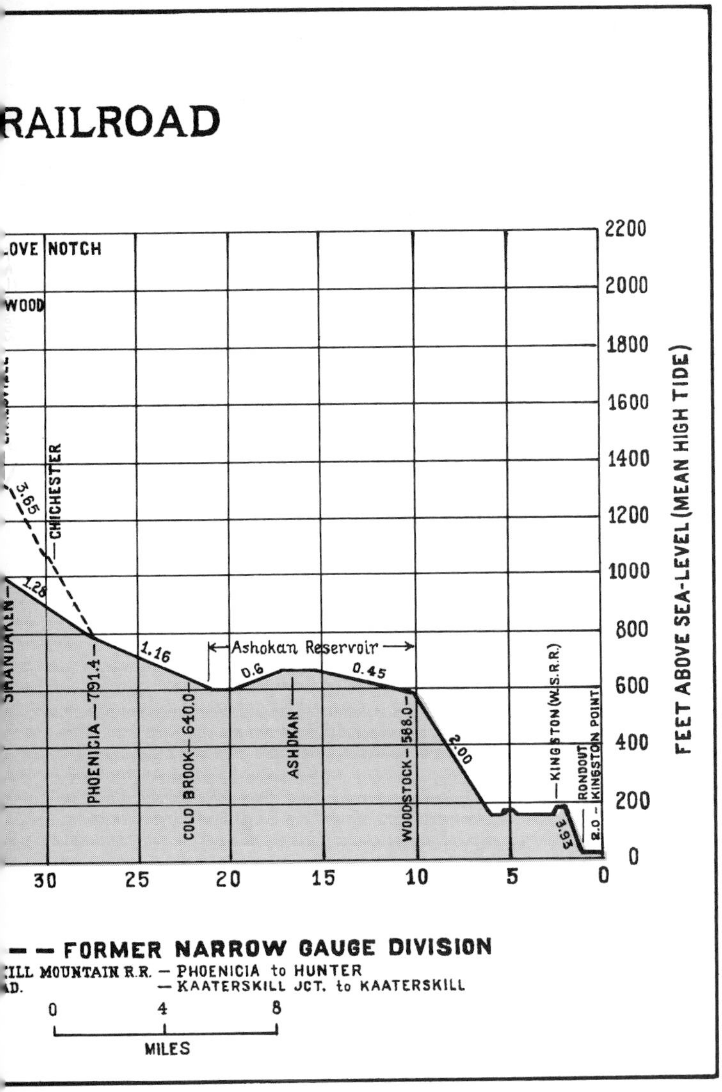

Chart labels (left diagram):

OVE NOTCH
WOOD
CHICHESTER
3.65
1.28
SHANDAKEN
PHOENICIA — 791.4
1.16
COLD BROOK — 640.0
Ashokan Reservoir
0.6
ASHOKAN
0.45
WOODSTOCK — 568.0
2.00
KINGSTON (W.S. R.R.)
RONDOUT
KINGSTON POINT
2.0
3.95

FEET ABOVE SEA-LEVEL (MEAN HIGH TIDE)

2200
2000
1800
1600
1400
1200
1000
800
600
400
200
0

30   25   20   15   10   5   0

— — FORMER NARROW GAUGE DIVISION

ILL MOUNTAIN R.R. — PHOENICIA to HUNTER
AD. — KAATERSKILL JCT. to KAATERSKILL

0   4   8
MILES

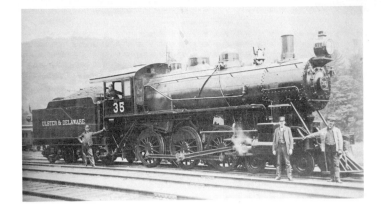

Ulster & Delaware No. 35 poses at Phoenicia in 1906, with Henry Sherman, engineer, in the cab and Perry McDonald standing by the cylinder. — AUTHOR'S COLLECTION

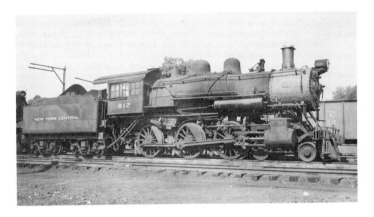

Old No. 35 as No. 812, at Kingston just before it was again renumbered in 1948. — AUTHOR'S COLLECTION

No. 35's last number was 1225 under which it operated for less than a year. — AUTHOR'S COLLECTION

a schedule, I walked through the picturesque old village to the New Hobart Inn, looking not so new in its coat of faded white paint, but for 75 cents I was served the most colossal (Hollywood expression), tasty banquet I had had in many a year. Seated at the long table were a dozen or more businessmen of the town, mostly from the Sheffield Farms Co. I heard, and all so occupied with eating that they scarcely gave me a glance. On the table were three or four kinds of vegetables, a soup tureen, fricasseed chicken, mashed potatoes, farm bread, a great pitcher of what the waitress called milk but which tasted like cream to me, apple pie and ice cream, with coffee afterwards. Not to mention jams and jellies, home-made pickles and a great chocolate layer cake on the sideboard in back of me — fare I dared not partake of by the time I saw them. When I was ready to leave, the gracious lady in charge wrapped up a huge piece of the cake and two giant apples, and though I felt as if I could never eat again that day, they did indeed come in handy later on.

171

Bloomville station in 1898, the start of this train's run to Rondout,
for it was the end of the line. — HAROLD L. GOLDSMITH COLLECTION
(BELOW) The same location in 1946. The station has changed very
little except for the siding to the right of engine No. 815. — GERALD
M. BEST

In the view above, West Shore train No. 25 northbound near Ulster Park is running on what was then high grade double track. — JOHN P. AHRENS At the left, No. 811 heads the second section of the *Catskill Mountain Limited*, while the cars for Kaaterskill are switched off. — EDWARD L. MAY COLLECTION (BELOW) Nos. 809 and 807 with No. 535 westbound, drifting into Arkville in July 1940. — T. A. GAY

Eastbound train No. 509 ready to leave Stamford with three cars of milk, a combo and several box cars. — RAYMOND S. BALDWIN COLLECTION (BELOW) After the Sheffield Farms milk car is coupled into the train, it will be on its way to Kingston, with a final destination of New York City. — WILLIAM D. EDSON

A train whistling in the distance proved to be the westbound train with engine No. 816 just pulling into the station. Our engine was backing down the line with three loaded milk cars which were soon coupled to our train. At this point conductor Baldwin, pointing out that my permit and signed release were good enough for him, suggested that I ride the engine the rest of the way into Kingston. Nothing loath, I lugged my eight-pound Graflex into the cab, where I met engineer George Burnett and fireman Wallace Effner, both of Kingston. The "highball" was not long in coming, and soon we were under way. I sat on the fireman's seat which was not in use, for Effner was very busy shoveling coal to keep No. 815 hot during the steady climb to Stamford. The West Branch of the Delaware looked wonderful in that early afternoon, with the leaves of the trees turned to the colors of Joseph's coat. At Stamford we added more cars of milk, then got down to the business of climbing the grade to the summit two miles east, and on the way downhill towards Grand Gorge, No. 815 gave us a very rough ride, for the spiralled and banked curves of yesteryear had been rebuilt with abrupt entrances with no bank, and the speed limit was 35 miles per hour. Gone were the days when the passenger trains negoti-

At Arkville, No. 812 will be turned by the enginemen and will help train No. 528 to Grand Hotel station. (BELOW) No. 815 takes water and No. 818 is backing down to the rear of the train, which will have two helpers to the summit. — BOTH GERALD M. BEST

Arkville was a busy yard, with train 528 on the right, No. 808 with the way freight in the center, and No. 811 on the left, waiting to help the freight to the summit. — GERALD M. BEST

ated these curves smoothly at over 50 m.p.h., and there were times when I was certain that we were going to take off into the woods when we hit the first rail of a curve. But No. 815 was sure-footed and I reasoned that the nonchalant engineer seemed not afraid, so why should I be? We rolled into Arkville about 3 P.M., nearly two hours late because of our delays at Hobart and Stamford. The Delaware & Northern's *Red Heifer* which was waiting at the station the last time I was in Arkville had been gone for four years, but the U. & D. yard was surprisingly active. As our engine took water, I watched two men turn No. 812 on the "armstrong" turntable and couple it behind No. 818, to make up our pair of helpers on the steep grade to Grand Hotel Summit. Waiting for us to get on our way was No. 808 with the eastbound way freight, so the Arkville yard was really busy.

We started out of town with 14 cars of milk and the two passenger cars. It was quite a sight to watch those two Ten-Wheelers on the rear of the

Dodging steam and heat waves, the author gets a fireman's view from engine No. 815, on the hill near Fleischmann's. — GERALD M. BEST

train, their stacks sending up almost vertical columns of smoke as the engines dug in on the hill. Fireman Effner kept up a steady stream of coal into the roaring hot firebox, and as we neared the summit there were times when our engine slipped its drivers and was practically down on its knees. All that saved us from stalling was George Burnett's expert hand on the throttle, and when we faltered those two engines on the rear would buck us past the danger point, until finally we reached the summit and stopped while the helpers were cut off.

Under a cloud of smoke and cinders, No. 811 moves westbound with the milk train, lucky to make 10 m.p.h. around Horseshoe Curve on Pine Hill. — EDWARD L. MAY

Kingston station from the northeast in 1946, with the Catskill Mountain branch crossing in the foreground. — EDWARD L. MAY

The rest of the journey was downhill through the beautiful valley of Esopus Creek, with the highest of the Catskills visible on both sides of the valley. Phoenicia station was deserted, a ghost of its former self, the yards and the start of the Kaaterskill branch now trackless and overgrown with weeds. As the sun began to set behind us, we came out on the shore of Ashokan Reservoir, where Burnett showed me that No. 815, though 39 years old, could still step out. We had a straight run for several miles, and reached what seemed to me to be a reckless speed after so many miles of crawling. We slowed down after passing West Hurley and finished the trip into Kingston well below the 35 m.p.h. limit, arriving exactly two hours late.

Raymond Baldwin brought me over to another combination coach standing by itself on the West Shore main line and introduced me to another conductor, with whom I was to ride to Weehawken. A few minutes later, heavy Pacific type No. 4709 started us on our way south, hauling our 14 cars of milk plus seven more added at Kingston. After a fast, non-stop run to Weehawken, we almost caught up with the local I had missed. Truly it was a memorable day.

The summer passenger trains of 1947 proved to be the last, and in 1948 the connecting train on the West Shore met the daily train from Oneonta if it was on time; otherwise, the alternative was a bus

Heavy Pacific type No. 4709, designed for fast running on level track between Kingston and Weehawken. — GERALD M. BEST

The Sheffield Farms plant in Hobart was a desolate ruin in 1970. (BELOW) The New Hobart Inn, after being used as a town meeting hall, was up for sale in 1970. — BOTH GERALD M. BEST

around at Oneonta and returning to Kingston the same day. The loss of the mail contract in 1953 sounded the death knell of even this lone train, and by early 1954 the New York Central's Catskill Mountain branch was relegated to the "Freight Service Only" portion of the timetable. The stations gradually fell into disuse as they were closed one by one and the agents pensioned, transferred to other jobs or laid off. Some of the stations were torn down, but many of them remain as relics of a bygone age, either abandoned or used as warehouses. In 1963 the New York Central petitioned the I.C.C. for permission to abandon the section from Oneonta to Bloomville — that 21 miles Cornell and Coykendall labored so hard to finance and build. Carload shipments to and from the D. & H. had reached the vanishing point, and the I.C.C. gave permission to abandon the line west of Bloomville in 1965. A 2.6 mile section of the line at the west end, from D. & H. Junction at Oneonta Station to Mickle Bridge across Charlotte Creek, was purchased by an Oneonta group which organized the Delaware Otsego Railroad. In 1966, pas-

connection. The milk business was gradually taken away as the highways improved and the glass-lined tank trucks carried milk in bulk shipments. After the death of Mr. Sheffield in Hobart, the creamery was sold to Sealtest, which began trucking milk to their other processing plants from Hobart, abandoning the old creamery until today it stands in ruins. There are empty houses today in Hobart village, and the New Hobart Inn, after being used by the town as a meeting hall for some years, is now for sale with no takers.

Coal shipments from the D. & H. at Oneonta dropped to a negligible amount as did any kind of carload freight. In 1950, as an economy move, the two trains which made the daily run and passed each other at Stamford were reduced to one train, leaving Kingston early in the morning, turning

With its throttle wide open, locomotive No. 817 charges up Pine Hill with westbound train No. 501. With a light load, engine No. 817 handled the three cars with ease. — EDWARD L. MAY

Weehawken terminal as seen from the air, in the last days of steam on the West Shore Route. The number of station tracks has decreased to 14. The Weehawken tunnel can be seen below and to the right of the highway intersection. — DEGOLYER FOUNDATION COLLECTION

Two former Ulster & Delaware Ten-Wheelers headed by No. 800 highball a freight drag near Montgomery on the Wallkill Valley branch. — M. B. COOKE

179

Mickle Bridge and the Delaware Otsego Railroad's end of track. The abandoned Ulster & Delaware right-of-way beyond the bridge is slowly disappearing into the forest. — GERALD M. BEST

senger service was begun as a summer tourist attraction, with a steam locomotive and passenger coaches purchased secondhand. Since then additional rolling stock including a dining car were added, the old station was converted into a railroad museum, and in the summer the western end of the old Ulster & Delaware remained active.

In 1970 the State of New York began proceedings to acquire most of the Delaware Otsego's western end for the proposed Susquehanna Expressway, and the odds were heavily in favor of the State Highway Department getting what it wanted in 1971. Then came the Delaware & Hudson's petition to abandon their Cooperstown branch, and in April 1971 a happy solution to the Delaware Otsego's predicament was found. The D. & H., with the consent of the I.C.C., sold their Cooperstown branch to the group which had formed the Delaware Otsego Railroad, at the scrap value, the DO Railroad agreed to turn over their three miles of former Ulster & Delaware trackage to the State for the expressway, and a new 16-mile shortline, the Cooperstown & Charlotte Valley was organized. The line will have bi-weekly freight service, with the DO Line's steam locomotive as motive power, and in the summer, daily passenger service over at least a part of the line.

The mainline of the Delaware Otsego Railroad was not scenic, but at least it was a tiny bit of the old Ulster & Delaware. (RIGHT) The Delaware Otsego Railroad train at Oneonta station in 1967. The engine was former U.S. Army No. 4038, later Virginia Blue Ridge No. 8, built in 1942. — GERALD M. BEST

The entire Catskill Mountain branch was fully dieselized in 1949 and by combining operations with the Wallkill Valley branch to Montgomery, considerable operating economies have been effected. The principal freight carried in 1971 was cattle feed, farm products, a small amount of coal for a cement plant, materials for the State Highway Department, steel pipe and other manufactured goods. The block signals which once regulated traffic on the busy main line between Kingston and Phoenicia have been removed, and the once proud Ulster & Delaware tracks are overgrown with weeds. The track repair gang is based at Kingston and goes out on the line only when a train crew reports a loose rail or other dangerous condition. The West Shore, now freight only, is single track on the Hudson River Division. The old Ulster & Delaware main line from Kingston to Rondout is operated by Kingston yard crews, and the diesels have just as hard a time getting up that grade past Hasbrouck Avenue tunnel as they did back in the 1870s when residents along the line complained of the noise made by the engines when they slipped their drivers and sometimes stalled on the grade and had to back all the way to Rondout to start over again.

Permission has been granted by the I.C.C. to abandon the five miles from Bloomville to South Kortright and an application is pending to abandon eight miles more from South Kortright to Stamford. A freight train makes the run to Stamford twice a week, laying overnight there, and if there is a car or two for Bloomville or South Kortright, they deliver them, picking their way gingerly through the weeds and hoping they won't derail. Delhi, with no railroad at all since the

Hasbrouck Avenue tunnel approaches are overgrown with weeds and the diesels have a hard time coming up from Rondout with a maximum load. — EDWARD L. MAY

abandonment of the N. Y. O. & W., cannot generate enough traffic to make the Bloomville-Stamford section worth maintaining. The speed limit west of Stamford is 15 m.p.h., the engine crew being very happy to keep below that speed for obvious reasons. When Schoharie power station near South Blenheim is completed four or five years hence, the railroad will lose one of its best customers, for large quantities of steel pipe have been delivered at Grand Gorge, the nearest siding, and much other construction material will come by rail. When the project is completed, the trucks will probably take the remaining business from the railroad, and its present owners, the Penn Central with the help of the I.C.C., will put an end to Thomas Cornell's dream.

The whole pattern of life in the Catskills had changed long before the 1960s, starting with the burning of the Hotel Kaaterskill in 1924, the demolishing of the Hotel Churchill and its satellites at Stamford, then the Grand Hotel and culminating in the demise of Catskill Mountain House and Laurel House in recent years. The Mountain House was closed for lack of patronage in 1942. Outmoded and wracked by storms and the efforts of vandals and wreckers, its remnants were burned by the New York State Conservation Department to remove the menace it presented to unwanted intruders. The Laurel House followed in 1967, and the area around North and South Mountains once served by the narrow gauge railroads has reverted to wilderness and State ownership. The nearest settlement of any sort is Haines' Falls, just west of the park entrance, where the Hotel Vista, almost the last of the old box-like boarding houses, was bulldozed to the ground in 1970. West of Haines' Falls there are a few of the old hotels and boarding houses, besides new motels and small lodges which cater to overnight or weekend guests in the summer and ski enthusiasts in the winter.

The same holds true of the area west of Phoenicia, where the motels have largely taken over from the hotels, though a few of the old timers still dot Pine Hill. Stamford's old hotels are mostly gone, although the Delaware Motor Inn, once the Delaware House, the Westholm, the Madison (now called the Scotch Mist Inn) and the Cold Spring Apartments cater to both summer and winter trade, in competition with ultra-modern Red Carpet Motor Inn. The old Rexmere is now a State Rural Supplementary Education Center, so it did

The Scotch Mist Inn, originally the Madison and now 90 years old, is another Stamford survivor in 1972. (BELOW) The Westholm, hardy pioneer of the 1880's, is a rendezvous for winter sports fans. — BOTH GERALD M. BEST

not share the fate of Dr. Churchill's other enterprises. The Churchill House and its two annexes were turned over to the village of Stamford in lieu of taxes by Herbert Mase, its last owner, who had called it the Maslynn. It cost the village $30,000 to tear down the buildings in 1944-45, but the land was sold for business purposes and the taxpayers got their money's worth.

The era of inexpensive holidays in far-away places is upon us. The central Catskills and the region from Haines' Falls west still attract large crowds in summer or winter, but except when the campers fill Pine Orchard camp grounds in the summer, a modern Rip Van Winkle could sleep undisturbed in the mythical vale on the slopes of the great wall of Manitou.

APPENDIX

LOCOMOTIVES OF THE RONDOUT & OSWEGO R. R.

No.	Name	Type	Builder and Construction No.		Year Built	Dimensions Dr.—Cyls.—Wt.	Remarks
—	*Pennsylvania*	4-4-0	Unknown		6-1869*	Inside-connected.	Wrecked 3-1871
1	*Wm. C. More*	2-6-0	Dickson	52	11-1869	49-18x24-79000	To U. & D. 1-1875 Note A
2	*Thomas Cornell*	4-4-0	Unknown		6-1870*		To U. & D. 2-1875. Retired 1896
3	*John C. Brodhead*	4-4-0	Danforth		12-1870	54-18x24	To U. & D. 3-1875. Note B
4	*William Lounsbury*	4-4-0	Danforth		1-1871	54-18x24	To U. & D. 4-1875. Retired 1889
5	*Orson N. Allaben*	4-4-0	Danforth	732	4-1871	54-18x24	To U. & D. 5-1875 Note A
6	*Lewis N. Heermance*	4-4-0	Danforth	749	7-1871	54-18x24	To U & D . 6-1875. Retired 1895
7	*Frank J. Hecker*	2-6-0T	Danforth	756	9-1871	48-17x22	To U. & D. 7-1875. To No. 9-1882

Note A.   Nos. 1 and 5 were sold to the New York Construction Co. 8-1893.

Note B.   No. 3 blew up at Rondout 8-23-1886 and was scrapped.

*Date Acquired.

Ulster & Delaware 2nd No. 1, built by Brooks in 1892, was of a type made famous by the Lake Shore & Michigan Southern. It became U. & D. 2nd No. 17 in 1898 and ended its days on the Atlanta & St. Andrews Bay Railroad.—EDWARD BOND COLLECTION

LOCOMOTIVES OF THE ULSTER & DELAWARE R. R.

No.	Type	Builder and Construction No.		Year Built	Dimensions Dr.-Cyls.-Wt.	Remarks

(For 1st Nos. 1 to 7 see Roster of Rondout & Oswego R.R.

No.	Type	Builder	Constr. No.	Year Built	Dimensions	Remarks
1	4-6-0	Brooks	2091	5-1892	56-18x24-104800	To 2nd No. 17, 1898
1	4-4-0	Dickson	519	5-1885	62-1/2-18x24-96500	Ex 1st No. 14. Retired 1903
2	4-4-0	Brooks	1539	5-1889	61-18x24-86300	Ex 2nd No. 16. Scrapped 7-9-1932
3	4-4-0	Brooks	1234	6-1887	61-18x24	Retired 1907. Sold Salisbury & Albert Ry. No. 5-1910
4	4-4-0	Brooks	1235	6-1887	61-18x24	Ex 1st No. 16. Retired 1907. To S. & A. Ry. No. 6-1910
5	4-6-0	Brooks	2425	4-1894	61-18x24-98000	To No. 18 in 1898
6	4-4-0	Danforth	749	7-1871	51-18x24	Ex Roundout & Oswego No. 6. Retired 1895
7	4-4-0	Dickson	360	7-1882	67-1/2-17x24	Retired in 1906
8	2-6-0	Rogers	3060	8-1882	54-17x24	Sold in 1888
8	2-6-0	Brooks	1538	5-1889	56-19x24	Renumbered 3rd No. 16-5-1899
8	4-4-0	Schenectady	5153	6-1899	66-19x24-129200	Scrapped 7-8-1932
9	2-6-0T	Danforth	756	9-1871	48-17x22	Ex 1st No. 7. Sold to New York Const. Co. 8-1893 for So. Jersey R.R.
9	4-4-0	Schenectady	4408	1-1896	62-19x24	Wrecked 8-31-11. Scrapped. Note 1
10	4-4-0	Dickson	424	5-1883	62-17x24	Scrapped or sold — 1903
11	4-4-0	Brooks	1014	4-1884	60-1/2-18x24	Scrapped or sold — 1903
12	4-4-0	Brooks	1068	6-1885	60-1/2-18x24	Scrapped or sold — 1896
12	4-4-0	Schenectady	4522	1-1897	66-19x24-129200	Scrapped 7-6-1932
13	0-6-0T	Brooks	1063	4-1885	44-17x24-95200	Scrapped 10-3-1932
14	4-4-0	Dickson	519	5-1885	62-1/2-18x24-96500	Renumbered 3rd No. 1 — 1899
14	0-6-0	Brooks	1701	7-1890	50-20x24-118700	Ex 1st No. 17. Scrapped 9-20-1932
15	2-6-0	Dickson	521	6-1885	56-1/4-19x24	Sold in 1907
16	4-4-0	Brooks	1235	6-1887	61-18x24	Renumbered 2nd No. 4, 5-1889
16	4-4-0	Brooks	1539	5-1889	61-18x24-86300	Renumbered 2nd No. 2, 1898
16	2-6-0	Brooks	1538	5-1889	56-19x24-107900	Ex 2nd No. 8. Retired 1907
17	0-6-0	Brooks	1701	7-1890	50-20x24-118700	Renumbered 2nd No. 14, 1898
17	4-6-0	Brooks	2091	5-1892	56-18x24-104800	Ex 2nd No. 1. Sold 1-1907. Note 2
18	4-6-0	Brooks	2425	4-1894	62-18x24-98000	Ex 2nd No. 5 Scrapped 7-11-1932
19	4-6-0	Schenectady	5106	4-1899	60-19x26-141000	1932 wt.-148300. To NYC 19-800 Scrapped 10-23-1946
20	4-4-0	Schenectady	4409	1-1896	62-14x22-80900	Inspection engine. Scrapped 9-22-1932
21	4-6-0	Schenectady	5107	4-1899	60-19x26-141000	1932 wt.-148300. To NYC 21-801-1216 Scrapped 4-1-1949
22	4-6-0	Schenectady	5108	4-1899	60-19x26-141000	Cyls. to 20x26; wt. 157000. To NYC 22-802. Scrapped 8-31-1948
23	4-6-0	Schenectady	6070	7-1901	60-19x26-141000	1932 wt.-148300. To NYC 23-803-1218. Scrapped 8-20-1949
24	4-6-0	Alco-Schenectady	25799	6-1902	60-19x26-141000	1924 wt.-148300. Blew up 8-23-30. Scrapped by NYC 5-6-32
25	4-6-0	Alco-Schenectady	25800	6-1902	60-19x26-141000	1932 wt.-148300. To NYC 25-804. Scrapped 9-27-1948
26	4-6-0	Alco-Schenectady	25801	6-1902	60-19x26-141000	1932 wt.-148300. To NYC 26-805-1220. Scrapped 8-3-1949
27	4-6-0	Alco-Schenectady	29450	4-1904	60-19x26-146500	1932 wt.-148300. To NYC 27-806-1221. Scrapped 3-28-1949
28	4-6-0	Alco-Schenectady	29451	4-1904	60-19x26-146500	1932 wt.-148300. To NYC 28-807. Scrapped 4-13-1946
29	4-6-0	Alco-Schenectady	29452	4-1904	60-19x26-146500	1932 wt.-148300. Scrapped by NYC 7-7-1932
30	4-6-0	Alco-Schenectady	39952	5-1906	63-20x26-164000	1932 wt.-167000. To NYC 30-808-1222. Scrapped 3-19-1949
31	4-6-0	Alco-Schenectady	39953	5-1906	63-20x26-164000	1932 wt.-167000. To NYC 31. Scrapped 7-28-1933
32	4-6-0	Alco-Schenectady	39954	5-1906	63-20x26-164000	Cyls. to 21x26-wt. 176500. To NYC 32-809. Scrapped 4-4-1945
33	4-6-0	Alco-Schenectady	39955	5-1906	63-20x26-164000	1932 wt.-167000. To NYC 33-810-1223. Scrapped 3-18-1949
34	4-6-0	Alco-Schenectady	39956	5-1906	63-20x26-164000	Cyls. to 21x26-wt. 176500. To NYC 34-811. Scrapped 7-12-1948
35	4-6-0	Alco-Schenectady	39957	5-1906	63-20x26-164000	1932 wt.-167000. To NYC 35-812-1225. Scrapped 3-14-1949
36	4-6-0	Alco-Schenectady	43061	6-1907	63-20x26-164000	1932 wt.-167000. To NYC 36-813-1226. Scrapped 5-12-1949
37	4-6-0	Alco-Schenectady	43062	6-1907	63-20x26-164000	Cyls. to 21x26-wt. 176500. To NYC 37-814-1227. Scrapped 5-14-1949
38	4-6-0	Alco-Schenectady	43063	6-1907	63-20x26-164000	Cyls. to 21x26-wt. 176500. To NYC 38-815-1228. Scrapped 2-13-1949
39	4-6-0	Alco-Schenectady	43064	6-1907	63-20x26-164000	1932 wt.-167000. To NYC 39-816-1229. Scrapped 3-25-1949
40	4-6-0	Alco-Schenectady	43065	6-1907	63-20x26-164000	Cyls. to 21x26-wt. 176500. To NYC 40-817-1230. Scrapped 2-10-1949
41	4-6-0	Alco-Schenectady	43066	6-1907	63-20x26-164000	Cyls. to 21x26-wt. 176500. To NYC 41-818-1231. Scrapped 5-21-1949

Note 1. No. 9 was numbered No. 11 at the factory. Became No. 9 on delivery.

Note 2. Sold to the Southern Iron & Equipment Co., Atlanta, Ga., their No. 558. The S.I.&E. records are incomplete, but photographs indicate the engine became Atlanta & St. Andrews Bay R. R. No. 110.

Note 3. New York Central 802, 804 and 811 were assigned 1200 series numbers, but were scrapped immediately. Engines 22, 24, 32, 34 37, 38, 40 and 41 were rebuilt with larger cylinders and piston valves as indicated, between 1915 and 1927. They were also superheated.

Discussion. In its entire history, the Ulster & Delaware owned a total of of 49 standard gauge locomotives, of four types. Using the Whyte's system of locomotive classification, these locomotives were the 4-4-0, or *American* type, with two pairs of driving wheels and a four-wheel pony truck supporting the front end of the engine; the 2-6-0, or *Mogul* type, with three pairs of driving wheels and a two-wheel pony truck; the 0-6-0, used for yard service and affectionately termed a *Goat,* and the 4-6-0, or *Ten-Wheel* type, with three pairs of drivers and a four-wheel pony truck. These latter engines were intended as all-purpose machines, and since the primary business in the summer was hauling passenger trains, the 4-6-0s were adequate for the job. After Labor Day, the heavy shipments of anthracite coal began, and with this nice balance between the rush summer traffic and the coal trains the other nine months of the year, it was easy for the railroad to carry on with only 30 locomotives after 1907. All the early engines burned anthracite coal, as it was available at Rondout at a very low price, but when the wide firebox, double-cab engines designed to burn anthracite more efficiently began to be very popular with the railroads hauling the hard coal, the Ulster & Delaware management wanted nothing to do with them, and converted all their engines to burn soft coal.

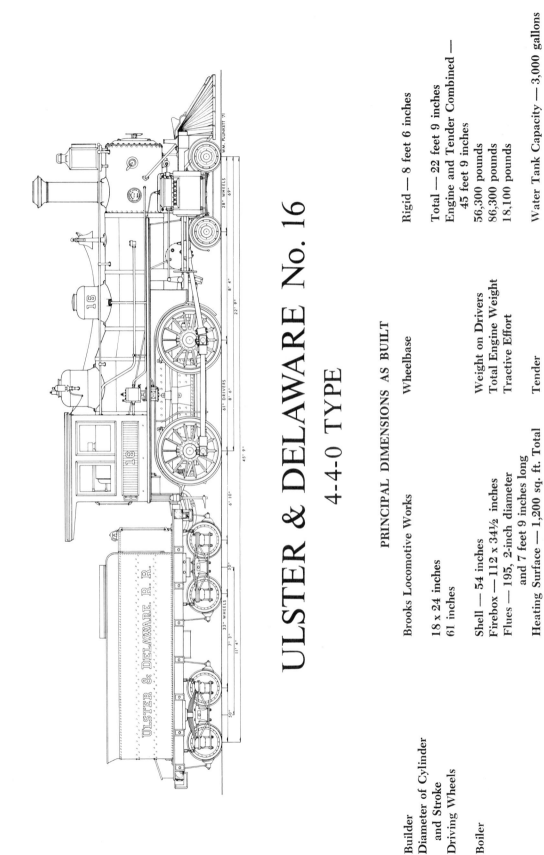

ULSTER & DELAWARE No. 16

4-4-0 TYPE

PRINCIPAL DIMENSIONS AS BUILT

Builder — Brooks Locomotive Works

Diameter of Cylinder and Stroke — 18 x 24 inches

Driving Wheels — 61 inches

Boiler
Shell — 54 inches
Firebox — 112 x 34½ inches
Flues — 195, 2-inch diameter and 7 feet 9 inches long
Heating Surface — 1,200 sq. ft. Total
Working Pressure — 165 pounds

Wheelbase
Rigid — 8 feet 6 inches
Total — 22 feet 9 inches
Engine and Tender Combined — 45 feet 9 inches

Weight on Drivers — 56,300 pounds
Total Engine Weight — 86,300 pounds
Tractive Effort — 18,100 pounds

Tender
Water Tank Capacity — 3,000 gallons
Fuel — Coal, 6 tons

SCALE — ¼ inch to the foot

U. & D. No. 14, built by Dickson in 1885, became 3rd No. 1 in 1899. It is shown here at Oneonta yard in 1902. — DEGOLYER FOUNDATION COLLECTION

U. & D. 2nd No. 2, ex 2nd No. 16 Brooks built in 1889, was being used as the Rondout switcher in 1924 and was the last 4-4-0 type on the road. — GEORGE M. SITTIG

U. & D. 2nd No. 4, ex 1st No. 16 Brooks 1887, at Arkville in 1889. The engine had just been renumbered, as the old number is still visible on the front number plate. — C. I. NEWMAN

U. & D. 2nd No. 5 photographed at the Brooks factory in 1894. It became No. 18 in 1898. — SCHENECTADY HISTORY CENTER

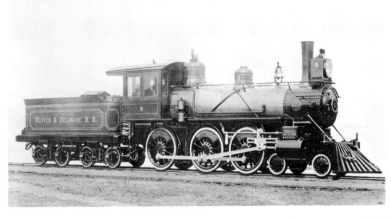

U. & D. 2nd No. 8, built by Brooks in 1889, replaced an unsatisfactory Rogers-built Mogul. It later became 3rd No. 16. — SCHENECTADY HISTORY CENTER

U. & D. 2nd No. 9, Schenectady-built in 1896, at Rondout shortly after it arrived on the road. It hauled the first train from Oneonta to Rondout in 1900. — HENRY P. EIGHMEY COLLECTION

U. & D. No. 10 retained the same number throughout its 20-year life. In this photo it still has its crosshead pump and no driving wheel brakes. — CHARLES E. FISHER COLLECTION

U. & D. No. 11 posing on the Kaaterskill turntable in 1900. It was the first Brooks built engine on the road. — DEGOLYER FOUNDATION COLLECTION

U. & D. 2nd No. 12, built by Schenectady in 1897, on the outbound track at Oneonta in 1915. In the summer when the trains were heavy, this class was used in helper service. — K. E. SCHLACHTER

U. &. D. No. 13, Brooks built in 1885, served as the Rondout yard switcher during its entire life of 47 years. — EDWARD BOND COLLECTION

U. & D. 2nd No. 14, former 1st No. 17, at Rondout yard. It was often used as a helper on passenger trains during weekends in the summer. — THOMAS NORRELL COLLECTION

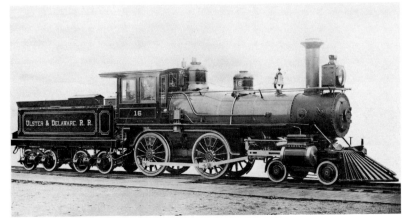

U. & D. 2nd No. 16 at the Brooks factory in 1889. As 2nd No. 2 in later years, it survived all its mates of the 1880-1890 era. — EDWARD BOND COLLECTION

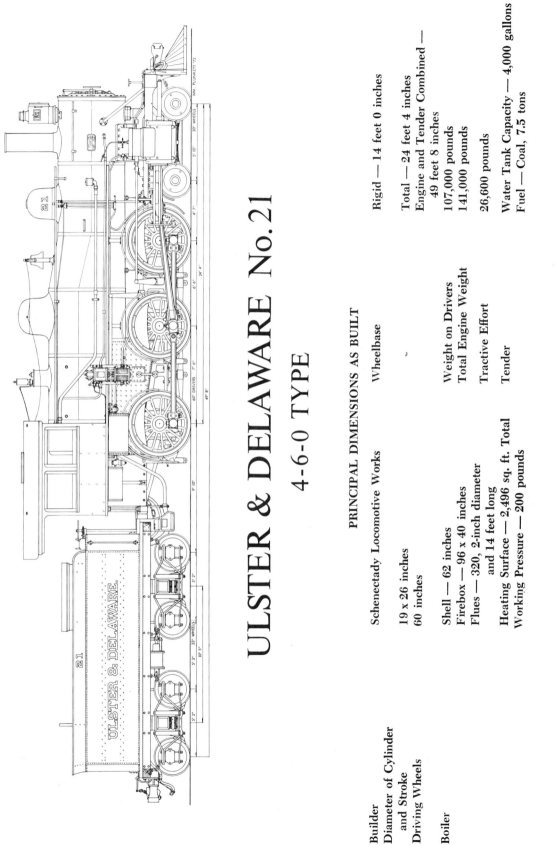

ULSTER & DELAWARE No. 21

4-6-0 TYPE

PRINCIPAL DIMENSIONS AS BUILT

Builder — Schenectady Locomotive Works

Diameter of Cylinder and Stroke — 19 x 26 inches

Driving Wheels — 60 inches

Boiler

Shell — 62 inches
Firebox — 96 x 40 inches
Flues — 320, 2-inch diameter and 14 feet long
Heating Surface — 2,496 sq. ft. Total
Working Pressure — 200 pounds

Wheelbase

Rigid — 14 feet 0 inches

Total — 24 feet 4 inches
Engine and Tender Combined — 49 feet 8 inches

Weight on Drivers — 107,000 pounds
Total Engine Weight — 141,000 pounds

Tractive Effort — 26,600 pounds

Tender

Water Tank Capacity — 4,000 gallons
Fuel — Coal, 7.5 tons

SCALE — ¼ inch to the foot

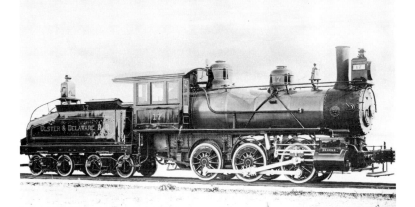

U. & D. No. 17 as turned out of the Brooks plant in 1890. As delivered it had link and pin couplers and no brakes on the engine. It had no air compressor, depending entirely on the tender brakes operated by hand. It became 2nd No. 14 in 1898.—EDWARD BOND COLLECTION

New York Central No. 22, ex Ulster & Delaware of the same number, was one of four Ten-Wheelers built by Schenectady as the first step towards modernizing the road's mainline power.—GERALD M. BEST

U. & D. No. 26, similar to No. 22 in dimensions, was one of a group of six engines built by the American Locomotive Company. Its tender piled high with coal, it is ready to head east with engine No. 12, visible behind it, as a helper. — K. E. SCHLACHTER

U. & D. No. 27, similar to No. 26 shown above, working as a switcher in Kingston yard in 1925. The oversized air tank was useful in handling long trains in the Catskills. — GEORGE M. SITTIG

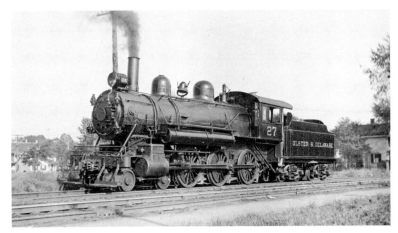

191

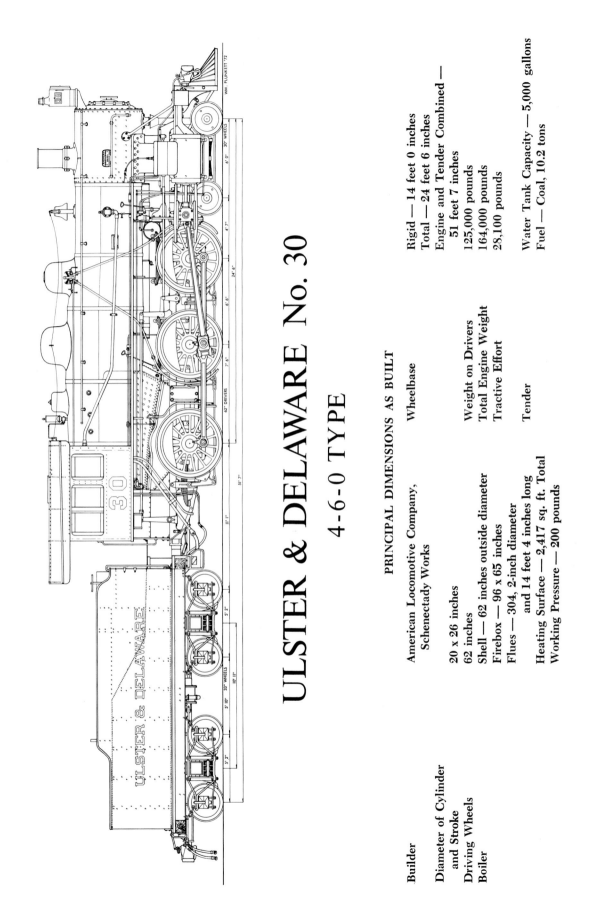

ULSTER & DELAWARE No. 30

4-6-0 TYPE

PRINCIPAL DIMENSIONS AS BUILT

Builder   American Locomotive Company, Schenectady Works

Diameter of Cylinder and Stroke   20 x 26 inches

Driving Wheels   62 inches

Boiler   Shell — 62 inches outside diameter
Firebox — 96 x 65 inches
Flues — 304, 2-inch diameter and 14 feet 4 inches long
Heating Surface — 2,417 sq. ft. Total
Working Pressure — 200 pounds

Wheelbase   Rigid — 14 feet 0 inches
Total — 24 feet 6 inches
Engine and Tender Combined — 51 feet 7 inches

Weight on Drivers   125,000 pounds
Total Engine Weight   164,000 pounds
Tractive Effort   28,100 pounds

Tender   Water Tank Capacity — 5,000 gallons
Fuel — Coal, 10.2 tons

SCALE — ¼ inch to the foot

U. & D. No. 31, one of the first group of heavy Alco-built Ten-Wheelers has just arrived in Oneonta on Memorial Day in 1915. — K. E. SCHLACHTER

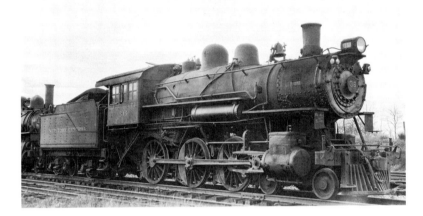

New York Central No. 36, former Ulster & Delaware No. 36, was one of the last order of heavy 4-6-0's built by Alco in 1907. The extra air tank on the right side was coupled to the main tank by a pipe curved over the top of the boiler.—GERALD M. BEST

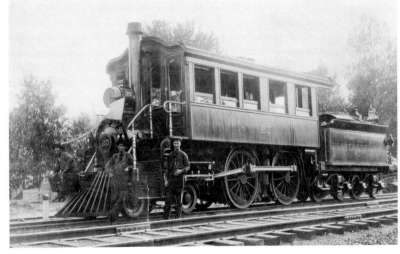

The pride and joy of the Ulster & Delaware was locomotive No. 20, the inspection engine. Built by Schenectady in 1896, Edward Coykendall used this engine on countless trips over the line as superintendent and then president. The bell was on the rear of the tender and the boiler jacket was heavily insulated so that the officials could ride in relative comfort in seats on each side of the boiler. — AUTHOR'S COLLECTION

ULSTER & DELAWARE

Passenger equipment — Built by Jackson & Sharp unless otherwise indicated.

Car Nos.	Type	Length	Pass. Capy.	Weight	Year Built	Remarks
1-3	Passenger	55'6"	62	20	1870	Open platform. Gone by 1914
4-9	Passenger	55'6"	62	23	1871	Open platform. Nos. 4-8 gone by 1914
10	Passenger	55'10"	62	23	1873	Open platform.
11-12	Passenger	55'10"	62	23	1882	Open platform. No. 12 gone by 1914
13-14	Passenger	56'0"	62	23	1882	Open platform. No. 13 gone by 1914
15-16	Passenger	55'6"	62	22	1882	Open platform. No. 16 gone by 1914
17-18	Passenger	56'3"	62	23	1883	Open platform.
19	Passenger	56'3"	62	23	1884	Open platform.
20-21	Passenger	57'0"	62	25	1885	Open platform.
22-25	Passenger	59'5"	64	27	1896	Open platform.
26-28	Passenger	68'4"	70	34.5	1899	Vestibuled.
30-39	Passenger	78'0"	82	52	1906	Vestibuled. Built by the Pullman Co.
40-43	Observation	38'0"	44	10	1897	Built by Rondout Shops. Converted to flat cars in 1902
51-53	Baggage-Passenger	56'0"	34	24	1899	Vestibuled.
54	Baggage-Passenger	50'9"	26	23	1899	Rebuilt from 1870-71 coach. Open platform.
1-2	Baggage	47'0"	—	19	1870	Gone by 1897.
61-62	Baggage	57'0"	—	23	1897	Ex 2nd Nos. 1-2. Closed ends.
63	Baggage	46'10"	—	19	1873	Ex No. 3. Open platform. Rebuilt 1891.
64-65	Baggage	41'5"	—	16	1891	Ex Nos. 4-5. Open platform.
66-67	Baggage	52'9"	—	22	1884	Ex Nos. 6-7. Open platform, flat roof.
71-73	Baggage-Mail	57'0"	—	22	1885	Ex Nos. 8-10. Open platform. No. 71 scrapped 1911.
74-76	Baggage-Mail	73'6"	—	67.5	1912	Built by Pullman Co. Closed ends. Steel.
81-83	Milk	42'0"	—	20	1879	Ex Nos. 1-3. Scrapped 1902-03.
84-85	Milk	42'0"	—	20	1881	Ex Nos. 4-5. No. 84 scrapped 1903; No. 85 scrapped 1909.
86-89	Milk	46'0"	—	21	1883	Ex Nos. 6-9. Scrapped 1902-03.
90-91	Milk	46'0"	—	21	1884	Ex Nos. 10-11. Scrapped 1899.
81, 83	Milk	46'8"	—	21	1902	Built Rondout Shops. Renumbered 1001, 1003 in 1921.
82, 84	Milk	46'8"	—	21	1903	Built Rondout Shops. Renumbered 1002, 1081 in 1921.
85	Milk	42'2"	—	23	1909	Built Rondout Shops. Renumbered 1082 in 1921.
86-90	Milk	46'8"	—	20	1903	Built Rondout Shops. Renumbered 1083-86, 1090 in 1921.
91-94	Milk	46'8"	—	23	1906	Built Rondout Shops. Renumbered 1091-1094 in 1921.

Freight equipment — builders unknown.

Car Nos.	Type	Length	Pass. Capy.	Weight	Year Built	Remarks
101-154	Box	33'6"	14	20	Prior 1901	Wood frame. See discussion.
150-199	Box	36'0"	19.5	40	1912	Steel underframe
201-338	Flat	34'0"	10.25	20	Prior 1900	Wood frame. See discussion
339-368	Flat	34'0"	10.25	20	1900	Wood frame.
401-499	Flat	40'0"	18.5	50	1912-14	Steel frame
501-532	Coal	31'10"	12	30	Prior 1900	Scrapped prior 1914.
500-501	Stock	34'10"	17.5	30	1908	
601-608	Stock	33'0"	16	25	1884-88	No. 602-08 Scrapped 1899; No. 601 scrapped 1908.
801-840	Coal	38'7"	19	50	1917	Steel underframe.
901-910	Coal	39'6"	17	50	1921	Low side, flat bottomed, for company service only.

Discussion. A renumbering of most rolling stock was made in 1898. The passenger cars were originally numbered 1 to 25 and these were not renumbered in 1898. Baggage type cars were originally numbered 1 to 10. Milk cars were originally numbered 1 to 11. Prior to 1898 there were 61 box cars numbered 2 to 122, even numbers only.

In 1895 ten of these cars were retired, and in 1900 three were added, for a total of 54 cars. Before 1898 there were 166 flat cars numbered 1 to 331, odd numbers only. This total had been reduced to 138 at the time of renumbering. An 1890 list shows the coal and stock cars with road numbers as given above.

The first two baggage cars on the Rondout & Oswego had gothic style windows which helped identify them in later photos. Almost. as interesting as the car is the unusual type of stub switch stand, at the Jackson & Sharp car works in Wilmington, Delaware in 1870. Unexplained is the road No. 3 on the side of the car, for the two cars of this type were numbered Nos. 1 and 2 in the earliest known roster.—DELAWARE STATE ARCHIVES

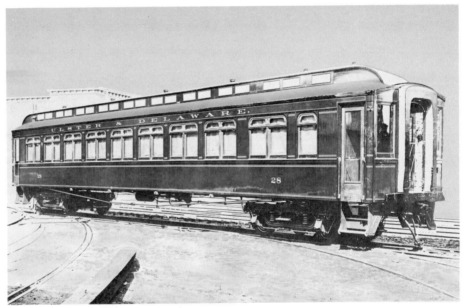

With shades lowered to make a better picture, Ulster & Delaware vestibuled coach No. 28 awaits delivery at the Jackson & Sharp works in 1899. (LEFT) The interior of the same coach shows the elaborate twin oil lamps which would be priceless museum pieces to any collector today. — DELAWARE STATE ARCHIVES

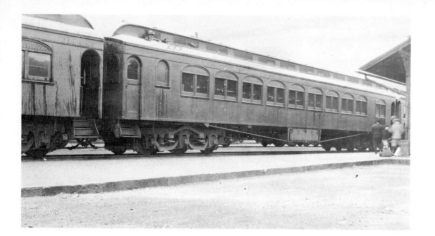

Pullman-built U. & D. coach No. 33, shown at the left, at Hunter on a rainy afternoon in 1923. — WALTER A. LUCAS (BELOW) Pullman parlor car *Marina*, with 22 chairs and three seats, was rebuilt in 1903 from an older car with open platforms. The trucks are of 1880 design. — ARTHUR DUBIN COLLECTION

Pullman parlor car *Ocean Grove*, with the narrow vestibules typical of 1890. The car had 18 chairs, six seats and a drawing room. — LUCIUS BEEBE COLLECTION

Cabooses

Car Nos.	Weight in Tons	No. of Wheels	Year Built	Remarks
626-629	8.75	4	1884	Ex Nos. 1-4. Scrapped by 1914.
630-632	17.5	8	1898	
633-635	9	4	1904	Built at Rondout Shops.
636	18.1	8	1907	
637-638	9.5	4	1905	Built at Rondout Shops.
639-640	9	4	1908	Built at Rondout Shops.
641	19	8	1924	Built at Rondout Shops.

Note. Cabooses in use after 1914 were rebuilt with steel underframes to comply with Federal laws.

Work Equipment

Car Nos.	Type Constr.	Type Service	Weight in Tons	Year Built	Description
1	Steel	Wreck	102	1911	Steam wrecking crane.
307	Wood	Work	10.5	1895	Flat to go with No. 675.
651	Wood	Wreck	28	1911	Commissary car, rebuilt from old coach.
652-653	Wood	Work	20	—	Maintenance of Way service.
654	Wood	Transfer	12	1882	Flat car equipped with 3 ft. gauge track.
655	Wood	Work	20	—	Maintenance of Way service.
656	Wood	Snow clearance	35	1902	Russell flanger-snowplow.
657	Wood	Wreck	19	1910	Tool car.
658,659	Wood	Work	23	—	Old coaches used as boarding cars.
675	Wood	Work	19	1895	Steam derrick-pile driver.

Note. No. 654 after 1899 was used in Maintenance of Way service.

Ulster & Delaware caboose No. 641 at Montgomery in 1933. This was the last caboose built at the Rondout shops. — THOMAS B. ANNIN

The cabooses used by the New York Central on the Catskill Mountain branch are of all-steel construction. — GERALD M. BEST

LOCOMOTIVES OF THE STONY CLOVE & CATSKILL MOUNTAIN R.R.

3 Foot Gauge

No.	Name	Type	Builder and Construction No.		Year Built	Dimensions Dr.–Cyls.–Wt.	Remarks
1		0-4-4	Rhode Is. Acq.		5-1881	-36000	Note 1
1	*Stony Clove*	2-6-0	Dickson	358	9-1882	36 1/2-15x18-56000	Renumb. U. & D. No. 2 -1894
2	*Gretchen*	2-6-0	Dickson		5-1882	36 1/2-15x18-56000	Note 2
2	*Hunter*	2-6-0	Dickson	530	5-1886	36 1/2-15x18-56000	Renumbered U. & D. No. 1 — 1894.

Note 1. Secondhand, probably from Worcester & Shrewsbury R. R. No. 4. Sold in 1886. Could have been a 4-4-0.

Note 2. On the road from May to November 1882. Probably Dickson No. 337, borrowed from the Chateaugay, R. R.

Stony Clove & Catskill Mountain Railroad *Stony Clove* No. 1, Dickson built in 1882, at Hunter in 1886. Frank Conerty is the engineer; William Van Valkenburg the fireman in the gangway, and switchman Shorty Hollow stands by the tender. (LEFT) The same engine as Ulster & Delaware No. 2 in 1895 at the Hunter station. Frank Conerty at the left is still the engineer, and the conductor with the watch chain is E. B. Van Demark.—
BOTH DEGOLYER FOUNDATION COLLECTION

U. & D. narrow gauge No. 5, former *Derrick Van Brummel* No. 2 of the Kaaterskill Railroad, stands in Hunter station with unidentified employees, a few days before the line was standard gauged in 1899. — HAROLD L. GOLDSMITH COLLECTION

LOCOMOTIVES OF THE KAATERSKILL R. R.

No.	Name	Type	Builder and Construction No.		Built	Dimensions Dr.–Cyls.–Wt.	Remarks
			3 Foot Gauge				
1	*Rip Van Winkle*	2-6-0	Dickson	423	5-1883	36 1/2-15x18-56000	Renumbered U. & D. 3-1894.
2	*Derrick Van Brummel*	2-6-0	Brooks	936	6-1883	37-15x18-55000	Renumbered U. & D. 5-1894.
3		2-6-0	Brooks		1882	37-15x18-55000	Note A

Note A. Acquired from New York Equipment Co. 7-6-1893. Renumbered U. & D. 4 in 1894.

DISPOSITION OF THE ULSTER & DELAWARE NARROW GAUGE LOCOMOTIVES

U. & D. No. 1 — Sold 1-1900 to F. M. Hicks; resold to Chateaugay R. R. 2nd No. 2 for $1,200. Scrapped by D. & H. 12-1903.

U. &. D. No. 2 — Sold 1-1900 to F. M. Hicks; resold to Chateaugay R. R. 2nd No. 8 for $1,200. Scrapped by D. & H. 12-1903.

U. & D. No. 3 — Sold 8-1899 to Empire Steel & Iron Co. for $3,252.17. Resold to Birmingham Rail & Loco. Co., 4-1905; to Crystal River Lumber Co., Crystal River, Fla. — 1905.

U. & D. No. 4 — Sold 8-1899. See discussion.

U. & D. No. 5 — Sold 8-1899. See discussion.

Discussion. The Stony Clove & Catskill Mountain R. R. had four locomotives, but only two at any one time. The first locomotive was purchased second hand when construction started in 1881, and another arrived shortly before the road was completed. The photo of the latter, named the *Gretchen* shows a No. 2 on the sandbox, so it can be assumed that the first engine on the road in 1881 was No. 1. Yet when the new Dickson engine, the *Stony Clove* was completed, it was given No. 1 at the factory and photos of it, in service, show this road number. On this basis, the first engine on the road was renumbered No. 2 when the *Stony Clove* arrived. The annual reports each year list two locomotives, and the 1886 report shows that one locomotive was sold and a new engine added, for an expenditure of $4,061.40 in addition to the money received from the sale of one locomotive.

The Kaaterskill Railroad bought two new engines when the road was opened, and these served the line until 1893. To operate the trains on the newly-built Catskill & Tannersville R. R., a secondhand Brooks 2-6-0 exactly like Kaaterskill R. R. No. 2 was purchased and operated the local service between Otis Summit and Tannersville until the end of the 1898 season. This engine is believed to be one of three Brooks 2-6-0s which were sold in the 1893 period by the Denver, Leadville & Gunnison R. R., a subsidiary of the Union Pacific in Colorado. These were Nos. 157, 158 and 160, sold to unknown buyers. Raymond Baldwin, retired conductor of the Ulster & Delaware was a brakeman on work trains during the standard gauging of the Kaaterskill R. R. in 1899 and states that he remembers that some of the narrow gauge equipment was left at Kaaterskill when the 3 foot gauge rails were pulled up. Presumably this equipment, probably two locomotives and two passenger cars plus a flat car were purchased by the contractors building the Catskill & Tannersville extension. Records of the sale of the U. & D.'s three narrow gauge Dickson engines are complete, but the two Brooks engines vanished.

From 1881 to 1899, the enginehouse and shop for running repairs to narrow gauge equipment was at Phoenicia. Engines needing heavy repairs were loaded on a specially equipped flat car and sent to the Rondout Shops. After standard gauging, all shop facilities at Phoenicia were removed.

NARROW GAUGE PASSENGER EQUIPMENT

Stony Clove & Catskill Mountain R. R.

Car Nos.	Type	Builder	Weight in Tons	Year Built	Remarks
1-2	Baggage	Jackson & Sharp	8	1882	No. 2 converted to combination coach.
3-4	Passenger	Jackson & Sharp	9	1881	
5	Passenger	Jackson & Sharp	9	1882	
6-9	Observation	Jackson & Sharp	9	1882	
10	Baggage-Passenger	Jackson & Sharp	11.5	1890	

Note. The road owned 2 box, 7 flat and 5 service cars, road numbers unknown.

Kaaterskill R. R.

Car Nos.	Type	Builder	Weight in Tons	Year Built	Remarks
1-2	Baggage	Jackson & Sharp	9.5	1883	
3-4	Passenger	Jackson & Sharp	11	1883	
5	Baggage-Passenger	Jackson & Sharp	11.5	1890	Probably converted from a coach.

Note. The Kaaterskill R. R. owned one box and three flat cars. The two narrow gauge roads jointly owned 21 sets of Ramsey transfer trucks. All narrow gauge equipment was sold in 1898-1899.

LOCOMOTIVES OF THE CATSKILL & TANNERSVILLE R. R.

No.	Type	Builder and Construction No.		Year Built	Dimensions Dr.—Cyls.	Remarks
1	2-6-0	Brooks		1882	37-15x18-55000	Note A
1	2-6-0	Baldwin	32715	3-1908	42-14x20-63000	Note B
2	2-6-0	Brooks		1882	37-15x18-55000	Note A
2	2-6-0	Baldwin	18884	4-1901	42-14x20-67160	Note B

Note A. See the remarks following the Ulster & Delaware narrow gauge roster for the possible origin of 1st Nos. 1 and 2. A good photo of No. 1 shows its unmistakeable Union Pacific narrow gauge origin, from one of their Colorado subsidiaries. No. 1 was retired in 1908, and No. 2 in 1901. The boiler of No. 2 was reported as being used in the Catskill Mountain House laundry, but a 1912 photo of the engine sitting derelict in back of the engine shed shows it was still intact except for the headlight, bell and the boiler lagging.

Note B. All four engines were equipped with vacuum brakes as well as air, so that if cars of the **Catskill Mountain Ry** were hauled up the Otis Railway to the summit, the vacuum brakes on the cars would work. According to several sources, the two Baldwins had names, but no photograph verifying this has been published or exhibited. The Baldwins were stored until purchased by the Birmingham Rail & Locomotive Co., which rebuilt both engines with steel cabs and other improvements. No. 1 was sold March 2, 1926 to the Chicago, Milwaukee, St. Paul & Pacific No. 3, and No. 2 followed on May 22, 1928 to become C.M. St.P & P. No. 2. These engines were operated on what was once the Bellevue & Cascade R. R., which the Milwaukee absorbed in 1899. Their life in Iowa was a short and merry one, for the Milwaukee sold the branch in 1933 to local residents who operated it for two years as the Bellevue & Cascade R. R., then closed it down for good.

The Catskill & Tannersville rolling stock consisted of a combination coach and a passenger coach, purchased secondhand in 1898-99, a box car and a flat car. Another coach was added in 1908 and these five cars were all the rolling stock the railroad ever owned.

Catskill & Tannersville 2nd No. 1 backing down to its train at Otis Summit. The fireman's shelter over the tender was installed at the Baldwin factory. — W. J. LANDON

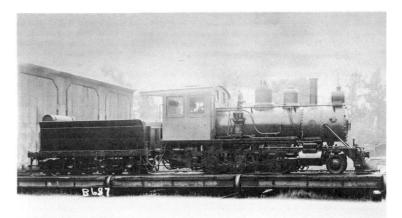

Catskill & Tannersville 2nd No. 1 for sale at the Birmingham Rail & Locomotive Co. in 1925. A new steel cab has been installed and the fireman's shelter removed. — AUTHOR'S COLLECTION

Catskill & Tannersville 2nd No. 2 was close to being a Mother Hubbard type, for the back boilerhead was exposed and the fireman worked in the open. Later he was protected by a shelter built over the forward end of the tender. — AUTHOR'S COLLECTION

The only close-up of a Catskill & Tannersville coach shows No. 2 with raised metal letters and number similar to those used on the Catskill Mountain Railway. — GEORGE PHELPS COLLECTION

LOCOMOTIVES OF THE CATSKILL MOUNTAIN RY.–CAIRO RAILROAD

Initial	No.	Name	Type	Builder and Construction No.		Year Built	Dimensions Dr.–Cyls.	Remarks
CMR	1	*S. Sherwood Day*	4-4-0	Dickson	335	5-1882	48-13x18	New boiler – 1909. Retired 1918
CMR	1	*John T. Mann*	4-4-0	Dickson	336	5-1882	48-13x18	New boiler – 1910. Retired 1918
CMR	3	*Alfred Van Santvoord*	4-4-0	Dickson	522	6-1885	48-13x18	Retired 1912
CMR	4	*Charles L. Beach*	4-4-0	Schenectady	4333	6-1895	49-13x18	Destroyed in enginehouse fire – 1908
CMR	4	*Charles L. Beach*	4-4-0	Alco-Schenectady	46045	6-1909	49-13x18	Note A
CMR	5	*Alfred Van Santvoord*	4-4-0	Alco-Rogers	51126	5-1912	49-13x18	Note A

Note A. Engines 2nd No. 4 and No. 5 were sold to the M. L. Davis Lumber Co., Oak Grove, Alabama for use on their Oak Grove & Georgetown R. R. in 1920.

CATSKILL MOUNTAIN RY. – CAIRO RAILROAD
Rolling Stock

The cars for the passenger trains consisted of four flat-roofed baggage cars, Nos. 1 to 4; four enclosed coaches, Nos. 5 to 8; six open excursion coaches, Nos. 9 to 14 and two enclosed coaches, Nos. 15 and 16. All were built by Jackson & Sharp in 1882 except the last two which were built by the same company in 1893. According to records given to the writer by A. Canton, purchasing agent for the F. C. Unidos de Yucatan, Merida, Yucatan, in 1952, the Catskill Mountain Railway passenger cars arrived in Merida in 1920 and were given the road numbers 105 to116 inclusive. There was no record of receiving any baggage cars

at that time. Since 1920 the cars were converted to the Tercero, or Third Class, with hard wooden seats along the sides, backless benches in the center, and no amenities whatsoever. No. 109 was sold to the Early West Railways of Pomona, California in 1963, and is now abandoned to the elements as the railroad was never built.

The freight rolling stock consisted of 10 platform cars and two box cars, all by Jackson & Sharp in 1882. Later two more cars were added, and some of the platform cars were converted to gondolas.

Catskill Mountain Railway No. 2 with the ever-present engineer Frank Ruf in front of the pilot. The beautiful polish on the Russian iron boiler jacket is probably the work of Frank's unidentified fireman. — AUTHOR'S COLLECTION

Cairo Railroad No. 3 in its prime, at Catskill Landing, with engineer Frank Ruf in the center. The fireman has a "hang-dog" expression as if to say, "What, another picture?"—COURTESY OF WINFIELD W. ROBINSON

Catskill Mountain Railway 1st No. 4, the *Charles L. Beach*, so new that the boiler jacket shines like silver. Frank Ruf, by the pilot as always, has as always, a very sober expression, but where is the oil can? — AUTHOR'S COLLECTION

Catskill Mountain Railway 2nd No. 4, also named the *Charles L. Beach*. Frank Ruf couldn't pose against this one because the locomotive was still at the factory. — AUTHOR'S COLLECTION

Catskill Mountain Railway No. 5, the *Alfred Van Santvoord*, at the Alco factory. The Walschaert valve gear replaced the older Stephenson type. — K. E. SCHLACHTER COLLECTION

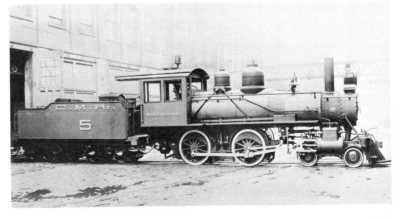

LOCOMOTIVES OF THE DELAWARE & EASTERN

No.	Name	Type	Builder and Construction No.		Year Built	Dimensions Dr.–Cyls.–Wt.	Remarks
1	F. F. Searing	4-4-0	Cooke	1591	6-1884	68-19x24-94000	Ex DL&W 482; earlier 947-M&E 133. To D&N 5
2	R. B. Williams	4-4-0	Dickson	476	5-1884	68-18x24-92800	Ex DL&W 484; earlier 949-124-181. To D&N 4
3	A. C. Fairchild	2-6-0	Dickson	312	11-1881	57-18x24-97572	Ex DL&W 285; orig. Buff. Divn. 24. Scr. 1911
4	H. M. George	4-4-0	Dickson	481	6-1884	68-18x24-92400	Ex DL&W 485; earlier 950-183-186. To D&N 6
5	Russell Murray	4-4-0	Dickson	395	12-1882	63-19x24-92400	Ex DL&W 499; earlier 969-NYL&W 76. Scr. 1912

LOCOMOTIVES OF THE DELAWARE & NORTHERN

No.	Type	Builder and Construction No.		Year Built	Dimensions Dr.–Cyls.–Wt.	Remarks
1	4-4-0	Baldwin	20736	7-1902	64-18x24-113000	Blt. as Sou. Indiana No. 16. Reblt. Baldwin 1911. Scr.
2	4-4-0	Baldwin	20964	9-1902	64-18x24-113000	Blt. as Sou. Indiana No. 18. Reblt. Baldwin 1911. Retired 1933
3	4-4-0	Baldwin	20737	7-1902	64-18x24-113000	Blt. as Sou. Indiana No. 17. Reblt. Baldwin 1911. Scr.
4	4-4-0	Dickson	476	5-1884	68-18x24-92800	Ex D.&E. No. 2. See above. Retired 1922
5	4-4-0	Cooke	1591	6-1884	68-19x24-94000	Ex D.&E. No. 1. See above. Retired 1929
6	4-4-0	Dickson	481	6-1884	68-18x24-92400	Ex D.&E. No. 4. See above. Retired 1930
7	4-6-0	Brooks	3556	6-1900	63-18x24-125000	Ex B.R.&P. No. 186. Acq. SI&E No. 1699 6-7-23. Scr.
10	2-6-0	Lima	1108	2-1910	56-19x26-138000	Ex Emporia Mfg. Co. No. 10. Acq. BR&L Co. 1-3-30. Scrapped
10	Motor	Brill		2-1926		250 h.p. Baggage–Mail–Passenger Motor Car Length 29 ft. Capacity 29 passengers. Sold 1942

DELAWARE & NORTHERN

ROLLING STOCK

Passenger Cars

No.	Type	Length	Capacity	Remarks
1-5	Passenger	55'0"	60	Open platform, wood construction, secondhand in 1906.
50-54	Baggage-Passenger	54'0"	28	Open platform, wood construction, secondhand in 1906.

Freight Cars

No.	Type	Length	Capacity	Remarks
101-108	Milk	52'0"	—	Wood construction. No. 108 wrecked 1908; rest sold in 1920.
501-557	Box	40'0"	30 tons	Wood construction. 47 cars sold 1912-1916.
1001-1110	Flat	40'0"	30 tons	Wood construction. 65 cars sold 1911-1918.
A, C, Z	Caboose			Cars C and Z sold by 1918.
MWA	Derrick and tool car.			Steel frame.
MWT	Tool and outfit car.			Rebuilt from an old box car.

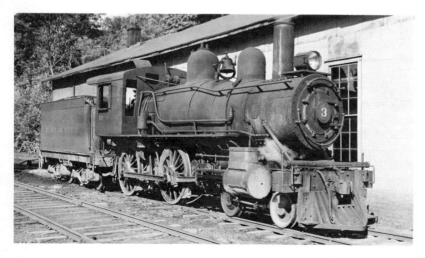

Delaware & Northern 2nd No. 3 had a true stovepipe stack in this 1941 picture. The relief valves on the front of the steamchest are reminiscent of the great East Branch locomotive fight of 1909.
— T. A. GAY

BIBLIOGRAPHY

Books

Beers, J. B., *Greene County, a history*, J. B. Beers & Co., New York, 1884.

Burgess and Kennedy, *History of the Pennsylvania Railroad*, Pennsylvania Railroad Co., 1949.

Buckman, D. L., *Old Steamboat Days on the Hudson*, Grafton Press, New York, 1907.

Clark, William, *Delaware County, a history*, William Clark, Delhi, New York, 1898.

Coughtry, W. J., *Delaware and Hudson Co., a history*, Delaware and Hudson Co., 1925.

DeLisser, Richard Lionel, *Picturesque Ulster, 1896-1905*. Reprinted by Twine's Catskill Bookshop, Woodstock, New York, 1968.

Green, Nelson, *The Valley of the Hudson, River of Destiny, Vol. II*, S. J. Clarke, Chicago, Ill. 1931.

Haring, H. A., *Our Catskill Mountains*, Putnam & Co., New York, 1931.

Harlow, Alvin F., *The Road of the Century*, Creative Age Press, New York, 1947.

Harris, Harold, *Treasure Tales of the Shawangunks and Catskills*, Harold Harris, Ellenville, New York, 1956.

Haskins, Vernon, *Canajoharie-Catskill Railroad*, Durham Center Museum, Durham Center, New York, 1967.

Hickey, Andrew S., *The Story of Kingston*, Stratford House, New York, 1952.

Longstreth, T. Morris, *The Catskills*, Century Co., 1918.

Lossing, Benson J., *The Hudson*, Virtue and Yorston, New York, 1866.

Moody's Manual of Railroads, 1900-1969, Moody's Investor Service, New York.

Poor, Henry V., *History of the Railroads and Canals of the U.S.*, Schultz & Co., New York, 1860.

Poor's Manual of Railroads, 1868-1927, Poor's R.R. Manual Co., New York.

Reynolds, Cuyler, *Genealogical History of Southern New York*, Lewis Historical Publication Co., New York, 1914.

Ringwald, D. C., *Hudson River Day Line*, Howell-North Books, Berkeley, Ca. 1965.

Rockwell, Rev. Charles, *The Catskill Mountains*, Taintor Bros. & Co., New York, 1867.

Schoonmaker, Marius, *The History of Kingston*, Burr Press, New York, 1888.

Van Deusen, W. J., *Ulster County, a history*, W. J. Van Deusen, Kingston, N. Y. 1907.

Van Zandt, Roland, *The Catskill Mountain House*, Rutgers University Press, New Brunswick, N. J., 1966.

Wakefield, Manville B., *Coal Boats to Tidewater*, Steingart Associates, South Fallsburg, N. Y., 1965.

Wakefield, Manville B., *To the Mountains by Rail*, Wakefair Press, Grahamsville, N. Y. 1970.

Travel Guides

America's Summer Resorts, New York Central & Hudson River Railroad, 1893-1912.

Appleton's Railroad and Steamboat Companion, D. Appleton & Co., New York, 1847.

Appleton's Illustrated Handbook of American Travel, D. Appleton & Co., New York, 1857.

Brooklyn Daily Eagle, Summer Resort Directory, Brooklyn, N.Y. 1903.

Handy Guide to the Hudson River and Catskill Mountains, Rand, McNally, New York, 1907.

Hudson River by Daylight, The, John Featherston, New York, 1874.

Hudson River Route, The, Taintor Bros., Merrill & Co., New York, 1883.

New York American, Summer Vacation Directory, New York, 1908.

Official Guide of the Railways and Steam Navigation Lines of the U.S., 1868-1970, National Railway Publishing Co., New York.

Summer Guide, New York, West Shore & Buffalo Railroad, 1883, 1884, 1885.

Summer Guide, Ulster & Delaware Railroad, 1891, 1896, 1900, 1906, 1910, 1916.

Van Loan's Catskill Mountain Guide, Walton Van Loan, Rogers & Sherwood, New York, Later Dudley Press, New York, 1891-1914.

Summer Guide, West Shore Railroad, 1890, 1896, 1900.

HISTORICAL PAPERS, PAMPHLETS, AND PERIODICALS

Berner, A. Kole, *Delaware & Northern Railroad, a history,* Margaretville, N.Y. 1969.

Board of Railroad Commissioners, State of New York, Annual reports, 1876 to 1903.

Kingston's 350th Anniversary, 1609-1959, Catskill Mountains Publishing Co., Kingston, N.Y. 1959.

Mack, Arthur C., "Reminder of the Past," *Railroad Magazine,* Feb. 1959, pp. 88-95.

Otis Incline Railways, Otis Elevator Co., New York, 1912.

Railroad Gazette, weekly, 1872-1908, New York.

Railway Age, weekly, 1909-1969, New York.

Railway Equipment Register, monthly, 1885-1932, Railway Equipment Publishing Co., New York.

Railway and Locomotive Historical Society, *Bulletin No. 37,* Capt. Winfield W. Robinson, The Catskill Mountain Lines, pp. 7-14.

Railway and Locomotive Historical Society, *Bulletin No. 43,* Capt. Winfield W. Robinson, The Delaware & Northern Railroad, pp. 23-29.

Railway Review, weekly, 1867-1892, Chicago, Ill.

Records of the County Clerks of Delaware, Greene and Ulster Counties, New York.

Records of the Town Clerk, Harpersfield, New York.

Ulster & Delaware Railroad, Annual reports, various years, 1876-1929.

NEWSPAPERS

Catskill Examiner, Catskill, N.Y.

Catskill Mail, Catskill, N.Y.

Catskill Mountain News, Margaretville, N.Y.

Kingston Daily Freeman

New York Herald

New York Times

Port Jervis Gazette

Port Jervis Union

Rondout Daily and *Weekly Freeman*

Rondout Weekly Journal

INDEX

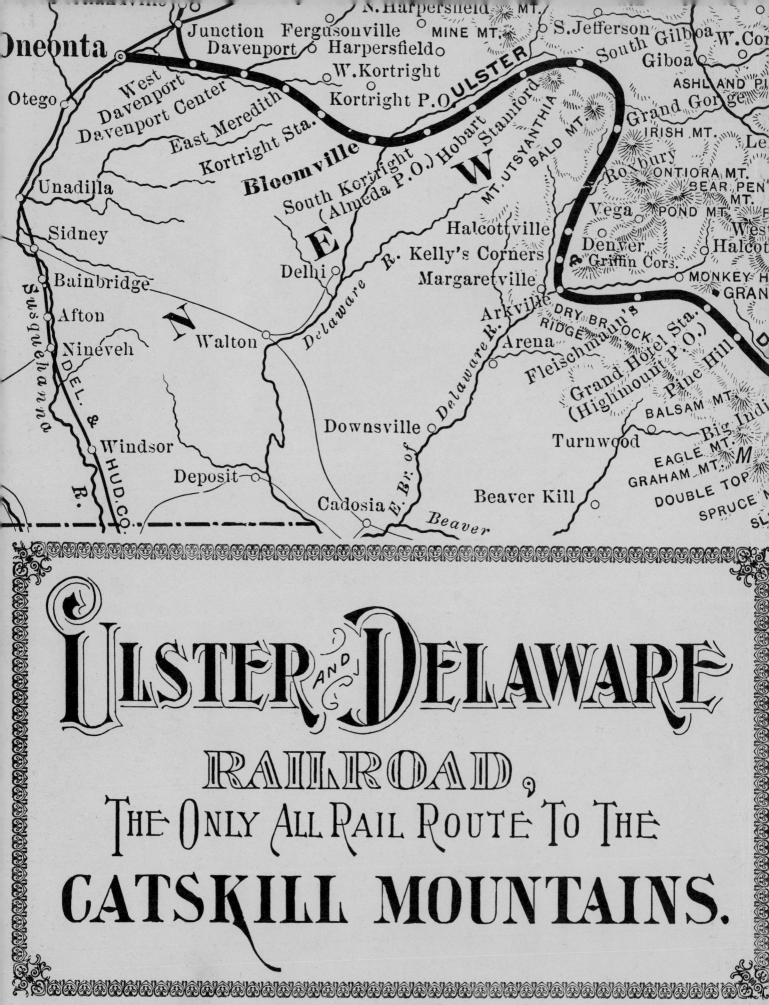

Oneonta
Otego
West Davenport
Davenport Center
Junction
Davenport
Fergusonville
Harpersfield
W. Kortright
Kortright P.O.
N. Harpersfield
MINE MT.
MT.
S. Jefferson
South Gilboa
Gilboa
W. Cor
W. Cor
ASHLAND PI
East Meredith
Kortright Sta.
Bloomville
South Kortright
(Almeda P.O.)
Hobart
Stamford
MT. UTSYANTHIA
BALD MT.
Grand Gor
Grand
IRISH MT.
Roxbury
ONTIORA MT.
BEAR PEN MT.
Unadilla
Delhi
Halcottville
Kelly's Corners
Margaretville
Vega
POND MT.
Wes
Halcot
Sidney
Denver
Griffin Cors.
MONKEY H
GRAN
Bainbridge
Afton
Nineveh
Walton
Arkville
Arena
DRY BROOK
RIDGE
D
Windsor
Downsville
Fleischmann's
Grand Hotel Sta.
(Highmount P.O.)
Pine Hill
BALSAM MT.
Big Indi
Deposit
Turnwood
EAGLE MT.
GRAHAM MT.
M
Cadosia
Beaver Kill
DOUBLE TOP
SPRUCE M
SL
Beaver
Susquehanna
DEL. & HUD. CO. R.
Delaware R.
Delaware R.
E. Br. of Delaware R.
N
E
W
ULSTER

ULSTER AND DELAWARE
RAILROAD,
THE ONLY ALL RAIL ROUTE TO THE
CATSKILL MOUNTAINS.

535731